READING AND VOCABULARY 4
Focus

Catherine Mazur-Jefferies

Series Consultant
Lawrence J. Zwier

NATIONAL GEOGRAPHIC LEARNING | **CENGAGE Learning**

Australia • Brazil • Japan • Korea • Mexico • Singapore • Spain • United Kingdom • United States

Reading and Vocabulary Focus 4
Catherine Mazur-Jefferies

Publisher: Sherrise Roehr

Series Consultant: Lawrence J. Zwier

Executive Editor: Laura Le Dréan

Contributing Editors: Bernard Seal, Jennifer Bixby, and Karen McAlister Shimoda

Director of Global Marketing: Ian Martin

Product Marketing Manager: Lindsey Miller

Director, Content and Media Production: Michael Burggren

Senior Content Project Manager: Daisy Sosa

Print Buyer: Mary Beth Hennebury

Cover Designers: Christopher Roy and Michael Rosenquest

Cover Image: Hidehiko Sakashita/Flickr/Getty Images

Text Design and Layout: Don Williams

Composition: Page Designs International

For product information and technology assistance, contact us at
**Cengage Learning Customer & Sales Support,
1-800-354-9706**
For permission to use material from this text or product,
submit all requests online at **www.cengage.com/permissions**.
Further permissions questions can be e-mailed to
permissionrequest@cengage.com.

Student Book ISBN: 978-1-285-17341-2

National Geographic Learning
20 Channel Center Street
Boston, MA 02210
USA

Cengage Learning is a leading provider of customized learning solutions with office locations around the globe, including Singapore, the United Kingdom, Australia, Mexico, Brazil and Japan.

Cengage Learning products are represented in Canada by Nelson Education, Ltd.

Visit National Geographic Learning online at **NGL.cengage.com**

Visit our corporate website at **www.cengage.com**

Printed in the United States of America
2 3 4 5 6 7 8   19 18 17 16 15 14

CONTENTS

Inside a Unit   vi

Series Introduction   xi

CITY SPACES   2

READING 1   **Above Manhattan**   4

     READING SKILL: Determining Chronology   10

READING 2   **Under Paris**   14

     READING SKILL: Annotating a Text   21

UNIT REVIEW   26

EXTREME JOBS   28

READING 1   **The Snow Patrol**   30

     READING SKILL: Dealing with Unknown Vocabulary   36

READING 2   **Into the Volcano**   40

     READING SKILL: Recognizing Causes and Effects   46

UNIT REVIEW   50

ANIMAL CONSERVATION   52

READING 1   **Path of the Jaguar**   54

     READING SKILL: Making Inferences   60

READING 2   **Champion of the Underdog**   64

     READING SKILL: Choosing the Correct Definition   71

UNIT REVIEW   76

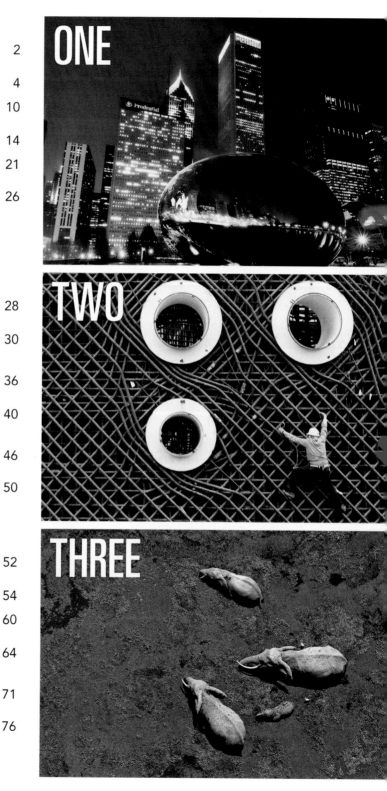

ONE

TWO

THREE

CONTENTS (CONTINUED)

FOUR NATURAL DISASTERS 78

READING 1 **Sun Struck** 80

READING SKILL: Understanding In-Text Definitions 86

READING 2 **Tracking Tsunamis** 90

READING SKILL: Connecting Visual Material to a Text 96

UNIT REVIEW 100

FIVE ART DETECTIVES 102

READING 1 **Finding Fakes** 104

READING SKILL: Assessing Problems and Solutions 110

READING 2 **The Lost Leonardo** 114

READING SKILL: Determining Certainty and Uncertainty in a Text 120

UNIT REVIEW 124

SIX SURVIVAL SKILLS 126

READING 1 **Mind over Matter** 128

READING SKILL: Understanding Argument and Finding Support 133

READING 2 **Journey to the North Pole** 138

READING SKILL: Recognizing Contrasts 144

UNIT REVIEW 148

NATURE'S MEDICINE 150

READING 1 **Golden Worms** 152

READING SKILL: Understanding Pronoun Reference 159

READING 2 **The Bite that Heals** 164

READING SKILL: Categorizing Information 170

UNIT REVIEW 174

LOST AT SEA 176

READING 1 **Treasures of the Titanic** 178

READING SKILL: Distinguishing Facts from Opinions 184

READING 2 **Shipwreck Discovery** 188

READING SKILL: Understanding Figurative Language 194

UNIT REVIEW 198

CULTURE AND IDENTITY 200

READING 1 **Kung Fu Battles** 202

READING SKILL: Analyzing the Pros and Cons of an Issue 208

READING 2 **Kwame Nyong'o: Film Animator** 212

READING SKILL: Recognizing Different Modes of Writing 218

UNIT REVIEW 222

Vocabulary Index 224

Credits 227

SEVEN

EIGHT

NINE

v

INSIDE A UNIT

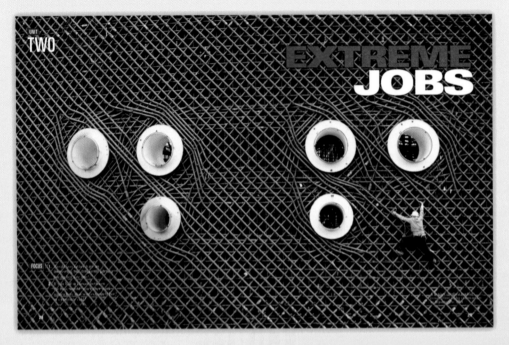

Each unit opens with an amazing **National Geographic** image that taps into learners' natural curiosity about the world while introducing the content that will be explored in the readings.

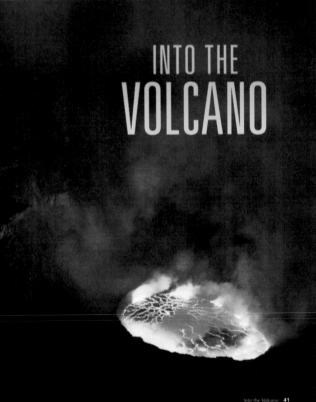

A comprehensive, three-part **vocabulary development program** builds student confidence as learners meet new or unfamiliar words in academic texts.

READING 2 INTO THE VOLCANO

Goma, in the Democratic Republic of the Congo, is quite possibly the most dangerous city in the world. It has an estimated population of one million and lies at the base of a two-mile high volcano, Nyiragongo. In 1977, eruptions sent lava racing down the mountain at more than 60 miles (96 kilometers) per hour, killing several hundred people. A subsequent eruption in 2002 shot lava into downtown Goma. It destroyed 14,000 homes, buried buildings to the top of the first floor, and forced 350,000 citizens to flee. The fact of the matter is that another eruption is inevitable, and scientists fear Nyiragongo is capable of much worse. They fear that it could transform Goma into a modern Pompeii.[1]

Nyiragongo is one of the most active volcanoes on the planet and one of the least studied. In 2011, U.S. volcanologist Ken Sims joined Dario Tedesco, an Italian volcanologist, on a three-week scientific expedition to study Nyiragongo's rocks and test its gases. Together with a team of scientists and porters,[2] their goal was to determine when the volcano might erupt again. Anticipating such an event could potentially save thousands of lives.

In order to reach the summit of Nyiragongo, the team followed the lava up the mountain, carrying camping gear, climbing equipment, scientific instruments, food, and water. After a full day of hiking, they reached the summit and looked down into the mouth of the volcano. High walls surrounded by ledges dropped down into the crater, which had an enormous, flat floor, black with hardened lava. In the middle of the crater, in a raised area shaped like a soup bowl, they saw an incredible sight: a lake of bubbling lava.

In 2002, an eruption from Nyiragongo destroys parts of the city of Goma in the Republic of the Congo.

A volcanologist takes gas samples from the rim of the Nyirangongo volcano.

[1] *Pompeii:* an ancient Roman city destroyed in the eruption of Mount Vesuvius in 79 CE
[2] *porters:* people whose job is to carry things

The lava lake was 700 feet (213 meters) across, making it one of the largest in the world. Shifting and swirling beneath them, it roared like an airplane and let out a thick white cloud of dozens of deadly gases. Even from the summit, they could feel the heat. The 1,800 degrees Fahrenheit (982.22 degrees Celsius) lava exploded in 100-foot sprays of electric orange that turned to black as they cooled in midair. The lake seemed to breathe. Rising and falling, its surface level changed several feet in a matter of minutes. It was both spectacular and terrifying.

Sims led the descent into the crater and secured the ropes carefully. Tedesco and the others followed. Stones fell from the walls, and massive rocks wobbled like loose teeth. They set up camp on a wide ledge 800 feet (244 meters) below the summit, a few hundred feet above the lake. The surface of the ledge was comfortably warm, but the air was toxic and gas masks[3] were essential.

Part of the team's dangerous mission was to obtain a zero-age sample, a piece of lava, freshly cooled from the edge of the boiling lake.

Based on data from a zero-age sample, scientists are able to accurately date all other rocks in a volcano. This, in turn, can help to predict volcanic eruptions. Sims, an avid rock climber, was well suited for the dangerous task. But he hesitated briefly, thinking of his wife and two young children. Volcano science has never been a safe occupation; more than 20 scientists have died on volcanoes in the past 30 years. Sims, himself, has a scar on his right arm from Sicily's Mount Etna, where his shirt melted into his skin. Nevertheless, he was one of only a handful of people with both the climbing skills and scientific knowledge to get exactly what was needed.

Sims made up his mind and rappelled[4] into the volcano. Standing on

[3] *gas masks:* devices worn over the face to protect it from poisonous gases
[4] *rappelled:* slid down a rock face in a controlled way, using a rope, with feet against the rock

---

Content-rich readings supported by real-world images, maps, charts, and informational graphics prepare learners for academic success.

After each reading . . .

READING COMPREHENSION

Reading Comprehension sections assess learner comprehension through a variety of activities.

Big Picture

A The following statements are the main ideas of some of the paragraphs in Reading 2. Write the correct paragraph number next to its main idea.

_____ **1.** Nyiragongo's next eruption could be even more deadly than the ones before it.

_____ **2.** Climbing into the crater requires special equipment.

_____ **3.** Retrieving a zero-age sample is dangerous.

_____ **4.** The heat of the lava lake is intense.

_____ **5.** Sims retrieves a zero-age sample.

_____ **6.** The reason for the mission is to be able to predict the volcano's next eruption.

B Reread the main ideas in Exercise A. How would you annotate (see page 21) the reading using this information? Remember to use key words. The first one is done for you.

1. *next eruption = more deadly?* ....

2. ....

3. ....

4. ....

5. ....

6. ....

Close-Up

A Choose the answer that best completes each of the following sentences.

1. In 2002, 350,000 people _____ when Nyiragongo erupted.
a. were killed
b. ran away quickly
c. moved to new houses

2. The goal of the 2011 scientific expedition to Nyiragongo was to _____.
a. predict the next eruption
b. stop the volcano from erupting
c. study a new volcano

3. The scientific team followed _____ to make their way to the summit.
a. guides
b. animal tracks
c. lava

4. The team set up their camp _____.
a. at the summit
b. between the summit and the lake
c. at the surface of the lake

5. Sims worried about his safety and thought about his _____.
a. family
b. colleagues
c. students

6. When Sims climbed the wall to the lava lake, _____ to communicate with the team.
a. he used a radio
b. he used a cell phone
c. it wasn't possible for him

7. Sims used his _____ to break off a piece of the lava.
a. gas mask
b. hammer
c. hands

Learners are taught an essential **reading skill** and then apply that skill meaningfully to the reading.

Reading Skill

Recognizing Causes and Effects

Writers often describe cause-and-effect relationships. These relationships connect a situation (the cause) and the result of that situation (the effect). Signal words and phrases such as *because*, *since*, and *as a result* are often used to highlight this information. However, writers don't always use signal words and phrases, so successful readers have to be able to recognize cause-and-effect relationships even when there are no signal words.

Look at the following example from Reading 2. The causes are underlined and the effects are circled. Note that some items are both both underlined and circled, because one cause can have an effect, and this effect can be a cause of a second effect.

In 1977, eruptions sent (lava) racing down the mountain at more than 60 miles (96 kilometers) an hour, (killing) several hundred people.

In order to show cause and effect when you annotate, one strategy is to draw an arrow from the cause to the effect.

1977 eruption → lava → death of 100s

A Read the following statements from Reading 2. Underline the causes and circle the effects. Note that some words might be both a cause and an effect.

1. A subsequent eruption in 2002 shot lava into downtown Goma. It destroyed 14,000 homes, buried buildings to the top of the first floor, and forced 350,000 citizens to flee.

2. Based on data from a zero-age sample, scientists are able to accurately date all other rocks in a volcano. This, in turn, can help to predict volcanic eruptions.

3. Sims, himself, has a scar on his right arm from Sicily's Mount Etna, where his shirt melted into his skin.

4. Suddenly, Sims's foot slipped and he smelled burning rubber. Looking down, he saw his shoe melting out from under him.

5. It [the piece of fresh lava] was shiny, black, and so hot that, even wearing thermal gloves, he had to juggle it from hand to hand.

Academic Vocabulary sections develop the language that students are likely to encounter in authentic academic readings.

VOCABULARY PRACTICE

Academic Vocabulary

A Find the words in the box below in Reading 2. Use the context to help you choose the correct words to complete the following sentences.

| subsequent (Par. 1) | toxic (Par. 5) | data (Par. 6) | briefly (Par. 6) |
| secured (Par. 5) | obtain (Par. 6) | accurately (Par. 6) | fluctuated (Par. 7) |

1. On March 1, a strong rainstorm _____ caused the Vistula River in Poland to flood. Although this only lasted a short time, it caused extensive damage.
2. The levels of the river _____ over the course of a month. At times, the water level was 5 feet (1.5 meters) higher than usual. This event made the banks of the river even weaker.
3. Engineers _____ predicted that _____ storms would cause more damage. The next storm proved that their predictions had been correct.
4. From their _____, the engineers estimated that the flood levels could be as high as three feet (close to one meter).
5. This could cause _____ waste from the sewers to be leaked into the environment, which could make people very ill.
6. Fortunately, the city was able to _____ the necessary funds from the government to prevent further damage. They _____ the riverbanks and were able to avoid a catastrophe.

B The words in bold are academic words from Exercise A and words they often appear with. Complete the sentences with your own ideas.

1. The teacher **briefly discussed** _____ before we started the new material.
2. Scientists usually **analyze data** in a _____ .
3. The best way to **accurately measure** your height is to _____ .
4. Newspaper reporters often try to **obtain information** about _____ .
5. At first, research showed that the medicine had no harmful effects. However, **subsequent studies** revealed that _____ .
6. Political events can cause _____ **prices** to **fluctuate**.
7. After the building collapsed, police tried to **secure the area** by _____ .
8. Make sure that cleaning products with **toxic chemicals** are _____ .

Into the Volcano **47**

Multiword Vocabulary sections identify words that are commonly grouped together and then prompt learners to work with them in different contexts for enhanced comprehension.

Multiword Vocabulary

A Find the multiword vocabulary in bold in Reading 2 and use the context to help you figure out the meaning. Then choose the best answer to complete each sentence.

1. When you use **the fact of the matter** (Par. 1), you want to emphasize _____.
   a. the scientific evidence
   b. the most important part of a discussion
2. If someone **is capable of** (Par. 1) doing something, it means that he or she _____.
   a. has the ability to do it
   b. has to do something quickly
3. A **scientific expedition** (Par. 2) is an organized trip that is made _____.
   a. in order to study something in the natural world
   b. for tourists to experience nature
4. The **surface level** (Par. 4) is the _____ of something that reaches a particular height.
   a. lowest layer
   b. top layer
5. You use **in a matter of minutes** (Par. 4) when you want to _____.
   a. emphasize how short a period of time is
   b. describe something that just happened
6. When someone is **well suited** (Par. 4) for a particular job, it means that _____.
   a. he or she is the right person for the job
   b. he or she is dressed appropriately
7. If he **made up his mind** (Par. 7) to do something, it means he _____.
   a. pretended to agree with another person's opinion
   b. decided which of a number of possible things he would do
8. If you do something **for the sake of** (Par. 9) your family, it means that you _____.
   a. are working with family members
   b. are acting in the best interest of your family

B Complete the following sentences with the correct multiword vocabulary in the box below from Exercise A. In some cases, you need to change the verb or noun form or the pronoun.

| capable of | for the sake of | make up his mind | surface level |
| the fact of the matter | in a matter of minutes | scientific expedition | well suited |

1. After Sergio _____ to become a firefighter, he trained for months, took the test, and made the cut!
2. Stephen is _____ for his job as a manager. He's patient, intelligent, and funny.
3. _____, the weather changed from hot and sunny to cold and rainy.
4. The _____ of the river is rising, and people who live along the river are worried about flooding.
5. You might not like hot weather, but if you're moving to Texas, _____ is that summer is very hot there. You'll need air-conditioning!
6. Maureen is an "armchair adventurer." She enjoys reading about _____, but she doesn't like to leave her comfortable house!

48 UNIT TWO *Extreme Jobs*

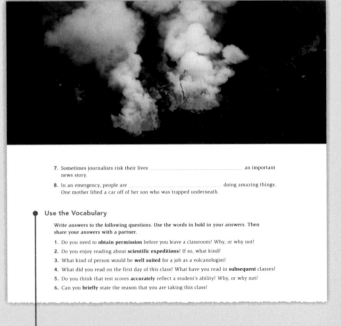

7. Sometimes journalists risk their lives _____ an important news story.
8. In an emergency, people are _____ doing amazing things. One mother lifted a car off of her son who was trapped underneath.

Use the Vocabulary

Write answers to the following questions. Use the words in bold in your answers. Then share your answers with a partner.

1. Do you need to **obtain permission** before you leave a classroom? Why, or why not?
2. Do you enjoy reading about **scientific expeditions**? If so, what kind?
3. What kind of person would be **well suited** for a job as a volcanologist?
4. What did you read on the first day of this class? What have you read in **subsequent** classes?
5. Do you think that test scores **accurately** reflect a student's ability? Why, or why not?
6. Can you **briefly** state the reason that you are taking this class?

In **Use the Vocabulary**, students get to activate the newly-learned vocabulary in new and interesting contexts.

THINK AND DISCUSS

Work in a small group. Use the information in the reading and your own ideas to discuss the following questions.

1. **Analyze purpose.** What do you think was going through Sims's mind when he made the decision to obtain the zero-age sample?

2. **Infer meaning.** Who said the following? When did the speaker say it? Why is it significant?
   Amazing. Incredible. I'll never see anything like this again.

3. **Identify problems and solutions.** How could this mission save lives? What other steps would need to occur after a prediction was made?

Into the Volcano **49**

Think and Discuss questions at the end of each reading require learners to discuss their opinions on the topic while making connections to their own lives.

The **Vocabulary Review** recycles the key vocabulary from the unit and offers meaningful, contextualized practice opportunities.

UNIT REVIEW

Vocabulary Review

A Complete the paragraphs with the vocabulary below that you have studied in the unit.

analyzing the data	simulate the experience
for the sake of	take this into consideration
have no chance	scientific expeditions
is capable of	toxic chemicals
morning routine	a viable option

At 9:45 a.m. each morning on the planet Mars, a rover (a robot the size of a car) asks: *What do I do today?* Bethany Ehlmann, a geologist and National Geographic Emerging Explorer, is one of the scientists in charge of the rover's daily _____1_____ on Mars. Guided by the scientists, the rover _____2_____ traveling around Mars to find rocks. The rocks on Mars can tell us a lot about the early history of our solar system. Less than 1 percent of the rocks on Earth date back to 3.5 billion years ago, but 50 percent of Mars's rocks are from that time period. _____3_____ from the rocks on Mars may help scientists understand Earth's early history as well.

It is not _____4_____ for scientists to test equipment on Mars because they would _____5_____ to make the physical adjustments that might be required by hand. There are no _____6_____ on Mars, but there is also no oxygen. This would affect humans but not a rover. So, _____7_____ equipment testing, Ehlmann leads _____8_____ to areas in Iceland and Hawaii, which have surfaces that are similar to Mars. This makes it possible to _____9_____ of being on Mars. If the equipment does not work, Ehlmann is able to _____10_____ and make changes before the equipment is sent into outer space.

B Compare answers to Exercise A with a partner. Then discuss the following questions.
   Would you be interested in Ehlmann's job? Why, or why not?

C Complete the following sentences in a way that shows that you understand the meaning of the words in bold.

1. During the interview, Ehlmann **briefly discussed** _____

2. One way to **obtain information** about exotic locations is to _____

3. I think **subsequent studies** of the rocks on Mars will show that _____

4. It is **virtually impossible** to climb a mountain in _____

Mars Rover

D Work with a partner and write sentences that include any six of the vocabulary items below. You may use any verb tense and make nouns plural if you wish.

accurately measured	eligible for	make the cut	originally anticipated
convince voters	first-aid	make up your mind	prices fluctuate
delay the inevitable	lighten the load		

Connect the Readings

A How are Sirius patrollers and volcanologists similar? How are they different? Discuss your answers with a partner or in a small group. Then fill in the Venn diagram. Think of at least three items for each circle. Compare diagrams with another group. The first items are done for you.

Sirius Patrollers — *cold*
Volcanologists — *hot*
dangerous

B With a partner or in a small group, compare answers to Exercise A. Then discuss the following questions.

1. Which career would you prefer, Sirius patroller or volcanologist? Explain your answer.

2. What are the personality traits that a patroller needs in order to be successful? Explain your answer.

3. What are the personality traits that a volcanologist needs in order to be successful? Explain your answer.

C Discuss the following questions with a partner. Use your understanding of the readings and your own ideas.

1. Imagine that you have been asked to join a scientific expedition. Where would you go? What would you study?

2. Discuss the following quotes from Reading 1. How could each quote apply to Reading 2? How could each quote apply to other adventure situations? Have you ever been in a situation where you had to keep this in mind? If so, explain.
   Whenever possible, out on the ice, it's best to continue moving.
   You'll be punished if you're not doing everything right.

3. Look back at your answers to the Focus questions on page 28. Have any of your answers changed after reading this unit? Why, or why not?

Connect the Readings sections at the end of each unit practice critical thinking skills as learners are guided to compare, contrast, and synthesize information from the two readings.

SERIES INTRODUCTION

Welcome to National Geographic Learning's new Reading and Vocabulary Focus *series. The series delivers memorable reading experiences, develops essential reading skills, and showcases a wide variety of high-utility vocabulary. The passages take readers to exciting new places where they can apply the skills of successful academic readers. While engaged with the content, readers encounter target vocabulary that is ample, diverse, and presented with a fresh, pragmatic view of what the term vocabulary item truly means.*

Great reading classes depend on top-of-the-line content. That's why we've taken such great care in selecting content for *Reading and Vocabulary Focus*. Through all four levels (high beginning to low advanced), *Reading and Vocabulary Focus* draws from the vast resources of National Geographic. High-interest reading content written by some of the world's most authoritative and thought-provoking reporters and explorers is presented in level-appropriate language and used to build reading skills and to promote vocabulary learning. Skill building is of course important, but not for its own sake. Our goal is always, first and foremost, for students to enjoy working with readings that are truly interesting and worth reading.

A BROADBAND APPROACH TO VOCABULARY

A distinctive feature of *Focus* is its broadband approach to vocabulary. For each reading passage, three groups of vocabulary are called out:

1) 10–12 topic-related vocabulary items to consider in pre-reading activities
2) 6–8 academic words—single word items essential to building an academic vocabulary
3) 6–8 multiword vocabulary items useful in academic reading

A systematic focus on multiword vocabulary sets *Reading and Vocabulary Focus* apart from most reading/vocabulary texts. Increasingly, more and more teachers and many textbooks recognize that some vocabulary items consist of more than one word, especially phrasal/prepositional verbs (*hurry up, take on*) and compound nouns (*glass ceiling, weather station*). However, the amount of effort and text space devoted to expanding students' multiword repertoires is typically minimal and the approach haphazard.

Our thinking in the *Reading and Vocabulary Focus* series has been influenced by numerous researchers who have examined the great importance to native speakers of conventionalized multi-word units, whether those units are called "chunks," "strings," or something else. Schmitt and Carter settle on the term *formulaic sequences* and point out a helpful description by Wray, that formulaic sequences "are stored and retrieved whole from memory at the time of use rather than being subject to generation and analysis at the time of use by the language grammar." (Schmitt & Carter, 2012, 13)[1]

It is not always easy to decide whether a group of words constitutes a unit so tight and useful that it should be taught as a discrete vocabulary item. In our item selection for *Focus*, we applied the criterion of "stored and retrieved whole." An item could make the cut if, in the expert judgment of our authors and editors, it was probably treated cognitively as a whole thing. In this way, we were able to judge that such diverse language as *pay attention to*, *on the whole*, *an invasion of privacy*, and *be the first to admit* are formulaic sequences that learners should study and learn as whole units. We checked our judgment against as many sources as possible, including corpora such as the Bank of English (part of the Collins COBUILD corpus) and the online version of the *Corpus of Contemporary American English* (COCA).[2]

UNIT STRUCTURE

Each unit of *Reading and Vocabulary Focus* begins with a high-impact photograph related to the unit theme to capture the students' imaginations and allow for pre-reading discussion. The unit theme encourages inquiry and exploration and offers opportunities for synthesis of information. Two reading passages, related to each other thematically, form the heart of the unit. Each reading is followed by stages of comprehension work, reading skill practice, formative vocabulary exercises, and discussion. Finally the unit ends with a comprehensive vocabulary review section and critical thinking synthesizing tasks.

Pre-Reading and Reading

For each reading passage, pre-reading activities include a task that activates content schemata and a vocabulary exercise that provides a set of clues to the content that the reader will encounter while reading. Each reading has been chosen for high-interest and conceptual challenge and is presented in the company of some of the world's most stimulating photography and other graphics.

Comprehension and Vocabulary Development

Comprehension exercises after each reading start out with a focus on main ideas ("Big Picture") and move to details ("Close-Up"). Then a concise treatment of a high-utility reading skill leads into practice of the skill applied to the reading passage. The vocabulary section after each reading proceeds from the broadband approach mentioned earlier. First come exercises in recognizing

---

[1] Norbert Schmitt and Ronald Carter, Introduction to Formulaic Sequences: Acquisition, Processing, and Use, in Norbert Schmitt, ed. (2004), *Formulaic Sequences: Acquisition, Processing, and Use*, John Benjamins.

[2] At corpus.byu.edu/coca/

academic words and placing them in context. Many of the items in this section are from the Academic Word List (AWL); whether from the AWL or not, every "academic word" is important in academic discourse. Then comes a section of multiword vocabulary, focusing on formulaic sequences as described earlier in this introduction.

Discussion

After studying the vocabulary, students are prompted to use it in discussion activities. Finally, Think and Discuss questions at the end of each reading prompt learners to discuss their opinions on the topic of the reading while making connections to their own lives.

Unit Review

The *Unit Review* consists of two parts: Vocabulary Review and Connect the Readings. The first section of the vocabulary review draws together vocabulary of all types into a richly contextualized exercise. Learners then encounter and practice the vocabulary from the unit, strengthening semantic networks and integrating a wide variety of items into their repertoires. The second section of the unit review, Connect the Readings, takes students' critical-thinking skills to a very high level as they analyze both readings and discover similarities/differences, agreement/disagreement, and other concept relationships.

Reading and Vocabulary Focus has been conceived to respect the wide-ranging curiosity and critical-thinking power of contemporary students. Every day these readers encounter a flood of information. They face unprecedented demands to sort the significant from the trivial and to synthesize information. We are delighted to help them do this by offering great readings, engaging skills development, and top-tier vocabulary learning all in an inviting, visually striking form.

Lawrence J. Zwier
Series Consultant

FOCUS

1. What are some pros and cons of living in a city?

2. Do you think it is important for cities to have public spaces for people to enjoy?

3. What types of public spaces do you enjoy visiting?

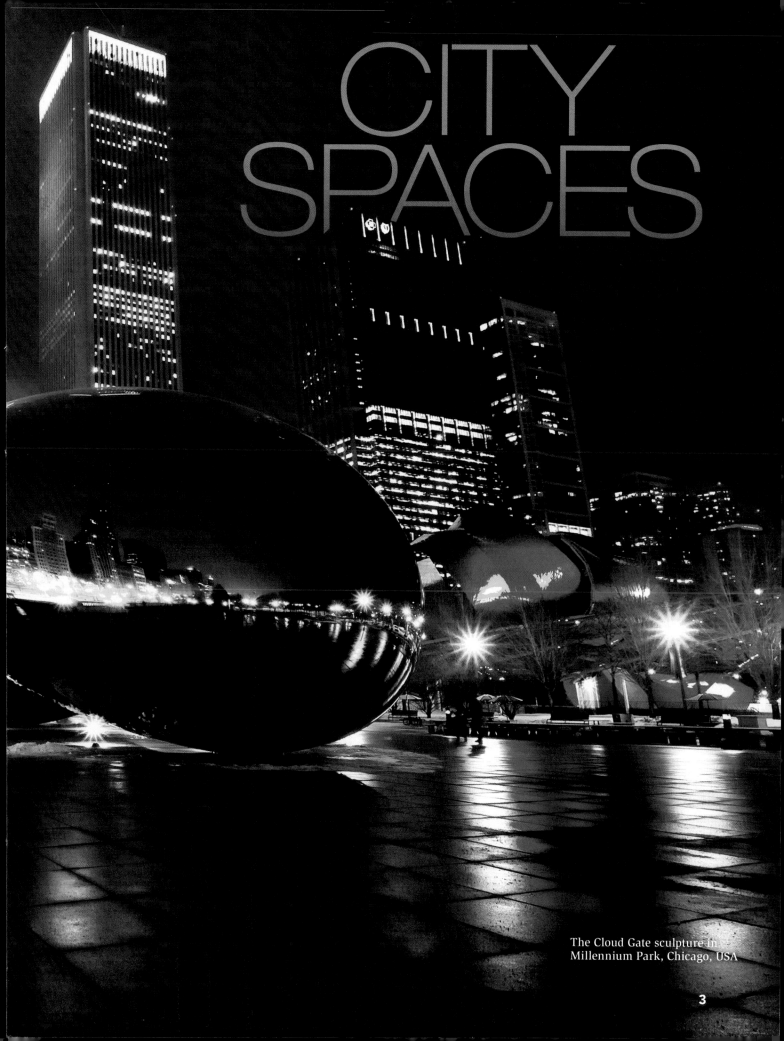

CITY SPACES

The Cloud Gate sculpture in
Millennium Park, Chicago, USA

Looking down on Manhattan skyscrapers, New York, USA

Academic Vocabulary

abandoned	to generate	persistence
annual	innovative	a transformation
to cease	to integrate	

Multiword Vocabulary

a charity event	a price tag
to come up with	to realize one's full potential
in a sense	to submit a proposal
precisely the opposite	surrounded by

Reading Preview

A **Preview.** Read the title of Reading 1. Look at the photos on pages 6–8 and read their captions. Then discuss the following questions with a partner or in a small group.

1. What do you think used to be where the High Line park is now?

2. Why is this park so unusual?

3. Why do you think this reading is called "Above Manhattan"?

B **Topic vocabulary.** The following words appear in Reading 1. Look at the words and answer the questions with a partner.

architect	residents
community	steel
elevated structure	tourists
grasses	tracks
officials	weeds
rails	wildflowers

1. Which words refer to people or groups of people?

2. Which words could be connected to trains?

3. Which words are types of plants?

C **Predict.** What do you think this reading will be about? Discuss each word in Exercise B and predict how it may relate to the reading.

Can cities be more than just "concrete jungles" of high-rise buildings? Discover how one group of community activists turned an old railway line into a place filled with natural beauty.

4 UNIT ONE *City Spaces*

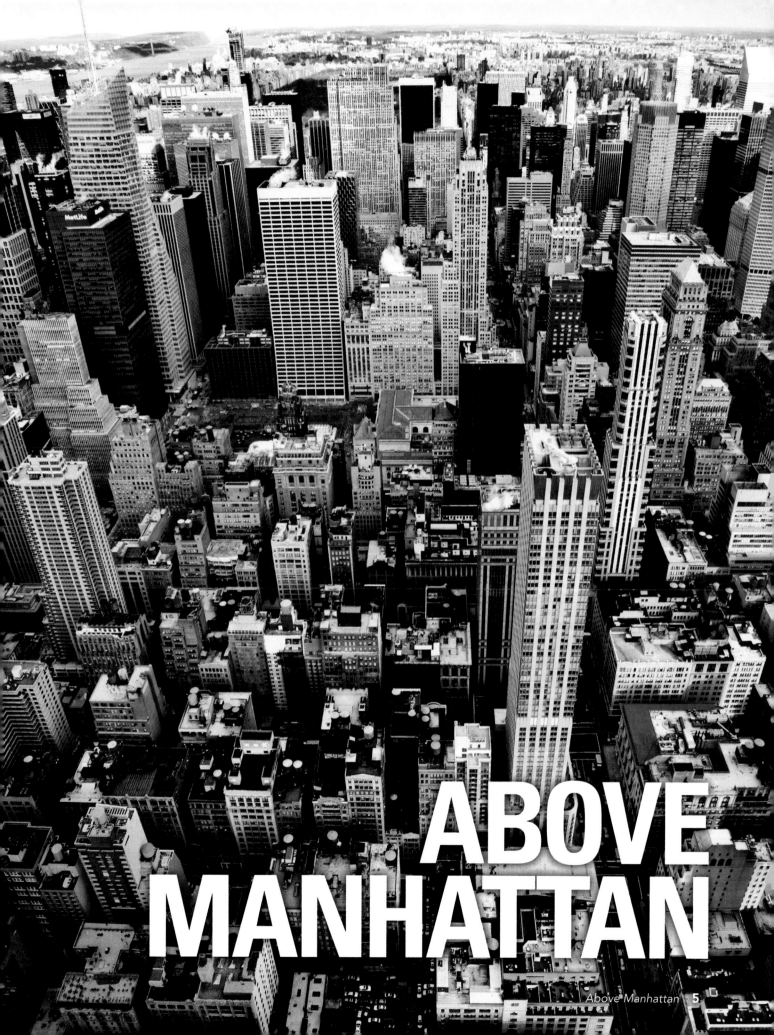

ABOVE
MANHATTAN

From a distance, the High Line in the Chelsea neighborhood of Manhattan does not look like a city park. In fact, it looks like precisely the opposite. The heavy, black elevated structure supports a railroad line that once brought supplies directly into factories and warehouses. However, moving closer, its true nature is revealed: It's an urban oasis,[1] high above the city. The High Line's transformation from a railroad line to a city park is a story of vision and persistence.

---

[1] *oasis:* a pleasant place or area that is surrounded by unpleasant ones

People stroll along the High Line on a sunny day in May.

Night view seen from below the High Line at its starting point

The railroad line, which opened in 1934, was 2 rarely used. Its final train traveled down the track in 1980. Then, in 1984, a rail enthusiast named Peter Obletz bought the abandoned structure for 10 dollars from the railroad company. Obletz died in 1996, but he is, in a sense, the "father" of the High Line. Photographer Joel Sternfeld also played an important role. As the railroad line stood unused, his striking images of the High Line as a ribbon of green showed that it really could look like a park.

In the 1990s, however, many of the residents 3 in the surrounding neighborhood couldn't wait to tear the rails down. Chelsea was becoming gentrified.[2] The area was becoming transformed into a neighborhood of art galleries, restaurants, and expensive apartments, and many residents felt that the High Line was an ugly reminder of Chelsea's industrial past. They argued that the abandoned railroad line was preventing the neighborhood from realizing its full potential as an upscale neighborhood.

Joshua David, a freelance writer, and Robert 4 Hammond, an artist, both lived close to the High Line. They met for the first time in 1999 at a community meeting to discuss the future of the railroad line. "I was in love with the steel structure, the rivets,[3] the ruin . . . ," Hammond said, "Josh was sitting next to me. We were the

---

[2] *gentrified:* to be changed from a poor neighborhood to one with housing and stores for wealthier people

[3] *rivets:* short metal pins used to hold two plates of metal together

only people at the meeting who were interested in saving it."

David and Hammond asked officials to take them to look at the High Line. "When we got up there," Hammond said, "we saw a mile and a half of wildflowers in the middle of Manhattan." David added, "New Yorkers always dream of finding open space—it's a fantasy when you live in a studio apartment." 5

Amazed by the elevated space, the two men were determined to keep the High Line from being destroyed. In the fall of 1999, they formed an organization called Friends of the High Line. 6

At first, their ambitions were modest. Their goal was to stop the High Line from being torn down. Then they began to realize that they could utilize the elevated area by transforming it into a new public space. After the attack on the World Trade Center in 2001, they thought that no one would care about the High Line project. However, this was not the case. As Hammond explains, "People felt this was one positive thing they could do."

In 2003, the group decided to hold an "ideas competition." They invited anyone to submit a proposal for what the High Line might become. They expected a few dozen ideas from New 7

High Line Public Park, Manhattan, New York

Yorkers. Instead, they received 720 entries from 36 countries. The winning designers were landscape architect James Corner and the architecture firm of Diller Scofidio + Renfro. They had designed a space that was part promenade,[4] part town square, and part botanical garden. Their design kept many of the original rails, which were cleverly integrated into the landscape, and they added plentiful seating areas. Tall grasses and reeds resembled the wildflowers and weeds that had sprung up during the years of the High Line's abandonment.

With the support of the new mayor of New York City, the project was approved. The price tag was just over $150 million. City and federal funds would cover about $130 million, but Friends of the High Line had to come up with approximately $20 million. They also had to agree to pay for the majority of the operating costs once the park was open. Celebrities also took up the cause and generated support. The Friends of the High Line's annual summer benefit party became one of New York's most popular charity events and one of the few with many supporters under age 40. By the spring of 2006, the funds were in place, and the first piece of rail was removed. Construction began.

More than two decades after the last train traveled down the line, the High Line is now one of the most innovative and inviting public spaces in all of New York City. From the day it opened in June 2009, it has been one of the city's major tourist attractions. It is unlike any other experience in the city. The black steel columns allow you to float 25 feet above the ground; without streets to cross or traffic lights to wait for, you can walk ten blocks[5] as quickly as two down below. You can sit surrounded by nature and take in the sun and the Hudson River views, or you can walk the line between old buildings and past striking new ones.

The High Line is visited by tourists from all over the world, and it is almost as common to hear German or Japanese spoken there as it is to hear English. Yet it is just as much a neighborhood park for the residents of Chelsea. This is a park that never ceases to amaze or delight. It represents one of those wonderful times when a creative solution has been even more successful than anyone had imagined.

---

[4] *promenade:* an area that is used for walking

[5] *block:* an area of land with streets on all its sides

READING COMPREHENSION

Big Picture

Ⓐ Choose the best answer for each of the following questions.

1. What is the main idea of Reading 1?
   a. Thanks to the vision of everyday citizens, a New York community was able to create a unique park.
   b. New York's High Line is one of the largest parks in the world.

2. What is the main idea of paragraph 3?
   a. Many people felt that the rail should be demolished because it was falling down.
   b. Many people felt that the rail should be demolished so that richer people would move to the area.

3. What is the main idea of paragraph 7?
   a. The group received 720 entries from 36 countries.
   b. The design of the park helps to tell the story of the High Line.

4. What would the best heading for paragraph 8 be?
   a. A New Mayor
   b. Money Talks

5. What is the purpose of paragraph 9?
   a. To describe the experience of walking on the High Line
   b. To explain the reason why the High Line was built

B Answer the following questions in your own words. Then discuss your answers with a partner or in a small group.

1. How would you describe the High Line?

2. How did it become a city park?

3. What do you think is the most interesting part of this reading? Explain your answer.

Close-Up

A Decide which of the following statements are true or false according to the reading. Write *T* (True) or *F* (False) next to each one.

_____ 1. The railroad line carried supplies to factories for 46 years.

_____ 2. Before the 1990s, many wealthy people lived in Chelsea.

_____ 3. At the community meeting in 1999, most people wanted to tear down the rails.

_____ 4. After September 11, 2001, there was less interest in the High Line project.

_____ 5. Hammond and David expected a lot of people to submit proposals for the competition.

_____ 6. The city of New York agreed to pay all of the operating costs of the park.

_____ 7. Many people under the age of 40 support the Friends of the High Line.

_____ 8. Tourists like to spend time relaxing on the High Line, but the locals only use it as a fast way to travel.

B Work with a partner or in a small group. Change the false statements in Exercise A to make them true.

Reading Skill

Determining Chronology

When a reading has time references, it is important to determine the chronology of the events, that is, the order of when things happened. One useful technique is to create a time line of the information. A time line maps out the events in the order of when they happened rather than in the order of when they are mentioned in the reading. When all of the information is in one place, it can help you better understand a text, study for a test, and use the information in a paper or presentation.

When you create your time line, you don't need to write complete sentences. Use your own words and write just enough to be able to understand the information later. The time line should have the events written from left to right in the order they occurred.

A Look back at Reading 1, and circle any dates you find in the text.

B Fill in the time line below, using five of the important dates you circled in Exercise A. Write the dates and brief notes about what happened on the blank lines. Then compare time lines with a partner.

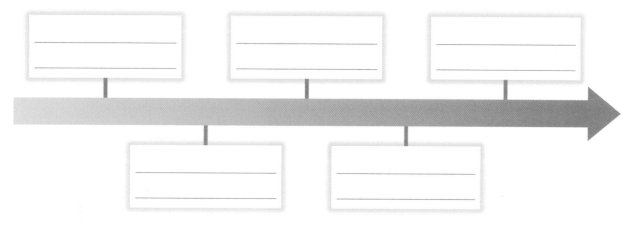

C Work with a new partner. Retell the story using the information in your time line.

VOCABULARY PRACTICE

Academic Vocabulary

A Find the words in bold in Reading 1. Use the paragraph numbers to help you. Then use the context to help you match each word to the correct definition.

_____ **1. transformation** (Par. 1)   **a.** new or improved

_____ **2. persistence** (Par. 1)   **b.** empty; deserted

_____ **3. abandoned** (Par. 2)   **c.** produced; created

_____ **4. integrated** (Par. 7)   **d.** continued action, even when difficult

_____ **5. generated** (Par. 8)   **e.** change from one appearance to another

_____ **6. annual** (Par. 8)   **f.** stops an action

_____ **7. innovative** (Par. 9)   **g.** combined two or more things so that they become a whole

_____ **8. ceases** (Par. 10)   **h.** occurring every year

B Choose the correct academic words from Exercise A to complete the following paragraph. Notice and learn the words in bold because they often appear with the academic words.

The city where I live has gone through **a period of** _____1_____ over the past few years. More people are moving to the area, and it has become a tourist destination. Twenty years ago, there were many _____2_____ **buildings** around the center of the city. Now these are home to some of the city's finest restaurants and stores. My community has worked hard despite many obstacles to make our city a success, and our _____3_____ **has paid off**. We have _____4_____ **interest** in the city by promoting tourism through advertisements. We have developed a variety of new, _____5_____ **approaches** to promote tourism such as encouraging companies from around the country to hold their _____6_____ **meetings** in the city every year. Artists _____7_____ **information about** our city's rich history into one large mural, and there is a now a festival celebrating the city's history every August. The city's largest employer, a shoe factory, _____8_____ **operations** during the festival so that the employees are free to enjoy the celebrations.

Multiword Vocabulary

A Find the words in bold in Reading 1. Use the paragraph numbers to help you. Then use the context to help you figure out the meaning, and match the sentence parts to complete each definition.

_____ **1.** When someone says that **precisely the opposite** (Par. 1) occurred, they mean

_____ **2.** We use **in a sense** (Par. 2) when we want to show that

_____ **3.** When something is **realizing** its **full potential** (Par. 3), it is

_____ **4.** When people **submit a proposal** (Par. 7), they

_____ **5.** A **price tag** (Par. 8) is

_____ **6.** When people **come up with** (Par. 8) something, it means they are able to

_____ **7.** **Charity events** (Par. 8) are

_____ **8.** When a person or place is **surrounded by** (Par. 9) something, it means

a. parties or other occasions that raise money for an organization that helps others.

b. successful because it is doing everything that it is capable of doing.

c. something is true in one way.

d. that thing is all around the person or place.

e. the amount you must pay for something.

f. give a formal explanation for approval of a possible future project.

g. it was completely different from what was expected.

h. find money or an idea for a specific purpose.

B Complete the following sentences with the correct multiword vocabulary from Exercise A. In some cases, you need to change the verb or noun form or change a pronoun.

1. The teacher motivates her students because she wants them to

_____.

2. Islands are _____ water.

3. Before you buy that new pair of jeans, check the _____. They look expensive!

4. Being a student isn't easy. It is, _____, a full-time job.

5. At the National Geographic Society, scientists can _____ for scientific expeditions.

6. When her boss asked her to meet with him, Maureen was worried that she might lose her job. However, _____ occurred—he gave her a promotion.

7. Last week, we went to a(n) _____ that was raising money for a new city park.

8. For some students, it can be hard to _____ the money to pay for college tuition.

Use the Vocabulary

Write answers to the following questions. Use the words in bold in your answers. Then share your answers with a partner.

1. What do you think is a good way for a teacher to **generate** interest in a subject?

2. What do you need to do in order to **realize your full potential** in school or in your job?

3. Would you prefer living in an area **surrounded by** water, trees, or buildings? Explain your answer.

4. How have you changed in the last 10 years? Describe your **transformation** into the person you are today.

5. If you organized a **charity event**, what charity would you raise money for? Explain your answer.

6. What are three items that often have large **price tags** attached to them?

7. What is an example of a time in your life when **persistence** has paid off?

8. Who is a person who never **ceases** to amaze you? What makes this person special?

THINK AND DISCUSS

Work in a small group. Use the information in the reading and your own ideas to discuss the following questions.

1. Use prior knowledge. Why did many New Yorkers want to tear down the High Line? What often changes when a place becomes gentrified? Explain your answers.

2. Infer meaning. Who said the following? What did the speaker mean? Why do you think this is true?

> New Yorkers always dream of finding open space—it's a fantasy when you live in a studio apartment.

3. Analyze. Why do you think so many young people support the High Line? Explain your answer.

4. Express an opinion. If you visited New York City, would the High Line be one of the sights that you would like to visit? Why, or why not?

Academic Vocabulary

to accompany	an inspector	specified
to commission	isolated	to stabilize
to evade	a network	

Multiword Vocabulary

as a consequence	of sorts
to come into contact with	to serve a purpose
in secret	to solve a mystery
in the open air	to spread out

Reading Preview

Ⓐ **Preview.** Scan Reading 2 to find answers to the following questions. Then discuss the answers with a partner or in a small group.

1. Who are *cataphiles*?

2. What are *catacombs*?

3. Where does the author go at six in the evening?

Ⓑ **Topic vocabulary.** The following words appear in Reading 2. Look at the words and answer the questions with a partner.

archaeologist	explore	police
art	flashlights	sewer worker
bones	mine	tour guide
cheesemaker	paint	tunnels

1. Which words are professions?

2. Which words name things that might be found under Paris?

3. Which words express what people might do underground?

Ⓒ **Predict.** What do you think this reading will be about? Discuss each word in Exercise B and predict how it may relate to the reading.

Under Paris

5:00 a.m.—My Day Begins

Early Saturday morning, the avenues are quiet; the shops are closed. As I pass a bakery, the smell of fresh bread fills the air. Suddenly, a man emerges from a manhole, with a lamp on his head, followed by a young woman. The man pushes the iron cover back over the hole, and they run grinning down the street. They must be *cataphiles*, people who love the Paris underground and who spend time below ground in secret. I watch them with interest because I am here in Paris to learn more about the world beneath this magnificent city.

"Paris has a deeper and stranger connection to its underground than almost any other city."

8:00 a.m.—A Café and a History Book

I find a small café, order a cappuccino, and open up a history book. Paris has a deeper and stranger connection to its underground than almost any other city. Hundreds of miles of tunnels make up some of the oldest subway and sewer networks in the world. Under Paris are spaces of all kinds: canals and reservoirs, crypts[1] and bank vaults, nightclubs and art galleries. How did this all begin?

Modern Paris sits above limestone and gypsum.[2] Over 2,000 years ago, the Romans were the first to mine these stones, leaving behind large holes in the ground and tunnels where the stones had been removed. In the beginning, these tunnels lay beyond the city limits, but as Paris grew, it spread out above them. In December 1774, a tunnel collapsed, swallowing houses and people. More holes opened up over the next few years, and King Louis XVI commissioned an architect named Charles Axel Guillaumot to explore, map, and stabilize the tunnels. Guillaumot's inspectors dug more tunnels to connect isolated networks. Then, when the king closed one of the city's cemeteries, Guillaumot was asked to find a place for bones. He decided

1

2

3

that Paris's underground networks could serve an additional purpose. Thus, some of the tunnels became *catacombs*, or underground cemeteries.

As late as the 19th century, the tunnels continued to be mined for stones. At one point, farmers raised mushrooms in them, sometimes producing hundreds of tons a year. During World War II, the French Resistance[3] hid in some of the tunnels. At the same time, the German occupiers built bunkers[4] in others. Today, only a few specified areas can be entered legally. Archaeologists are allowed underground to study Paris's past, tour guides can lead tourists through this hidden part of Paris, and sewer workers are able to search for water leaks. Cataphiles, on the other hand, have to evade the police as they explore under the city.

4

11:00 a.m.—Exploring with Cataphiles

I have been told that cataphiles make some of the best guides to the world under Paris. Two guides, young men in blue coveralls, wait for me on a park bench. They have agreed to accompany me underground. Dominique is a repairman. Yopie (who will only give his cataphile nickname) is a computer graphics designer and father of two. We spend several hours wandering through crypts and galleries of bright murals.[5] I ask Yopie what draws him underground. "No boss, no master," he tells me. As a consequence, many people come to the catacombs to party or to paint. Yopie continues, "Some people [come] to destroy or to create or to explore. We do what we want here. We don't have rules. At the surface . . ." He smiles. "We say, 'To be happy, stay hidden.'"

5

Yopie explains that cataphiles have been exploring the catacombs for decades. In 1955, it became illegal to go underground without a

6

---

[1] *crypts:* underground rooms, usually under a church or cathedral, that are used for burying people

[2] *limestone and gypsum:* two types of stone that are often used as building materials

[3] *The French Resistance:* French civilians who opposed the Nazi German army occupying France during World War II

[4] *bunkers:* places, usually underground, with strong walls to protect them against heavy gunfire and bombing

[5] *murals:* pictures painted on walls

Cataphiles gather in a quarry tunnel under Paris for a party.

permit. However, cataphiles discovered that they could simply walk in through forgotten doors in school basements. They could then move through tunnels to places only they knew about. Throughout the 1970s and 1980s, the cataphiles had parties, gave performances, and created art. By the end of the 1980s, however, the city and private property owners had shut most of the entrances and police began patrolling the tunnels. Despite the increase of police presence, many cataphiles continued their adventures below the city. Decades later, my guides tell me, cataphiles still forge friendships underground.

Some even meet their future husbands and wives in the tunnels, trading phone numbers by flashlight. I think back to the man and woman I saw early this morning and wonder about their story.

3:00 p.m.—A Cheesemaker and Many More

After lunch, I explore the catacombs legally. On a typical day, the walls would echo with the voices and uneasy laughter of tourists. But today the place is closed. I am here with Philippe Charlier, an archaeologist and forensic pathologist at the University of Paris. Charlier is a detective of sorts, solving mysteries of the past. This is

LES MISÉRABLES

While most of us have never actually been under Paris, audiences around the world caught a glimpse of the famous Paris underground sewers in the 2013 movie, *Les Misérables*. The award-winning movie was a huge success and is based on the French novel of the same name. Written by Victor Hugo and published in 1862, the novel tells the story of people living in poverty in 19th century Paris. The main character, Jean Valjean, is an ex-convict who saves a little girl after her mother dies. At one point in the story, Valjean evades the chief of police by going into the sewers. Hugo writes, "In the very heart of the city, Jean Valjean had escaped from the city . . ." Looking at the world under Paris, it is easy to see how this is possible.

Jean Valjean played by Hugh Jackman in the 2013 movie

Figure 1.
Paris's Underground History

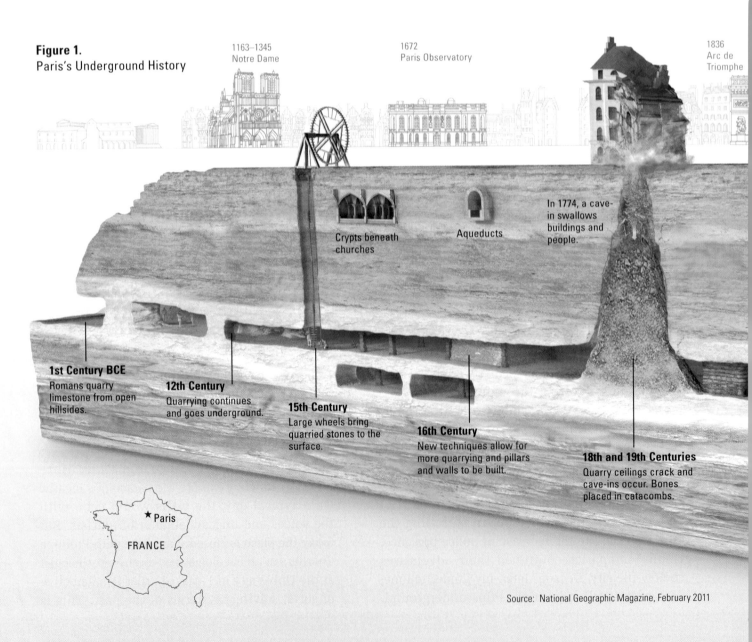

1163–1345
Notre Dame

1672
Paris Observatory

1836
Arc de Triomphe

Crypts beneath churches

Aqueducts

In 1774, a cave-in swallows buildings and people.

1st Century BCE
Romans quarry limestone from open hillsides.

12th Century
Quarrying continues and goes underground.

15th Century
Large wheels bring quarried stones to the surface.

16th Century
New techniques allow for more quarrying and pillars and walls to be built.

18th and 19th Centuries
Quarry ceilings crack and cave-ins occur. Bones placed in catacombs.

★ Paris

FRANCE

Source: National Geographic Magazine, February 2011

what forensic pathologists do; they study bones in order to gain a better understanding of diseases and causes of death. As we look around, the air smells of mold[6] and damp earth. It may be dark, but Charlier insists that from down here, he can see how people once lived.

The remains of some six million Parisians 8 rest down here. All are anonymous. However, Charlier explains that he is able to learn their stories from their bones—the diseases and accidents they suffered, the wounds that healed or did not, the food they ate. "Ah!" Charlier says, looking at a vertebra.[7] "Malta fever!" He explains that Malta fever is caused by people coming into contact with diseased animals or their secretions, such as milk. "This person was maybe a cheesemaker," Charlier says. We stand surrounded by bones in a kind of library; 10 thousand more stories like the cheesemaker's lie within view.

6:00 p.m.—Diamonds in the Sewers

After exploring the catacombs with Charlier, 9 my final trip underground is to the Parisian sewers. In *Les Misérables*, Victor Hugo called the

---

[6] *mold:* a soft, gray, green, or blue substance that sometimes forms on damp walls or old food

[7] *vertebra:* one of the small bones that form the spine, or backbone, of a human or animal

1889
Eiffel Tower

1900
Grand Palais

1989
Grande Arche de la Défense

— 0 meters

Gas, telephone, electrical lines

Parking garage

— 5

After two cholera epidemics, the sewer system is improved.

The early Metro lines run close to the surface.

Regional Express trains link the suburbs to the Metro system.

Water lines

— 10

— 15

— 20

World War II bunkers

— 25

Inspection tunnels

— 30

19th Century
Bones are re-arranged neatly in the catacombs.

20th Century
The Paris subway opens in 1900 and grows in size throughout the century.

Late 20th Century
Automated Meteor trains extend subway system deep underground.

— 35

Paris sewers the "conscience of the city," because from them, all humans look equal. In a small van, sewer workers tell me about the pockets of explosive gas, the diseases, and stories of enormous rats. They put on white bodysuits, white gloves, and white helmets. Wearing so much white in the sewers seems unwise.

Pascal Quignon is a 20-year veteran of the 10 sewers whose father and grandfather worked here before him. He says he only notices the smell when he comes back from vacation. I follow Quignon underground as he shines a flashlight to find leaking pipes. Sewer workers say they have found jewelry, wallets, and guns. Once Quignon found a diamond. I find no treasure today. Instead, I watch as water pours over my feet from one of the pipes.

9:00 p.m.—Above Ground, But for How Long?

After my adventures underground, I walk in 11 the open air. However, I haven't gone far before I notice a manhole. It must lead to a tunnel. The tunnel may follow the street or move in a different direction. My mind moves along that passage, imagining its path and its many branches. Cataphiles tell me this sort of thing is perfectly normal when you return to the surface. You picture the cool, quiet freedom of the underground with all its possibilities.

READING COMPREHENSION

Big Picture

A Choose the best answer for each of the following questions.

1. Where can you find the main idea of Reading 2?
   a. Paragraph 1, sentence 2
   b. Paragraph 2, sentence 2
   c. Paragraph 3, sentence 2
   d. Paragraph 4, sentence 2

2. Paragraph 2 asks the following question: *How did this all begin?* What does "this" refer to?
   a. Paris's connection to the underground
   b. Tunnels for subways and sewers
   c. Underground spaces such as canals and crypts
   d. All of the above

3. What is the purpose of paragraph 3?
   a. To explain what the catacombs are
   b. To describe why Paris has catacombs
   c. To introduce King Louis XVI
   d. To describe the work of Charles Axel Guillaumot

4. Which sentence contains the main idea of paragraph 8?
   a. The first
   b. The second
   c. The third
   d. The fifth

5. In paragraph 11, what does the author want to illustrate?
   a. He is back above ground.
   b. He has fallen under the spell of the underground.
   c. He wants to include maps of the tunnels in his article.
   d. All of the above

B Using information from Reading 2 and from the short extra reading, *"Les Misérables,"* on page 18, write a brief sentence about each of the following people.

1. Yopie _____ .

2. Philippe Charlier _____ .

3. Pascal Quignon _____ .

4. Jean Valjean _____ .

Close-Up

A Scan Reading 2 and *"Les Misérables"* to find answers to the following questions.

1. Why did Guillaumot's team build more tunnels?

2. Why are there so many bones in the catacombs?

3. Have the catacombs always been strictly patrolled?

4. How can tourists visit the catacombs legally?

5. Why does Jean Valjean go into the sewers?

B Complete the following sentences with your own ideas. Then discuss your answers with a partner.

1. "Yopie" doesn't want the author to use his real name because _____ .

2. When the author describes a "library" of bones, he means that _____ .

3. The author thinks the sewer workers' white outfits are unwise because _____ .

4. Pascal Quignon doesn't usually notice the smell because _____ .

Reading Skill

Annotating a Text

Successful readers often *annotate*, or take notes, to remind themselves where they can find important information in a text. One benefit of annotating a text is that you don't have to reread the text from beginning to end when you have specific questions. Your annotations will signal where the answers are. Annotating can also help you stay focused. If you aim to write notes next to each paragraph, you will need to read the text carefully.

Here are some guidelines for annotating:

- Don't copy an entire sentence from the text. Instead, write key words next to each paragraph, or on paper next to the words. Key words are important words that will help you remember the information later. For example, for the first paragraph in Reading 2, you could write: *P1: Paris early morning*.

- Using symbols in the margin can be helpful. For example, writing a question mark (?) can remind you that you need to ask the teacher because you don't understand something. Writing an asterisk (*) can signify that this is an important idea in the text and that you will need to read that paragraph again. For example: *P2 ?? (How is everything under the city?)* or *P3 ** (good explanation)*.

A Read the following key words from Reading 2. Match them to the correct paragraphs in the reading. Write the paragraph numbers on the lines.

_____ **1.** Cataphiles: surface rules vs. underground

_____ **2.** Description of underground

_____ **3.** Cheesemaker

_____ **4.** History of catacombs

_____ **5.** Parisian sewers

_____ **6.** Quignon—diamond!

_____ **7.** Who uses tunnels?

_____ **8.** Forensic pathology

B Discuss the following questions with a partner.

1. Do you think the key words in Exercise A are useful annotations, or would you use different key words instead?

2. Are there any places in the reading in which you would write a question mark (?)?

3. Are there any places in the reading in which you would write an asterisk (*)?

VOCABULARY PRACTICE

Academic Vocabulary

A Find the words in bold in Reading 2. Use the paragraph numbers to help you. Then use the context and the sentences below to help you choose the correct definition.

1. When lightning hit the building, all of the communications **networks** (Par. 2) in the neighborhood went down for an hour, so no one could do any work.
  a. jobs in the computer industry that are related to communication
  b. systems of connected travel routes or communication lines

2. The city **commissioned** (Par. 3) a number of artists to paint murals in the subway stations.
  a. arrested someone for doing something illegal
  b. ordered or requested someone to make or do something

3. After the revolution, the new leaders worked hard to **stabilize** (Par. 3) the government.
  a. make something safe and secure
  b. use strength to make a new government

4. After construction was completed, the building **inspectors** (Par. 3) made sure that the building was safe.
  a. people whose job it is to find out whether other people are obeying official regulations
  b. people whose job it is to create the plan for what a building will look like

5. There have been a number of robberies over the last few days, but the police believe they are **isolated** (Par. 3) incidents; they do not think the same thieves are responsible for all of the robberies.
  a. separate
  b. dangerous

6. During construction, please walk only in the **specified** (Par. 4) areas. This is for your own protection.
  a. special for tourists
  b. clearly stated

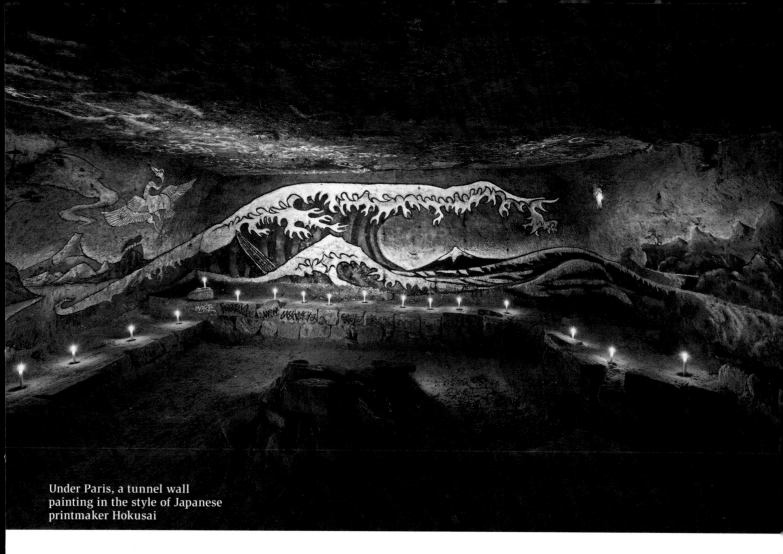

Under Paris, a tunnel wall painting in the style of Japanese printmaker Hokusai

7. The bank robbers ran through a railroad tunnel in order to **evade** (Par. 4) the police.

   a. avoid   **b.** hide

8. The writer's wife agreed to **accompany** (Par. 5) him on his trip to Paris, but she did not want to visit the catacombs.

   a. plan something in advance   **b.** go somewhere with someone else

B Choose an academic word from Exercise A that can go on both lines to make frequently used combinations of words. The first one is done for you.

1. a(n) _____*isolated*_____ incident   a(n) _____*isolated*_____ area

2. health _____   weapons _____

3. _____ responsibility   _____ the questions

4. _____ the situation   _____ the economy

5. a(n) _____ amount   a(n) _____ date

6. _____ a study   _____ a painting

7. extensive _____   social _____

8. _____ the president   _____ me

C Choose the best phrase from Exercise B to complete each of the following sentences.

1. Security officers _____ wherever he or she goes. Whether it is to important meetings or fast food restaurants, safety is always an issue.

2. When reporters try to interview people about scandals, the people often _____ and walk away.

3. If you go hiking in _____ , be sure to tell someone before you leave and bring supplies with you. You might not see anyone on your trip.

4. When people began fighting in the streets, peacekeepers came in to try to _____ as much as possible.

5. The letter ordered Chris to pay the bill by _____ or he would have to pay a fine.

6. Central Park in New York City has _____ of walking paths so that visitors can experience nature, even in the middle of the city.

7. The city council _____ to find out the best ways to attract tourists.

8. When _____ visit a restaurant, they make sure that the food is prepared and served in a clean and safe way.

Multiword Vocabulary

A Find the words in bold in Reading 2. Use the paragraph numbers to help you. Then write the words that come before and/or after them to complete the multiword vocabulary.

1. _____ **secret** (Par. 1)

2. **spread** _____ (Par. 3)

3. **serve** an additional _____ (Par. 3)

4. _____ _____ **consequence** (Par. 5)

5. _____ **sorts** (Par. 7)

6. _____ **mysteries** (Par. 7)

7. **coming into** _____ **with** (Par. 8)

8. _____ _____ **open air** (Par. 11)

B Complete the following sentences with the correct multiword vocabulary from Exercise A. Use the information in parentheses and the context from Reading 2 to help you. In some cases, you need to change the verb or noun form or the article.

1. It is harmful to _____ (touch) certain chemicals.

2. If you have been inside for too long, it's a good idea to take a walk _____ (outside).

3. Maria missed classes for two weeks and, _____ (because of this), she wasn't prepared for the quiz today.

4. Who has been looking through my desk drawer? I am determined to

_____ (find the answer).

5. The party turned into a concert _____ (or something similar) when three different musicians agreed to perform.

6. As more and more people moved to the area, the city _____ (grew and covered more space), and farmland disappeared.

7. The students planned the party for their teacher, but they did it

_____ (without telling her). She was very surprised!

8. The music was loud, but it _____ (was actually helpful)—it made it harder to hear the noise of the construction project next door.

Use the Vocabulary

Complete the following sentences with your own ideas. Then share your answers with a partner.

1. If a table is uneven, one way to **stabilize** it is to _____ .

2. It isn't a good idea to **come into contact with** _____ .

3. The most **isolated area** that I have ever been to is _____ .

4. In today's world, families are often **spread out** over _____ .

5. Today people often communicate using **social networks** such as _____ .

6. If children want to _____ , an adult needs to **accompany** them.

7. Many students stay up late the night before a test. **As a consequence**, they may be

_____ .

8. If someone asks you a question you don't want to answer, one way to **evade** the question is to

_____ .

THINK AND DISCUSS

Work in a small group. Use the information in the reading and your own ideas to discuss the following questions.

1. Summarize. Imagine you are speaking to a friend who has not read "Under Paris." Explain how the catacombs came into existence.

2. Infer meaning. Who said the following? What did the speakers mean?

We say, "To be happy, stay hidden."

The Paris sewers [are] the "conscience of the city," because from them, all humans look equal.

This person was maybe a cheesemaker.

3. Express an opinion. Do you think cataphiles would be as interested in going underground if it were legal? Why, or why not?

4. Relate to personal experience. Have you ever been underground? If so, what was it like? If not, would you like to go? Why, or why not?

Vocabulary Review

A Complete the paragraphs with the vocabulary below that you have studied in the unit.

as a consequence	in a sense
came up with	in the open air
ceased operations	innovative approach
extensive network	precisely the opposite
generate interest	price tag

Underground exhibit to promote the Low Line on New York's Lower East Side

The success of the High Line on the West Side of New York City has some New Yorkers hoping that they can _____ 1 among the public in an equivalent park on the Lower East Side. This time, there's a new twist—it's underground. Two of the key figures in this project, Dan Barasch and James Ramsey, _____ 2 a plan for an abandoned trolley terminal, which _____ 3 in 1948. They want to transform this into an underground park. This park has similarities to the High Line project, and _____ 4 , has been nicknamed the "Low Line."

This city park may sound like a dark place without any plants at all. However, Barasch and Ramsey say that _____ 5 will occur. Thanks to new technology, the Low Line will be bright, with natural sunlight and vegetation. Although visitors will be underground, _____ 6 , it will feel as if visitors are still outside _____ 7 . Ramsey, an architect and former NASA engineer, has proposed a plan, which would use solar technology underground. This exciting, _____ 8 would allow natural light to travel downward, through an _____ 9 of fiber optic cables, to provide sunlight for the trees and plants underground. A plan like this has an enormous _____ 10 , but Barasch and Ramsey hope that New Yorkers will decide that it is worth the cost.

B Compare answers to Exercise A with a partner. Then discuss the following question.

Would you prefer to visit the High Line or the Low Line? Explain your answer.

C Complete the following sentences in a way that shows that you understand the meaning of the words in bold.

1. City parks are often **surrounded by** _____.

2. Most people don't like living in an area with **abandoned buildings** because _____.

3. I would like to **commission a study** that _____.

4. One way that a city park **serves a purpose** is _____.

D Work with a partner and write sentences that include any six of the vocabulary items below. You may use any verb tense and make nouns plural if you wish.

annual meetings	in secret	persistence paid off	specified date
come into contact with	integrate information	solve the mystery	submit a proposal
health inspectors	isolated incident		

Connect the Readings

A How are the High Line and the Paris Underground different? How are they the same? Fill out the chart below. Put a check (✓) in the column indicating if the statement describes the High Line, the Paris Underground, or both.

	The High Line	The Paris Underground
1. It's illegal to visit without a permit.		
2. Tourists and locals enjoy it.		
3. It tells a story of the past.		
4. It changes during different seasons.		
5. It's dangerous.		
6. It is ugly in parts.		
7. People feel passionately about it.		
8. It was in danger of disappearing.		

B With a partner or in a small group, compare answers to Exercise A. Then discuss the following questions.

1. Look at the chart above. Which items make each space inviting and interesting?

2. Which would you prefer to visit, the High Line or the Paris Underground? If you chose the Paris Underground, would you want to go with the cataphiles, the forensic pathologist, or the sewer workers? Explain your answers.

C Discuss the following questions with a partner. Use your understanding of the readings and your own ideas.

1. As cities grow and change, is it important to preserve their history? Why, or why not?

2. How are the stories in this unit about persistence? How are the stories about transformation? Explain your answers.

3. If you were able to create a new public space in your city or town, where would it be? Why would you choose this place?

FOCUS

1. Would you rather have an interesting but dangerous job or a boring but safe one?

2. If you had to choose between the two, would you rather work somewhere that was extremely hot or extremely cold?

EXTREME JOBS

A worker climbs a nuclear power plant under construction in Washington, USA.

Academic Vocabulary

to anticipate	inevitable	to simulate
to convince	reliable	virtually
eligible	a routine	

Multiword Vocabulary

at the very least	to make the cut
first-aid	to set out
to have no chance	to take into consideration
to lighten the load	a viable option

A dogsled team on patrol in whiteout conditions in Greenland

Reading Preview

A **Preview.** Scan Reading 1 to find answers to the following questions. Then discuss the answers with a partner or in a small group.

1. Where and when does this story take place?

2. What is the Sirius Patrol?

3. Who are Johan, Sally, Indy, and Armstrong?

B **Topic vocabulary.** The following words appear in Reading 1. Look at the words and answer the questions with a partner.

brutal	polar bears	tent
fog	ropes	unruly
frostbite	sled dogs	wind
injuries	supplies	

1. Which words could be classified as equipment?

2. Which words could refer to problems in the wild?

3. Which words are adjectives? Which of the other vocabulary items could they describe?

C **Predict.** What do you think this reading will be about? Discuss each word in Exercise B and predict how it may relate to the reading.

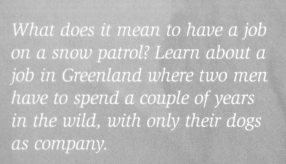

What does it mean to have a job on a snow patrol? Learn about a job in Greenland where two men have to spend a couple of years in the wild, with only their dogs as company.

The Snow Patrol

THE SNOW PATROL

I t was dark and cold when Jesper Olsen fell.   1

In wintertime in northern Greenland,   2
there's not a single ray of sunlight for more
than three months. The average temperature is 25
degrees below zero, Fahrenheit (32 degrees below
zero, Celsius), and the wind is brutal. As a Sirius
patroller, traveling by dogsled across Greenland,
Jesper had taken the weather into consideration.
He was also prepared for unruly dogs, a heavy
sled, and the difficult landscape. What he hadn't
anticipated was that his knife would come loose
and that he would land on it, the blade cutting
into his thigh.

"You OK?" his partner, Rasmus Jørgensen,   3
asked.

"Yeah." Jesper replied.   4

Jesper and Rasmus were 500 miles (805 kilo-   5
meters) north of the Arctic Circle, in one of the
most isolated places on Earth. It was four days into
his first trip as a Sirius patroller, and he lay on the
snow, pain washing over him. He convinced himself, within a few moments, that he would be all
right. During his intense training, he'd learned to
remain calm no matter how difficult the situation,
and he remembered the Sirius motto:[1] Whenever
possible, out on the ice, it's best to continue
moving. So, Jesper Olsen rose to his feet, picked up
the ropes to the dogsled, and continued on.

The desire to explore Greenland, a Danish   6
protectorate[2] since 1721, came to Jesper Olsen
when he was a sergeant in the Danish Royal
Life Guards, working at the Queen of Denmark's
palaces. Twenty-three year old Jesper yearned for
something different, something more adventur-
ous. "I like to push myself," he says. In 2008, he
applied for a job with an elite special forces unit,
famous for driving soldiers to the limits of human
capabilities: The Sirius Patrol.

Sirius is the world's only military dog-   7
sled patrol. For more than 60 years, it has

patrolled northeast Greenland's 8,699-mile
(14,000-kilometer) coast. Six two-man teams
visit each inch of the coastline at least once
every five years. They act as the only rangers in
Northeast Greenland National Park, maintaining
Denmark's sovereignty[3] in the region. They also
support scientific and sporting expeditions in
the world's largest park, home to herds of musk
oxen and hundreds of polar bears. The job—low
pay, no holidays—means working with a partner
and a dog team for 26 months and traveling more
than 5,000 miles (8,047 kilometers). Injuries are
virtually inevitable, as are hunger and exhaustion
and frostbite. Sirius patrollers also have to watch
out for polar bears. Patrollers have no chance to
visit family or friends; they never even get to see
a tree.

---

[1] *motto:* a short sentence, phrase, or word that expresses
a belief or rule for sensible behavior, especially a way of
behaving in a particular situation

[2] *protectorate:* a country that is controlled and protected by
a more powerful country

---

[3] *sovereignty:* the power that a country has to govern itself
or another country or state

A sled team goes past a giant iceberg on a frozen sea near Station Nord, Greenland.

Becoming a patroller is highly competitive. 8 Although half the patrollers are replaced every year, this still means that only six spots open up each year for new patrollers. Women are eligible, though none have yet applied, and everyone must be under 30 to try out. Jesper came close to being chosen when he first applied, but he didn't make the cut. He was devastated. "I was never going to apply again," he says. However, when he could not stop thinking about Greenland's beauty, he decided to try once more. This time he studied everything from meteorology[4] to hunting skills to veterinary medicine. He memorized the shape of more than 600 fjords[5] and points along the Greenland coast in case he lost his map.

[4] *meteorology:* the study of the processes in Earth's atmosphere that cause particular weather conditions, especially in order to predict the weather

[5] *fjords:* strips of sea that come into the land between high cliffs

On his second attempt, Jesper got the job. As 9 part of his final training, he had to jump into icy water to simulate a sledding disaster. He had to survive in the wild for five days with only a small bag of emergency supplies, sleeping in a snow cave that he dug with a tin cup and hunting arctic hare and musk ox for food. At last, in July 2010, Jesper reported to the Sirius base camp[6] in northeastern Greenland. He was officially a Sirius patroller.

Jesper's partner, Rasmus, is a 28-year-old 10 second-year patroller and former Air Force sergeant. Before they set out on patrol, the two men built a 14-foot (4-meter) sled, named it Black Sun, and worked with their dogs until they felt like a cohesive unit. In mid-October, they loaded Black Sun with 815 pounds (370 kilograms) of supplies

[6] *base camp:* a place where people begin a journey to explore a remote area and can return to for rest

A rare red aurora borealis (the northern lights)

and left the base, following a route determined by Danish military officers.

Sirius patrollers travel by dogsled. In this modern age of Humvees and tanks, there's still no better way than dogsledding to travel long distances in Greenland, where the engine failure of a motor vehicle can be deadly. Not only are sled dogs reliable, there have been many instances where they have saved patrollers' lives. Sledding during the endless night, especially in fog, is often performed half blind. The dogs have stopped short at cliff edges and refused to move. They also make a specific polar bear warning sound—a hissing growl—that lets patrollers know when to be alert.

Any mistake in the far north can be dangerous; if you put your gloves down in the wrong spot for an instant, they'll blow away. "You'll be punished if you're not doing everything right," Rasmus warns. The only fatality in Sirius history occurred in 1968 when a patroller became separated from his partners on a training ride and died. Lost in a snowstorm, he hadn't been able to survive alone.

Relationships between patrollers aren't always friendly, but separation is not a viable option. Fortunately, Jesper and Rasmus are a good match. While some Sirius pairs prefer traveling light and fast, Jesper and Rasmus have chosen a slower and warmer approach. Other teams cut off the tags from their T-shirts and the handles off of their toothbrushes in order to lighten the load. Jesper and Rasmus, on the other hand, don't worry as much about speed, and they bring all the clothing they need to keep warm.

At the end of the day, Jesper and Rasmus stop the sled and start their nighttime routine. While the northern lights[7] blaze overhead in bright pinks and greens, Jesper sets up the tent. Rasmus takes care of the dogs, spending a little time with each one. "They become your family," Jesper explains. Rasmus hugs their proud lead dog, Johan; their cheerful female, Sally; their resident troublemaker, Indy; and their legend, Armstrong, who is in his tenth winter as a sled dog. Armstrong has pulled a sled at least 25,000 miles (40,236 kilometers), which is the equivalent of more than once around the equator.

Inside the tent, Jesper and Rasmus finally warm up. As their dinner cooks, Jesper finally has time to take care of his wound. He climbs out of his ski pants and examines the deep gash in his leg and the blood that continues to ooze. For most people, this would require a doctor's visit at the very least. However, Jesper simply takes out the first-aid kit and patches himself up, ready to continue his work. He is, after all, a Sirius patroller.

---

[7] *northern lights:* colored lights that appear in the sky in far northern parts of the world; also called the aurora borealis

READING COMPREHENSION

Big Picture

A Choose the answer that best completes each of the following sentences.

1. The main idea of Reading 1 is to _____ .
   a. explain how Jesper Olsen applied to become a Sirius patroller
   b. talk about the harsh but beautiful landscape of Greenland
   c. describe what it is like to be on the Sirius Patrol
   d. discuss why it's better to use dogs than motor vehicles in Greenland

2. The main idea of paragraph 6 is that _____ .
   a. Jesper was a guard at a palace in Denmark
   b. Jesper likes to try new things and have adventures
   c. Jesper was 23 years old
   d. Jesper's interests led him to apply to be on the Sirius Patrol

3. The purpose of paragraph 7 is to describe _____ .
   a. the dogs of the Sirius Patrol
   b. the life of a patroller
   c. Greenland's coastline
   d. Possible injuries to a patroller

4. The main idea of paragraph 8 is that Jesper _____ .
   a. was not chosen to be a Sirius patroller
   b. was devastated when he was not chosen to be a Sirius patroller
   c. didn't give up his dream
   d. was one of six people who wanted to be Sirius patrollers

5. The main idea of paragraph 13 is that _____ .
   a. once you have a partner, you need to find a way to get along
   b. Jesper and Rasmus are a good match
   c. there is only one way to travel by dogsled
   d. T-shirt tags and toothbrush handles add to the weight of the sled

6. The purpose of paragraph 14 is to show all of the following except _____ .
   a. the beauty of the nighttime routine
   b. that patrollers love their dogs
   c. the challenge of the nighttime routine
   d. that dogs have different personalities

B Order the following events from 1 to 10, based on when they happened in Jesper's life.
Compare answers with a partner. The first one is done for you.

_____ **a.** becomes a patroller

_____ **b.** ignores his injury and sets up the tent

_____ **c.** falls on his knife

_____ **d.** is not accepted to the program

_____ **e.** starts his first trip on patrol

_____ **f.** studies intensely

_____ **g.** applies to be part of the Sirius Patrol

_____ **h.** builds his sled with his partner, Rasmus

_1_ **i.** works at a Danish palace

_____ **j.** patches up his wound

Close-Up

(A) Decide which of the following statements are true or false according to the reading. Write *T* (True) or *F* (False) next to each one.

_____ **1.** When he cut his leg, Jesper was on his first trip as a patroller.

_____ **2.** Patrollers have a difficult job, but they are paid a lot of money.

_____ **3.** Every year, six patrollers leave Greenland.

_____ **4.** Sirius patrollers make their own sleds before they go out on patrol.

_____ **5.** Jesper and Rasmus don't have a friendly relationship.

_____ **6.** Almost all patrollers experience hunger and frostbite.

_____ **7.** On the Sirius Patrol, there has been only one death per year.

_____ **8.** The dog Armstrong is a legend because he has pulled a sled around the equator.

(B) Work with a partner or in a small group. Change the false statements in Exercise A to make them true.

Reading Skill

Dealing with Unknown Vocabulary

When you are reading, it is common to see new words that you don't know. Successful readers know when to use a dictionary and when to ignore unknown words. Often, if you read to the end of a sentence or paragraph, it is possible to figure out the meaning of the text even if some words are still unknown. If you can understand a sentence even when you omit an unknown word, then you probably don't have to look the word up.

Read the following sentence from the second paragraph of Reading 1. One word is underlined. Can you still understand the sentence, even without this word?

> In wintertime in northern Greenland, there's not a single <u>ray</u> of sunlight for more than three months.

The idea in this sentence is that there is no sunlight in Greenland in the winter. Because it says "not a single," we can guess that whatever "ray" means, it refers to the sunlight.

(A) Continue reading the second paragraph below from Reading 1. Look at the underlined words. You should be able to ignore three of these words. Circle the three words that you will probably want to look up. Discuss your choices with a partner.

The average temperature is 25 degrees below zero, Fahrenheit (32 degrees below zero, Celsius), and the wind is <u>brutal</u>. Jesper had taken the weather into consideration. He was also prepared for <u>unruly</u> dogs, a heavy <u>sled</u>, and the difficult landscape. What Jesper hadn't <u>anticipated</u> was that his knife would come loose and that he would land on it, the <u>blade</u> cutting into his <u>thigh</u>.

B Read the following passages from Reading 1. Underline the new words that you can ignore. Circle the words that you think you need to look up in a dictionary.

1. . . . sleeping in a snow cave that he dug with a tin cup and hunting arctic hare and musk ox for food.

2. They also make a specific polar bear warning sound, a hissing growl—that lets patrollers know when to be alert.

3. He climbs out of his ski pants and examines the deep gash in his leg and the blood that continues to ooze.

C Compare answers to Exercise B with a partner.

VOCABULARY PRACTICE

Academic Vocabulary

A Find the words in bold in Reading 1. Use the context to help you figure out the meaning. Then match each word to the word that is closest in meaning.

_____ 1. **anticipated** (Par. 2)   **a.** almost

_____ 2. **convinced** (Par. 5)   **b.** qualified

_____ 3. **virtually** (Par. 7)   **c.** schedule

_____ 4. **inevitable** (Par. 7)   **d.** expected

_____ 5. **eligible** (Par. 8)   **e.** certain

_____ 6. **simulate** (Par. 9)   **f.** trustworthy

_____ 7. **reliable** (Par. 11)   **g.** pretend

_____ 8. **routine** (Par. 14)   **h.** persuaded

B Choose an academic word from Exercise A to complete each of the following sentences. Notice and learn the words in bold because they often appear with the academic words.

1. Stephen drives to work every day, so he bought a(n) _____ **car**. He can't afford to miss work because of engine trouble.

2. During her successful campaign, the presidential candidate clearly _____ **voters** that she would act in their best interest.

3. The zero-gravity machine allows users to _____ **the experience** of being in outer space.

4. People who are over 65 years old are _____ **for** a discount on their bus fare.

5. More people came to the concert than had been **originally** _____, and as a result, the lines to get in were very long.

6. It is _____ **impossible** to learn a new language in one week.

7. **Don't delay the** _____. At some point, you will have to study for this test!

8. My father's **morning** _____ never varies. He wakes up, gets dressed, and reads the newspaper while he eats breakfast.

Multiword Vocabulary

Ⓐ Find the multiword vocabulary in bold in Reading 1 and use the context to help you figure out the meaning. Then match each item to the correct definition.

_____ **1. taken** the weather **into consideration** (Par. 2)

_____ **2. have no chance** (Par. 7)

_____ **3. make the cut** (Par. 8)

_____ **4. set out** (Par. 10)

_____ **5. a viable option** (Par. 13)

_____ **6. lighten the load** (Par. 13)

_____ **7. at the very least** (Par. 15)

_____ **8. first-aid** (Par. 15)

a. a good possibility

b. start a journey

c. make something less heavy

d. have no possibility

e. relating to immediate medical attention in an emergency

f. thought about something because it is relevant to what you are doing

g. be asked to be part of a team

h. not less than this

Ⓑ Complete the following paragraph with the correct multiword vocabulary from Exercise A. In some cases, you need to change the verb or noun form or pronoun.

Congratulations! You tried out for the exploration team, and you

_____ . You are now about to spend a week in the wild. Before
             1

you _____ on your journey, be sure you are prepared for a
             2

medical emergency. Always remember to bring a _____ kit. If
                                                          3

your backpack is heavy, you might be tempted to _____ by
                                                            4

removing the kit. However, be sure to _____ that driving to a
                                                  5

hospital might not be _____ , and you will
                               6

_____ to run to
             7

a store. _____ ,
             8

this kit should include bandages, antiseptic

cream, and a pain reliever.

Use the Vocabulary

Complete the following sentences with your own ideas. Then share your answers with a partner.

1. It's important for everyone to have a **reliable** _____.

2. It's a good idea to have **first-aid** supplies such as _____ in your house.

3. When you are studying for a test, it's a good strategy to **anticipate** _____.

4. Before you **set out** on a trip to the desert, be sure to bring _____ and _____. **At the very least**, make sure that you have enough _____.

5. It is **virtually impossible** to convince children to _____.

6. When a student applies to a college or university, the admissions department **takes** the student's _____ and _____ **into consideration**.

7. There is a saying, "Change is **inevitable**." This means that _____.

THINK AND DISCUSS

Work in a small group. Use the information in the reading and your own ideas to discuss the following questions.

1. Analyze. Who said the following? When did the speaker say it? What changed the speaker's mind?

I was never going to apply again.

2. Infer meaning. Who said the following? Who does *they* refer to? Why do you think this is true?

They become your family.

3. Evaluate the author's opinion. Who said the following? What does *this* refer to? Why do you think the author ends the reading with this observation?

For most people, this would require a doctor's visit at the very least.

Academic Vocabulary

accurately	to fluctuate	subsequent
briefly	to obtain	toxic
data	to secure	

Multiword Vocabulary

to be capable of	to make up one's mind
the fact of the matter	a scientific expedition
for the sake of	surface level
in a matter of minutes (seconds, etc.)	well suited

Reading Preview

A **Preview.** Read the first sentence of each paragraph in Reading 2. Then put the following topics in the order in which they appear in the reading.

_____ **1.** A description of a lava lake

_____ **2.** Traveling into a volcano

_____ **3.** The history of Nyiragongo

_____ **4.** An attempt to get a lava sample

B **Topic vocabulary.** The following words appear in Reading 2. Look at the words and answer the questions with a partner.

crater	lake	research
eruption	lava	sample
fresh	ledge	summit
hardened	mission	volcanologist

1. Which words relate to areas in and around a volcano?

2. Which words are adjectives? Which of the other words could they describe?

3. Which words relate to scientific study?

C **Predict.** What do you think this reading will be about? Discuss each word in Exercise B and predict how it may relate to the reading.

Looking down into the Nyiragongo volcano in the Democratic Republic of Congo

The Nyiragongo volcano in Africa is one of the most active volcanoes in the world. Join a team of scientists on their dangerous mission into its fiery heart.

INTO THE
VOLCANO

INTO THE VOLCANO

Goma, in the Democratic Republic of the Congo, is quite possibly the most dangerous city in the world. It has an estimated population of one million and lies at the base of a two-mile high volcano, Nyiragongo. In 1977, eruptions sent lava racing down the mountain at more than 60 miles (96 kilometers) per hour, killing several hundred people. A subsequent eruption in 2002 shot lava into downtown Goma. It destroyed 14,000 homes, buried buildings to the top of the first floor, and forced 350,000 citizens to flee. The fact of the matter is that another eruption is inevitable, and scientists fear Nyiragongo is capable of much worse. They fear that it could transform Goma into a modern Pompeii.[1]

Nyiragongo is one of the most active volcanoes on the planet and one of the least studied. In 2011, U.S. volcanologist Ken Sims joined Dario Tedesco, an Italian volcanologist, on a three-week scientific expedition to study Nyiragongo's rocks and test its gases. Together with a team of scientists and porters,[2] their goal was to determine when the volcano might erupt again. Anticipating such an event could potentially save thousands of lives.

In order to reach the summit of Nyiragongo, the team followed the lava up the mountain, carrying camping gear, climbing equipment, scientific instruments, food, and water. After a full day of hiking, they reached the summit and looked down into the mouth of the volcano. High walls surrounded by ledges dropped down into the crater, which had an enormous, flat floor, black with hardened lava. In the middle of the crater, in a raised area shaped like a soup bowl, they saw an incredible sight: a lake of bubbling lava.

---

[1] *Pompeii:* an ancient Roman city destroyed in the eruption of Mount Vesuvius in 79 CE

[2] *porters:* people whose job is to carry things

A volcanologist takes gas samples from the rim of the Nyirangongo volcano.

In 2002, an eruption from Nyirangongo destroys parts of the city of Goma in the Republic of the Congo.

The lava lake was 700 feet (213 meters) across, making it one of the largest in the world. Shifting and swirling beneath them, it roared like an airplane and let out a thick white cloud of dozens of deadly gases. Even from the summit, they could feel the heat. The 1,800 degrees Fahrenheit (982.22 degrees Celsius) lava exploded in 100-foot sprays of electric orange that turned to black as they cooled in midair. The lake seemed to breathe. Rising and falling, its surface level changed several feet in a matter of minutes. It was both spectacular and terrifying. 4

Sims led the descent into the crater and secured the ropes carefully. Tedesco and the others followed. Stones fell from the walls, and massive rocks wobbled like loose teeth. They set up camp on a wide ledge 800 feet (244 meters) below the summit, a few hundred feet above the lake. The surface of the ledge was comfortably warm, but the air was toxic and gas masks[3] were essential. 5

Part of the team's dangerous mission was to obtain a zero-age sample, a piece of lava, freshly cooled from the edge of the boiling lake. 6

Based on data from a zero-age sample, scientists are able to accurately date all other rocks in a volcano. This, in turn, can help to predict volcanic eruptions. Sims, an avid rock climber, was well suited for the dangerous task. But he hesitated briefly, thinking of his wife and two young children. Volcano science has never been a safe occupation; more than 20 scientists have died on volcanoes in the past 30 years. Sims, himself, has a scar on his right arm from Sicily's Mount Etna, where his shirt melted into his skin. Nevertheless, he was one of only a handful of people with both the climbing skills and scientific knowledge to get exactly what was needed.

Sims made up his mind and rappelled[4] into the volcano. Standing on 7

---

[3] *gas masks:* devices worn over the face to protect it from poisonous gases

[4] *rappelled:* slid down a rock face in a controlled way, using a rope, with feet against the rock

the crater floor, he couldn't see the lake itself. The lake was high above him and contained within a cone of cooled lava—the soup bowl that he had seen from the summit. However, he could hear the hiss of its gases and smell its fumes as he put on a silver-colored thermal suit, a full-body oven mitt.[5] He approached the cone, the lava crunching beneath his feet. The cone was 40 feet (12 meters) high, and the wall was nearly vertical, requiring his rock-climbing skills. Tedesco communicated with Sims by radio, describing the lava as it fluctuated—where it was exploding and where it was spilling over. Conditions changed by the minute. Suddenly, Sims's foot slipped, and he smelled burning rubber. Looking down, he saw his shoe melting out from under him.

Sims kept going. Climbing steadily, he 8 reached the top of the rim, inches away from the boiling lava. This was beyond science. This was personal. It was the culmination of a lifetime of exploration and adventure and curiosity. Over the radio, Tedesco and the team could hear the emotion in Sims's voice. "Amazing. Incredible. I'll never see anything like this again."

With a hard slam of his fist, Sims broke off 9 a piece of fresh lava. It was shiny, black, and so hot that, even wearing thermal gloves, he had to juggle it from hand to hand. As he carried it up to the team, they cheered. Up a mountain, down a crater, to the edge of a lava lake, Sims had come face-to-face with the fiery inferno[6] for the sake of science. Thanks to the zero-age sample, the next stage of the volcanologists' research could begin, and Goma is more likely to be prepared for Nyiragongo's next eruption.

---

[5] *oven mitt:* protective glove used when cooking

[6] *inferno:* place of extreme heat and destruction

Volcanologists preparing to go down into Nyirangongo

READING COMPREHENSION

Big Picture

A The following statements are the main ideas of some of the paragraphs in Reading 2. Write the correct paragraph number next to its main idea.

_____ **1.** Nyiragongo's next eruption could be even more deadly than the ones before it.

_____ **2.** Climbing into the crater requires special equipment.

_____ **3.** Retrieving a zero-age sample is dangerous.

_____ **4.** The heat of the lava lake is intense.

_____ **5.** Sims retrieves a zero-age sample.

_____ **6.** The reason for the mission is to be able to predict the volcano's next eruption.

B Reread the main ideas in Exercise A. How would you annotate (see page 21) the reading using this information? Remember to use key words. The first one is done for you.

1. _next eruption = more deadly?_

2. _____

3. _____

4. _____

5. _____

6. _____

Close-Up

A Choose the answer that best completes each of the following sentences.

1. In 2002, 350,000 people _____ when Nyiragongo erupted.
   a. were killed   **b.** ran away quickly   **c.** moved to new houses

2. The goal of the 2011 scientific expedition to Nyiragongo was to _____.
   a. predict the next eruption   **b.** stop the volcano from erupting   **c.** study a new volcano

3. The scientific team followed _____ to make their way to the summit.
   a. guides   **b.** animal tracks   **c.** lava

4. The team set up their camp _____.
   a. at the summit   **b.** between the summit and the lake   **c.** at the surface of the lake

5. Sims worried about his safety and thought about his _____.
   a. family   **b.** colleagues   **c.** students

6. When Sims climbed the wall to the lava lake, _____ to communicate with the team.
   a. he used a radio   **b.** he used a cell phone   **c.** it wasn't possible for him

7. Sims used his _____ to break off a piece of the lava.
   a. gas mask   **b.** hammer   **c.** hands

B Complete the following sentences in your own words. Write at least two details for each one. Then discuss your answers in a small group.

1. Goma is a city that _____

    _____.

2. The lava lake is _____

    _____.

3. Ken Sims is a man who _____

    _____.

4. A zero-age sample is a _____

    _____.

Reading Skill

Recognizing Causes and Effects

Writers often describe cause-and-effect relationships. These relationships connect a situation (the cause) and the result of that situation (the effect). Signal words and phrases such as *because*, *since*, and *as a result* are often used to highlight this information. However, writers don't always use signal words and phrases, so successful readers have to be able to recognize cause-and-effect relationships even when there are no signal words.

Look at the following example from Reading 2. The causes are underlined and the effects are circled. Note that some items are both underlined and circled, because one cause can have an effect, and this effect can be a cause of a second effect.

In 1977, <u>eruptions</u> sent ⟨lava⟩ racing down the mountain at more than 60 miles

(96 kilometers) an hour, ⟨killing⟩ several hundred people.

In order to show cause and effect when you annotate, one strategy is to draw an arrow from the cause to the effect.

1977 eruption → lava → death of 100s

A Read the following statements from Reading 2. Underline the causes and circle the effects. Note that some words might be both a cause and an effect.

1. A subsequent eruption in 2002 shot lava into downtown Goma. It destroyed 14,000 homes, buried buildings to the top of the first floor, and forced 350,000 citizens to flee.

2. Based on data from a zero-age sample, scientists are able to accurately date all other rocks in a volcano. This, in turn, can help to predict volcanic eruptions.

3. Sims, himself, has a scar on his right arm from Sicily's Mount Etna, where his shirt melted into his skin.

4. Suddenly, Sims's foot slipped and he smelled burning rubber. Looking down, he saw his shoe melting out from under him.

5. It [the piece of fresh lava] was shiny, black, and so hot that, even wearing thermal gloves, he had to juggle it from hand to hand.

B Annotate each sentence in Exercise A, using key words and arrows to show cause and effect.

C Work with a partner. In your own words, explain why Sims retrieved the lava sample and how he was able to do so. Tell the story by describing as many causes and effects as possible.

VOCABULARY PRACTICE

Academic Vocabulary

A Find the words in the box below in Reading 2. Use the context to help you choose the correct words to complete the following sentences.

subsequent (Par. 1)	toxic (Par. 5)	data (Par. 6)	briefly (Par. 6)
secured (Par. 5)	obtain (Par. 6)	accurately (Par. 6)	fluctuated (Par. 7)

1. On March 1, a strong rainstorm _____ caused the Vistula River in Poland to flood. Although this only lasted a short time, it caused extensive damage.

2. The levels of the river _____ over the course of a month. At times, the water level was 5 feet (1.5 meters) higher than usual. This event made the banks of the river even weaker.

3. Engineers _____ predicted that _____ storms would cause more damage. The next storm proved that their predictions had been correct.

4. From their _____, the engineers estimated that the flood levels could be as high as three feet (close to one meter).

5. This could cause _____ waste from the sewers to be leaked into the environment, which could make people very ill.

6. Fortunately, the city was able to _____ the necessary funds from the government to prevent further damage. They _____ the riverbanks and were able to avoid a catastrophe.

B The words in bold are academic words from Exercise A and words they often appear with. Complete the sentences with your own ideas.

1. The teacher **briefly discussed** _____ before we started the new material.

2. Scientists usually **analyze data** in a _____.

3. The best way to **accurately measure** your height is to _____.

4. Newspaper reporters often try to **obtain information** about _____.

5. At first, research showed that the medicine had no harmful effects. However, **subsequent studies** revealed that _____.

6. Political events can cause _____ **prices** to **fluctuate**.

7. After the building collapsed, police tried to **secure the area** by _____.

8. Make sure that cleaning products with **toxic chemicals** are _____.

Multiword Vocabulary

(A) Find the multiword vocabulary in bold in Reading 2 and use the context to help you figure out the meaning. Then choose the best answer to complete each sentence.

1. When you use **the fact of the matter** (Par. 1), you want to emphasize _____.
   a. the scientific evidence
   b. the most important part of a discussion

2. If someone **is capable of** (Par. 1) doing something, it means that he or she _____.
   a. has the ability to do it
   b. has to do something quickly

3. A **scientific expedition** (Par. 2) is an organized trip that is made _____.
   a. in order to study something in the natural world
   b. for tourists to experience nature

4. The **surface level** (Par. 4) is the _____ of something that reaches a particular height.
   a. lowest layer
   b. top layer

5. You use **in a matter of minutes** (Par. 4) when you want to _____.
   a. emphasize how short a period of time is
   b. describe something that just happened

6. When someone is **well suited** (Par. 6) for a particular job, it means that _____.
   a. he or she is the right person for the job
   b. he or she is dressed appropriately

7. If he **made up** his **mind** (Par. 7) to do something, it means he _____.
   a. pretended to agree with another person's opinion
   b. decided which of a number of possible things he would do

8. If you do something **for the sake of** (Par. 9) your family, it means that you _____.
   a. are working with family members
   b. are acting in the best interest of your family

(B) Complete the following sentences with the correct multiword vocabulary in the box below from Exercise A. In some cases, you need to change the verb or noun form or the pronoun.

capable of	for the sake of	make up his mind	surface level
the fact of the matter	in a matter of minutes	scientific expedition	well suited

1. After Sergio _____ to become a firefighter, he trained for months, took the test, and made the cut!

2. Stephen is _____ for his job as a manager. He's patient, intelligent, and funny.

3. _____, the weather changed from hot and sunny to cold and rainy.

4. The _____ of the river is rising, and people who live along the river are worried about flooding.

5. You might not like hot weather, but if you're moving to Texas, _____ is that summer is very hot there. You'll need air-conditioning!

6. Maureen is an "armchair adventurer." She enjoys reading about _____, but she doesn't like to leave her comfortable house!

7. Sometimes journalists risk their lives _____ an important news story.

8. In an emergency, people are _____ doing amazing things. One mother lifted a car off of her son who was trapped underneath.

Use the Vocabulary

Write answers to the following questions. Use the words in bold in your answers. Then share your answers with a partner.

1. Do you need to **obtain permission** before you leave a classroom? Why, or why not?

2. Do you enjoy reading about **scientific expeditions**? If so, what kind?

3. What kind of person would be **well suited** for a job as a volcanologist?

4. What did you read on the first day of this class? What have you read in **subsequent** classes?

5. Do you think that test scores **accurately** reflect a student's ability? Why, or why not?

6. Can you **briefly** state the reason that you are taking this class?

THINK AND DISCUSS

Work in a small group. Use the information in the reading and your own ideas to discuss the following questions.

1. **Analyze purpose.** What do you think was going through Sims's mind when he made the decision to obtain the zero-age sample?

2. **Infer meaning.** Who said the following? When did the speaker say it? Why is it significant?
   Amazing. Incredible. I'll never see anything like this again.

3. **Identify problems and solutions.** How could this mission save lives? What other steps would need to occur after a prediction was made?

Vocabulary Review

A Complete the paragraphs with the vocabulary below that you have studied in the unit.

analyzing the data	simulate the experience
for the sake of	take this into consideration
have no chance	scientific expeditions
is capable of	toxic chemicals
morning routine	a viable option

Mars Rover

At 9:45 a.m. each morning on the planet Mars, a rover (a robot the size of a car) asks: *What do I do today?* Bethany Ehlmann, a geologist and National Geographic Emerging Explorer, is one of the scientists in charge of the rover's daily _____ on Mars. Guided by the scientists, the rover _____ traveling around Mars to find rocks. The rocks on Mars can tell us a lot about the early history of our solar system. Less than 1 percent of the rocks on Earth date back to 3.5 billion years ago, but 50 percent of Mars's rocks are from that time period. _____ from the rocks on Mars may help scientists understand Earth's early history as well.

It is not _____ for scientists to test equipment on Mars because they would _____ to make the physical adjustments that might be required by hand. There are no _____ on Mars, but there is also no oxygen. This would affect humans but not a rover. So, _____ equipment testing, Ehlmann leads _____ to areas in Iceland and Hawaii, which have surfaces that are similar to Mars. This makes it possible to _____ of being on Mars. If the equipment does not work, Ehlmann is able to _____ and make changes before the equipment is sent into outer space.

B Compare answers to Exercise A with a partner. Then discuss the following questions.

Would you be interested in Ehlmann's job? Why, or why not?

C Complete the following sentences in a way that shows that you understand the meaning of the words in bold.

1. During the interview, Ehlmann **briefly discussed** _____.

2. One way to **obtain information** about exotic locations is to _____.

3. I think **subsequent studies** of the rocks on Mars will show that _____.

4. It is **virtually impossible** to climb a mountain in _____.

D Work with a partner and write sentences that include any six of the vocabulary items below. You may use any verb tense and make nouns plural if you wish.

accurately measured	eligible for	make the cut	originally anticipated
convince voters	first-aid	make up your mind	prices fluctuate
delay the inevitable	lighten the load		

Connect the Readings

A How are Sirius patrollers and volcanologists similar? How are they different? Discuss your answers with a partner or in a small group. Then fill in the Venn diagram. Think of at least three items for each circle. Compare diagrams with another group. The first items are done for you.

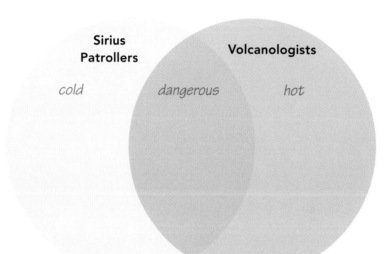

Sirius Patrollers | **Volcanologists**

cold | dangerous | hot

B With a partner or in a small group, compare answers to Exercise A. Then discuss the following questions.

1. Which career would you prefer, Sirius patroller or volcanologist? Explain your answer.

2. What are the personality traits that a patroller needs in order to be successful? Explain your answer.

3. What are the personality traits that a volcanologist needs in order to be successful? Explain your answer.

C Discuss the following questions with a partner. Use your understanding of the readings and your own ideas.

1. Imagine that you have been asked to join a scientific expedition. Where would you go? What would you study?

2. Discuss the following quotes from Reading 1. How could each quote apply to Reading 2? How could each quote apply to other adventure situations? Have you ever been in a situation where you had to keep this in mind? If so, explain.

Whenever possible, out on the ice, it's best to continue moving.

You'll be punished if you're not doing everything right.

3. Look back at your answers to the Focus questions on page 28. Have any of your answers changed after reading this unit? Why, or why not?

FOCUS

1. What are some animals that are in danger of extinction?

2. Why are these animals in danger?

3. Why is it important to protect endangered animals?

52

Animal Conservation

Elephants feed in a swamp in
Amboseli National Park in Kenya.

READING 1

Academic Vocabulary

ambitious	genetic	to regulate
astounding	an incentive	shelter
crucial	prime	

Multiword Vocabulary

to become a reality	let alone
a buffer zone	out of the picture
just around the corner	a stepping stone
to keep something in check	to write something off

Reading Preview

A Preview. Look at the map on page 58 of Reading 1. Then discuss the following questions with a partner or in a small group.

1. What do the different colored areas on the map represent?

2. Where are most of the jaguar populations located?

3. Based on information in the map, what do you think conservationists want to do to help the jaguar?

B Topic vocabulary. The following words appear in Reading 1. Look at the words and answer the questions with a partner.

blind	habitat
cattle ranches	jaguar
conservationists	predator
disease	prey
endangered species	villagers
epidemiologists	wounded

1. Which words refer to people or groups of people?

2. Which words are related to the animal world?

3. Which words are related to health?

C Predict. What do you think this reading will be about? Discuss each word in Exercise B and predict how it may relate to the reading.

Jaguars are some of the most impressive big cats in the world. But their habitat is being threatened. Read how one organization is trying to find a solution to this problem.

Path
of the Jaguar

PATH OF THE JAGUAR

One evening, deep in a Costa Rican forest, 1 a young male jaguar silently leaves the place where he was born, forever. There's shelter, plenty of food, and females. But there's an older male jaguar in the forest as well, a fierce rival who wants him out of the picture. The young jaguar's mother, so comforting to him when he was a cub, can no longer protect him. So he goes.

In just a few miles, the young jaguar reaches 2 the edge of the forest. Pushed by instinct and necessity, he keeps moving, hiding among the trees along the border of the open land. Soon, though, shelter consists of only small bushes and a few trees, and he can't find anything to eat. He's now in a land of cattle ranches. One night, his hunger and the smell of a newborn calf[1] are so powerful that he moves out of the forest, into the open areas. Creeping close, he instantly kills the calf with one snap of his powerful jaws.

The next day, a rancher finds the remains of 3 the calf and the tracks of the jaguar. He gathers some of his neighbors and their dogs. When they find the young jaguar, they shoot anxiously, from a distance. The bullets blind the jaguar in one eye and hurt his left leg. Wounded now, he is unable to even find his normal prey, let alone stalk[2] and kill it. His hunger drives him to easier meals; he kills another calf, and then a dog outside a nearby town. He stays too long, and a group of villagers shoot him again. This time, they kill him. Jaguars, the villagers say, are nothing but killers. They should be shot on sight, anytime, anywhere.

Similar stories could be told about thou- 4 sands of other young jaguars, from Mexico to Argentina. In recent decades, over half of the big cat's prime habitat has been taken over by ranching, farming, and development. The jaguars are threatened. Conservationists are concerned and working to protect these powerful animals from extinction. Epidemiologists are also concerned

Mother jaguar and her cub

about the jaguar population. Why? Because new research shows that when the health of the jaguar population is in danger, human health is in danger as well.

Alan Rabinowitz, who is generally agreed 5 to be the world's leading jaguar expert, explains that diseases such as HIV, West Nile virus, and avian influenza are transmitted by certain animals. In the past, many of these diseases have been kept in check by predators such as the jaguar. Without predators, the animals grow in numbers, and the diseases that they carry can become stronger. Some diseases become zoonotic, that is, they jump from animal species to humans. As predators, jaguars can play an essential role in preventing the spread of these diseases as well as future pandemics that could be just around the corner. Rabinowitz hopes that this knowledge will provide an incentive for local people to tolerate jaguars.

---

[1] *calf:* baby cow or bull

[2] *stalk:* follow someone or something, usually waiting for a chance to attack

However, in order for humans to peacefully coexist with jaguars, there has to be a way for the animals to kill their prey in the wild, not on the cattle ranches. Rabinowitz dreams of a different ending to the story of the young male jaguar. He imagines a young male leaving his birthplace and passing, unnoticed by humans, through an almost continuous corridor of sheltering vegetation. Within a couple of days, the young jaguar finds a small forest with enough prey so that he can stop, eat, and rest before he continues on his way. Eventually, he'll reach a national park or wildlife preserve where he'll find a home, room to roam, plenty of prey, and females looking for a mate. This dream is becoming a reality, thanks to the Panthera Foundation.

Rabinowitz is the head of the Panthera Foundation, a conservation group dedicated to protecting the world's 36 species of wild cats. Rabinowitz works to conserve the jaguar's habitats through a program called *Paseo del Jaguar* (Path of the Jaguar). This is a vast network of interconnected corridors and refuges[3] extending from the U.S.–Mexico border into South America. It aims to keep the jaguar from joining lions and tigers on the endangered species list. This, in turn, may keep diseases in check.

In the 1990s, Rabinowitz wanted to expand preserves, or protected areas, for jaguars and secure them with surrounding buffer zones. "I felt that the best thing we could hope to do was to lock up these great populations in these fragmented areas," he said. However, he changed his mind after DNA fingerprinting—studying genetic material to understand family and species relationships—revealed an astounding fact: The jaguar is the only large, wide-ranging carnivore[4] in the world with no subspecies. This means that jaguars in northern Mexico are identical to those in southern Brazil. Therefore, the jaguars need to be able to wander between populations in order to successfully breed.

Rabinowitz and his colleagues went back to their data to see whether the preserves could be connected in order to support traveling jaguars. Rabinowitz explained, "While good jaguar

___
[3] *refuges:* places of safety from danger and discomfort

[4] *carnivore:* animal that eats meat to survive

Alan Rabinowitz, head of the Panthera Foundation

habitat, where the cats can live and breed, has decreased by 50 percent since the 1900s, habitat a jaguar can use to travel through has decreased only by 16 percent. These places are like little oases—very small patches that jaguars will come to, use a while, and then leave. We were writing these places off because they're not habitat where a permanent jaguar population can live. Now they're turning out to be crucial."

The Panthera Foundation hopes to convince 10 national governments to maintain this network of habitats through land-use planning. Studies have shown that even areas that are smaller than one and a half square miles can serve as temporary, one- or two-day homes, each one a stepping stone for wandering jaguars. This network will need to be protected, especially in certain areas of Central America and Colombia, where some sections of the path are already in danger of disappearing (see Figure 1). Rabinowitz and his

team are working to identify the areas most in need of protection by studying satellite photographs and airplane surveys. On the ground, they talk to local people and walk the areas of the proposed corridor in order to get a sense of what is needed.

Paseo del Jaguar is one of the world's most 11 ambitious conservation programs. Rabinowitz is focusing first on Mexico and Central America, where officials in all eight countries have approved the project. Costa Rica has already incorporated protection of the jaguar corridor into laws that regulate land development. This is an enormous project, but Rabinowitz is encouraged by his audiences' positive responses when he talks about jaguars. People are drawn to the animal's beauty, strength, and mystery. As conservation efforts increase and awareness grows about the jaguar's role in preventing diseases, hopefully these "killers" will be saved.

Figure 1. Networks of Jaguar Populations in Central and South America

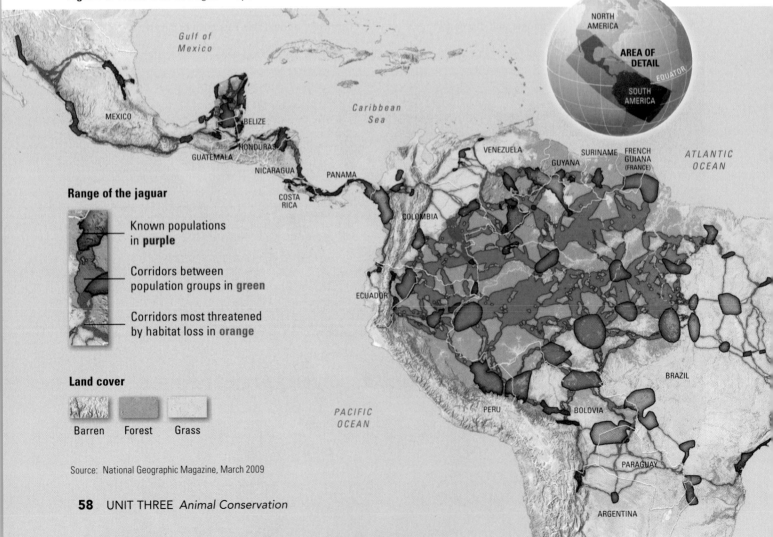

Range of the jaguar

— Known populations in **purple**

— Corridors between population groups in **green**

— Corridors most threatened by habitat loss in **orange**

Land cover

Barren   Forest   Grass

Source: National Geographic Magazine, March 2009

READING COMPREHENSION

Big Picture

A Read the following statements. Check (✓) the four statements that express the main ideas of Reading 1.

_____ **1.** A young male jaguar silently leaves the place where he was born, forever.

_____ **2.** Diseases such as HIV, West Nile virus, and avian influenza can be transmitted by animals.

_____ **3.** As predators, jaguars can prevent the spread of certain diseases.

_____ **4.** Jaguars need to be able to travel in order to successfully breed.

_____ **5.** The Panthera Foundation works with different governments to preserve land for jaguars.

_____ **6.** In the 1990s, Rabinowitz wanted to expand protected areas and keep jaguars in these areas.

_____ **7.** As conservation efforts increase and awareness grows about the jaguar's role in preventing diseases, hopefully these "killers" will be saved.

_____ **8.** Costa Rica has already incorporated protection of the jaguar corridor into its laws.

B Which statement in Exercise A best expresses the main idea of the _whole_ reading?

Close-Up

A Decide which of the following statements are true or false according to the reading. Write _T_ (True) or _F_ (False) next to each one.

_____ **1.** The young jaguar leaves his home in the forest because there is not enough food.

_____ **2.** The rancher sees the young jaguar before he kills a calf.

_____ **3.** The Panthera Foundation has 36 programs around the world.

_____ **4.** All jaguars live in Mexico and Argentina.

_____ **5.** A zoonotic disease can be spread from animals to humans.

_____ **6.** Jaguars all over South America look similar.

_____ **7.** Jaguars only need one and a half square miles of habitat to live on.

_____ **8.** The goal of Paseo del Jaguar is now to create a jaguar preserve in one large area.

_____ **9.** Rabinowitz's team uses technology to find areas that are in need of protection.

_____ **10.** Paseo del Jaguar has the support of many government officials in Central America.

B Work with a partner or in a small group. Change the false statements in Exercise A to make them true.

Reading Skill

Making inferences, or "reading between the lines," is an important part of being a successful reader. When you make inferences, you try to understand more about the topic than what is simply stated in a text. To do so, think about the reasons for or consequences of a particular statement. In the real world, we do this all the time. If you see classmates walking into class with wet hair, you will probably infer, or guess, that it is raining outside. They don't have to tell you this information. The same is true when you read a text. You make inferences, based on the information in the text and your own background knowledge.

Look at the following example from Reading 1:

When they [the ranchers] find the young jaguar, they shoot anxiously, from a distance.

With your background knowledge, you can guess that the jaguar has the ability to harm the ranchers. The adjective *anxiously* and the phrase *from a distance* add to the clues that the ranchers don't want to get too close because the jaguar could hurt them as well.

A Read the following statements from Reading 1. What inferences can you make about each one? Complete the inference statements in your own words.

1. *But there's an older male jaguar in the forest as well, a fierce rival who wants him out of the picture.*

   Inference: If the younger jaguar stays, the older jaguar will most likely _____
   _____.

2. *As predators, jaguars can play an essential role in preventing the spread of these diseases . . .*

   Inference: If jaguars don't keep the animal population under control, humans will _____
   _____.

3. *The Panthera Foundation hopes to convince national governments to maintain this network of habitats through land-use planning. Studies have shown that even areas that are smaller than one and a half square miles can serve as temporary, one- or two-day homes, each one a stepping stone for wandering jaguars.*

   Inference: The fact that small areas are important to jaguars could be useful when Rabinowitz is talking to governments about conservation. Governments might prefer to _____
   _____.

4. *On the ground, they [Rabinowitz and his team] talk to local people and walk the areas of the proposed corridor in order to get a sense of what is needed.*

   Inference: Rabinowitz and his team want to involve local people with this project because _____
   _____.

B What else can you infer from Reading 1? Write one inference about each of the following topics. Discuss your answers with a partner.

1. Alan Rabinowitz _____.

2. Young jaguar cubs _____.

3. Villagers _____.

4. The country of Costa Rica _____.

VOCABULARY PRACTICE

Academic Vocabulary

(A) Find the words in bold in Reading 1. Use the context to help you match each word to the correct definition.

_____ **1. shelter** (Par. 1)

_____ **2. prime** (Par. 4)

_____ **3.** an **incentive** (Par. 5)

_____ **4. genetic** (Par. 8)

_____ **5. astounding** (Par. 8)

_____ **6. crucial** (Par. 9)

_____ **7. ambitious** (Par. 11)

_____ **8.** to **regulate** (Par. 11)

a. main, typical

b. a reason for doing something

c. related to the part of a cell that is characteristic of one's parents

d. amazing; surprising

e. extremely important

f. any type of cover that provides physical protection

g. to control something through government rules

h. challenging and requiring a lot of effort

(B) Choose the correct academic word from the box below to complete each of the following sentences. Notice and learn the words in bold because they often appear with the academic words.

| ambitious | crucial | incentives | regulate |
| astounding | genetic | prime | shelter |

1. Clean water **plays a** _____ **role** in children's health. In many places around the world, water is unsafe to drink.

2. By studying your _____ **material**, scientists are able to make predictions about your health.

3. If you are caught in a thunderstorm, **seek** _____ and wait for the weather to clear.

4. I had no idea that animals in the rainforest were becoming endangered at such a(n) _____ **rate**. We need to act quickly to save these creatures.

5. A movie about the disappearing rainforest is a(n) _____ **example** of using media to send an important message.

6. In the new plan, the government has the **ability to** _____ the costs of health care so that everyone is able to receive care at a lower cost.

7. The prime minister wants to create **economic** _____ such as lower tax rates to keep businesses in local communities.

8. This is a(n) _____ **project**. It won't be easy, but with effort and determination, we can make it work.

Multiword Vocabulary

A Find the multiword vocabulary in bold in Reading 1 and use the context to help you understand the meaning. Then match each item to the correct definition.

_____ 1. **out of the picture** (Par. 1)

_____ 2. **let alone** (Par. 3)

_____ 3. **kept in check** (Par. 5)

_____ 4. **just around the corner** (Par. 5)

_____ 5. **becoming a reality** (Par. 6)

_____ 6. **buffer zones** (Par. 8)

_____ 7. **writing** these places **off** (Par. 9)

_____ 8. **a stepping stone** (Par. 10)

a. not present or involved in a situation

b. coming true

c. a way of getting from one place to another

d. or even more unlikely

e. happening very soon

f. saying something isn't important

g. areas created to separate two different groups and that belong to neither group

h. stopped before it became too large or unmanageable

B Complete the following paragraph with the correct multiword vocabulary in parentheses.

The TOEFL is one of the most common English language exams, and it is an important _____ (stepping stone / buffer zone) for many English language
¹
students because it can lead to acceptance into a university in an English-speaking country. In order for this to _____ (become a reality / write off), students
²
need to get a good score on the exam. Preparation for the exam can be stressful, but it's important to _____ (keep anxiety in check / let anxiety alone). Stress can
³
make it hard to concentrate, _____ (write off / let alone) study
⁴
for a difficult exam. Some students try to create a _____
⁵
(stepping stone / buffer zone) to protect themselves from the distractions of the outside world. For example, they might go to the library and wear headphones so that they won't be disturbed. Any late-night parties should _____ (be out of the picture / become a
⁶
reality). Even if you are nervous, don't _____ (keep in check /
⁷
write off) your chances of success. Remember, there is also a chance that the TOEFL will be easier than you think, and an English-language university education might be
_____ (out of the picture / just around the corner)!
⁸

Use the Vocabulary

Complete the following sentences with your own ideas. Then share your answers with a partner.

1. _____ is **crucial** to a person's health and well-being.

2. Many people have a hard time running for 10 minutes, **let alone** for _____ .

3. Even if you _____ , you don't have to **write off** all physical exercise.
   One simple exercise is to _____ .

4. _____ can be a stepping stone to a better life.

5. It might help to give yourself **incentives** such as _____ each time you exercise.

6. When you are tired or stressed, it can be hard to **keep** _____ **in check**.

7. Many countries **regulate** the sale of _____ to children. You have to be
_____ years old to buy _____ .

8. Most people would agree that it takes _____ and _____
to make your dreams **become a reality**.

THINK AND DISCUSS

Work in a small group. Use the information in the reading and your own ideas to discuss the following questions.

1. **Summarize.** In Reading 1, Rabinowitz found out new information based on DNA fingerprinting. What did he discover? How did this change the Panthera Foundation's approach to conservation? Explain your answers.

2. **Analyze author's purpose.** Why does this reading begin with the story of the young jaguar? What purpose does this serve? Explain your answers.

3. **Use prior knowledge.** What other predators keep animal populations in check? Explain your answer.

4. **Express an opinion.** Did the reading change your opinion of jaguars? Explain your answer.

Academic Vocabulary

charismatic	funding	a tactic
to engage	humor	vulnerable
to expose	to process	

Multiword Vocabulary

at the end of the day	a key to success
to be onto something	on the brink of
to go viral	to stick around
in the spotlight	a wide audience

Reading Preview

A Preview. Skim Reading 2 by reading the first sentence of each paragraph. Then check (✓) each topic you think will be in the reading.

_____ 1. Why cute animals are so important

_____ 2. Online blogs

_____ 3. A sloth video

_____ 4. Big cats such as jaguars and lions

_____ 5. A panda video

_____ 6. Frogs in danger

_____ 7. Protecting endangered species

B Topic vocabulary. The following words appear in Reading 2. Look at the words and answer the questions with a partner.

amphibian	frog	sloth
blog	odd	support
cute	research	unlovable
fluffy	shiny	

1. Which words could be used to describe an animal?

2. Which words refer to animals?

3. Which words might be related to the work of an animal conservationist?

C Predict. What do you think this reading will be about? Discuss each word in Exercise B and predict how it may relate to the reading.

Cute animals aren't the only animals that deserve our attention. Conservationist Lucy Cooke wants to show the world that ugly animals are just as interesting as their cute counterparts.

Champion of the Underdog

Which species would you want to protect first, a tiger cub or a sloth? A panda or a frog? A lion or a dung beetle? When it comes to an emotional response, the cuter creatures get more attention. They also get more research funding, global popularity, and conservation support. If you're an animal, the fluffier your fur and the bigger your eyes, the better your chances for protection. That is, unless zoologist Lucy Cooke has a vote. She's on a mission to show the world why some of the most unlovable animals are actually the most interesting and why they deserve our attention—and our protection.

Cooke's popular blogs, online videos, films, and TV programs all include humor and quirky[1] stories, but they have a serious message: At the end of the day, if we only care for the best-known and best-loved species, other enormously crucial parts of the web of life[2] could disappear forever. With her unique approach combining funny encounters with interesting facts, Cooke uses the Internet to bring her message to a wider audience than to people who watch more traditional wildlife programs on television.

Cooke explains that "a lot of conservation messages are difficult to hear; they make people feel guilty. I think humor is the sugar coating that helps people swallow the pill. If you manage to make someone laugh while you tell them something important, they'll stick around and listen to more." Judging by the positive responses to her videos and blogs, she must be onto something. Cooke often jokes about the animal interactions and her not-so-glamorous work environment. For example, when baboons throw their waste on her favorite jacket, she wonders if perhaps they really are evil animals. As with all of her animal encounters, she comes to appreciate the

---

[1] *quirky:* unusual, strange

[2] *web of life:* the relationships between different species in nature such as predators and their prey.

Three-toed tree sloth

baboons and leads her audience to a better understanding of the animals.

Cooke worries about what she calls "the tyranny[3] of the cute." "There are so many television shows about koala bears and kittens," she observes. "All the attention seems focused on a handful of charismatic "celebrity" animals." She argues that scientists are given more funding for cute animals, citing the fact that there are 500 times more published papers about large mammals as there are about threatened amphibians. Cooke adds: "I've always loved an underdog. Weird, freaky creatures fascinate me because they tell an amazing evolutionary story. I'm interested in all of nature, not just the shiny, fluffy bits."

Amphibians, particularly frogs, are at the top of Cooke's underdog list. "Over a third of amphibians are going extinct; it's the worst extinction crisis since the dinosaurs were wiped off the planet. Yet I couldn't convince anyone to commission a film about it. That motivated me to start my Amphibian Avenger[4] blog." The widely read blog talks about creatures that are not usually in the spotlight. "Frogs are a miracle of evolution

---

[3] *tyranny:* a dictatorship enforced by power and terror

[4] *avenger:* someone who takes revenge for a wrongdoing; also the name of a fictional group of superheroes

that come in myriad[5] forms and every color of the rainbow. You literally can't get bored with them."

Amphibians occupy a crucial spot in the middle of the food chain. "If you remove them, everything else goes haywire,[6]" Cooke explains, describing the web of life, "When amphibians go extinct, birds and snakes that eat them also disappear. Since amphibians breathe through their delicate skin; they are very vulnerable to pollution, climate change, and disease. . . . If amphibians aren't doing well, chances are their overall environment is sick."

Cooke's blog and videos take you around the world. At one of the world's highest lakes, the endangered Lake Titicaca frog survives huge variations in temperature and intense UV rays[7] by permanently living on the lake's floor. Since the frog never comes to the surface, it breathes only through its skin. As a consequence, it evolved with many folds and flaps to increase its surface area. "Tragically, I've only seen this frog in a blender,[8]" Cooke reports. "People have decided he's a medicinal cure." Cooke's videos expose frog juice bars, which have caused the ancient species to be on the brink of extinction.

"It's exciting to tell stories that haven't been told," Cooke says. One story she tells is of Wallace's flying frog, which lives on top of the rainforest canopy in Borneo. Rather than going all the way up and down, it glides from tree to tree using its flaps of skin as wings. Cooke also shows her audience the golden poison dart frog, which measures only one centimeter, but has enough poison to kill 10 men. Yet another frog is Darwin's frog, which is one of only two known species where the male gets pregnant.

Cooke reached her widest audience when her online video about sloths went viral. Millions of viewers have watched the film about baby sloths that were orphaned after power lines and roads were built in Costa Rica's jungles. Cooke is pleased to help change people's opinions of

6

7

8

9

---

5 *myriad:* many, referring to a great number of things
6 *goes haywire:* goes wrong or badly
7 *UV rays:* ultra-violet rays. Rays that can be harmful because of radiation, and are transmitted from the sun
8 *blender:* small kitchen machine used to cut and mix foods together

Lake Titicaca frog

Wallace's flying frog

Proboscis monkey

sloths. "They've always had a reputation for being lazy, stupid, and dirty. The first European to describe a sloth said, 'If there was one more thing wrong with it, it wouldn't survive.'"

In fact, "slothfulness" is the key to the ani- 10 mal's success. A slow metabolism[9] allows the sloth's body to process toxins found in the leaves it eats. Moving slowly also keeps it hidden from predators. "My video showed the world how cute

---
[9] *metabolism:* the processes in the body that digest, use, and expel nourishment

and interesting these babies are," Cooke says. "I'll use any tactic to make people like things."

Through her videos, Cooke introduces her 11 audience to the proboscis monkey, dung beetles, bats, and many other animals. "It's about championing animals that don't have a voice and telling their stories in a way that engages a wider audience. I want people to share my sense of wonder, amazement, and love for these creatures. Once you understand why they're ugly or odd, I hope you'll appreciate and want to save them as much as I do."

SAVING THE SEA TURTLE

Sea turtles around the world are now close to extinction. Sea turtles come ashore to lay their eggs, but in many places their eggs, meat, and shells are in high demand. Nicaragua is one country where poaching—illegal hunting of the turtles and their eggs—has been a major threat to the creatures. Here, where many people live on $1 a day, they can make $5 a day by selling 12 sea turtle eggs. Conservation groups have been working to end poaching through education and finding alternative sources of income for the people living in these areas.

Local people are also encouraged to join in the 24-hour beach patrols and monitor the turtles' movements. A media campaign in Nicaragua raises awareness of the issue by featuring celebrities who state publicly that they don't eat sea turtle eggs. The results have been impressive. Now, according to some estimates, approximately 90% of sea turtle nests on key beaches in Nicaragua are protected. Thanks to these ongoing conservation efforts, the sea turtles may have a chance at survival.

READING COMPREHENSION

Big Picture

Ⓐ Choose the answer that best completes each of the following sentences.

1. The main idea of Reading 2 is stated in the _____.
   a. first sentence of paragraph 1   b. last sentence of paragraph 1

2. The main idea of paragraph 2 is that _____.
   a. Cooke's blogs are stories about well-known species of endangered animals
   b. Cooke uses humor to bring her conservation message to as many viewers as possible

3. The main idea of paragraph 4 is that _____.
   a. Cooke doesn't like cute, fluffy animals as much as amphibians
   b. cute, fluffy animals receive more funding than amphibians

4. The purpose of paragraph 5 is to explain why Cooke _____.
   a. started a blog about amphibians   b. became interested in amphibians

5. The main idea of paragraph 9 is found in the _____ sentence.
   a. first   b. fifth

Ⓑ Read the following ideas. Check (✓) the one that expresses the author's purpose for writing Reading 2.

_____ 1. To describe Lucy Cooke's mission to save cute animals

_____ 2. To tell the story of Lucy Cooke's life

_____ 3. To describe how Lucy Cooke raises awareness of endangered creatures

_____ 4. To talk about amphibians and other "ugly" animals

_____ 5. To describe why there are differences between different types of animals

Close-Up

Ⓐ Complete the following sentences in your own words, using information from Reading 2 and the short extra reading, "Saving the Sea Turtle," on page 69.

1. The reading implies that Cooke thinks amphibians would get more attention if they were

   _____.

2. Cooke explains that more than _____ of all amphibians are going extinct, which means that this is the worst extinction crisis since _____.

3. Cooke's blog and videos feature animals from _____.

4. Conservation groups in Nicaragua try to protect sea turtles by _____.

Ⓑ Write one detail about each of the following animals, based on the information in Reading 2 and "Saving the Sea Turtle."

1. Lake Titicaca frog (Par. 7) _____

2. Wallace's flying frog (Par. 8) _____

3. Golden poison dart frog (Par. 8) _____

4. Darwin's frog (Par. 8) _____

5. Sloth (Par. 9) _____

6. Sea turtles (Extra reading) _____

Reading Skill

Choosing the Correct Definition

As you learned in Unit 2 on page 36, sometimes you can ignore a word you don't know and still figure out the meaning of the sentence. There are other times, however, when you will need to look up the definition of a word in order to better understand the text. Many words in English have more than one meaning, and it is important to determine which definition is appropriate in the context of the reading. Ask yourself the following questions about each word in order to choose the correct definition:

- What is its part of speech? Focus on the definitions for the part of speech that is used in the reading. Dictionary definitions begin with *n.* for noun, *v.* for verb, *adj.* for adjective, *adv.* for adverb, etc.

- Does the definition make sense in the context of the sentence? Reread the sentence in the text and substitute each dictionary definition in place of the vocabulary word.

- Do more than one of the definitions make sense? If so, read the example sentences. These can also help you determine which is the better definition by giving more of a context to each meaning.

Look at the following sentence from Reading 2. The highlighted word has more than one meaning.

With her unique approach combining funny encounters with interesting facts, Cooke uses the Internet to bring her message to a wider audience than to people who watch more traditional wildlife programs on television.

Now read the dictionary entry from Heinle's *Newbury House Dictionary of American English* for *approach.*

> Approach *n.* -es 1. a course of action, a way of handling a situation: *She took a quiet, friendly approach in dealing with her daughter about the problem.* 2. means of access: *The pilot made a slow, gradual approach to the airport runway. v.* [T] -es 1. to go near, move toward: *As I approached the house, I noticed that the door was open.* 2. to begin to handle a situation or work on st: *I approached the problem of reducing costs by making a list of them.*

We know that *approach* in the sentence from Reading 2 is a noun because it follows an adjective (*unique*). If we substitute both noun meanings, we can see that it must be the first meaning. This is about a course of action: Lucy Cooke is bringing her conservation message to the public. The second meaning might be a possibility until we look at the example sentence for meaning 2. We can see that it is very different from the meaning in the sentence in the reading.

A Read the dictionary entries for each word. Choose the correct definitions based on the reading. Write the definition number on the line.

1. support (Par. 1) _____

> *n*. support: 1. [C] st that holds up or bears the weight of s.t. else: *If you take away the supports, the wall will fall down. (fig) She is his sole support in life.* 2. [U] the act of supporting (helping) st *Can we have your support at the next meeting?* 3. money used for the necessities of life: *When he lost his job, he was suddenly without support.* 4. moral, emotional, or financial assistance. *Her family always gave her lots of support.*

2. observes (Par. 4) _____

> *v*. observe [T] -served, -serving, -serves 1. to view, watch, esp. for anything unusual: *A policeman observed the activity on the street.* 2. to remark, express an opinion: *Our professor observed that we all did well on the examination.* 3. to see, notice: *She observed a man with a large suitcase getting into a car. Did you observe anything unusual?* 4. to respect or follow laws, rules, or customs: *We observed Memorial Day by going to church and praying for the dead.*

B Circle each of the following words in Reading 2. Based on the context in the reading, write the correct part of speech on the line.

1. response (Par. 1) _____

2. message (Par. 2) _____

3. handful (Par. 4) _____

4. folds (Par. 7) _____

5. cure (Par. 7) _____

6. measures (Par. 8) _____

7. appreciate (Par. 11) _____

C Look in a dictionary and find the correct definition for each of the words in Exercise B.

VOCABULARY PRACTICE

Academic Vocabulary

A Find the words in bold in Reading 2. Use the context to help you choose the definition that is closest to the meaning in the reading.

_____ **1. funding** (Par. 1)
    a. money for a specific purpose
    b. a new building

_____ **2. humor** (Par. 2)
    a. something healthy
    b. something funny

_____ **3. charismatic** (Par. 4)
    a. attractive and charming
    b. interesting and informative

_____ **4. vulnerable** (Par. 6)
    a. unprotected
    b. impossible

_____ **5. expose** (Par. 7)
    a. reveal something
    b. define something

_____ **6. process** (Par. 10)
    a. plan a way to use something in the future
    b. transform something into something else in order to use it

_____ **7. tactic** (Par. 10)

    a. a method of doing something

    b. a way to finish something

_____ **8. engages** (Par 11)

    a. describes something or someone in a particular situation

    b. gets and holds the attention of something or someone

B Choose the best answer for each of the following questions. Notice and learn the words in bold because they often appear together.

1. Which of the following people need to have a **charismatic personality**?

    a. computer programmers   **b.** public speakers   **c.** passport control officers

2. If you want to **engage** a child's **interest**, which of the following would probably NOT be an **effective tactic**?

    a. singing a song   **b.** explaining academic vocabulary   **c.** telling a story

3. Which of the following people are most likely to **expose corruption**?

    a. teachers   **b.** politicians   **c.** journalists

4. Which of the following usually rely on **public funding**?

    a. universities   **b.** clothing stores   **c.** restaurants

5. When someone has a good **sense of humor**, what is the usual outcome?

    a. Their friends cry.   **b.** Their friends laugh.   **c.** Their friends make money.

6. In which of the following situations do people usually worry that they are more **vulnerable to danger**?

    a. with friends   **b.** at a restaurant   **c.** alone in the dark

7. Thousands of students apply to universities each year. Which is the most likely amount of time needed for a university to **process** an **application**?

    a. three hours   **b.** three months   **c.** three years

Dung beetle

Multiword Vocabulary

A Find the multiword vocabulary in bold in Reading 2 and use the context to help you understand the meaning. Then match each item to the correct definition.

_____ 1. **at the end of the day** (Par. 2)

_____ 2. **a wider audience** (Par. 2)

_____ 3. **stick around** (Par. 3)

_____ 4. **be onto something** (Par. 3)

_____ 5. **in the spotlight** (Par. 5)

_____ 6. **on the brink of** (Par. 7)

_____ 7. **went viral** (Par. 9)

_____ 8. **key to** the animal's **success** (Par. 10)

a. became very popular on the Internet

b. stay somewhere and not leave

c. getting a lot of public attention

d. appearing to be the case after all the facts are considered

e. the way to achieve something

f. more people who watch, listen, or read something than previously

g. very close to doing something

h. be aware of or discover important information that leads to thinking or acting correctly

B Complete the following paragraph with the correct multiword vocabulary from Exercise A. In some cases, you need to change the verb or noun form.

When a video _____ on the Internet, the actors and actresses
                              1
in the video can become instantly famous. Once a video is a success, a natural human response is

to try to attract _____ than before. However, sudden fame isn't
                              2
always positive. It can be very stressful. Some actors, when they suddenly become famous, may

even find themselves _____ a nervous breakdown. There are
                              3
some older movie stars who advise the younger generation to spend time away from the fancy

parties and paparazzi. They say that it isn't good to _____
                                                              4
Hollywood for too long. Instead, they say that the _____ is to
                                                              5
live a quiet life. These stars think that, _____ , the most
                                                  6
important thing is to have close family and friends. What do you think? Do you think that movie

stars who live quiet lives _____ , or is it a better idea to live a
                              7
glamorous life and stay _____ ?
                              8

Use the Vocabulary

Write answers to the following questions. Use the words in bold in your answers. Then share your answers with a partner.

1. What are some common **tactics** that advertisers use in order to sell a product?

2. After most of your classes, do students **stick around** and ask the teacher for help, or does everyone leave immediately?

3. What are some examples of organizations or projects that receive **funding** from your government?

4. How do journalists often **engage** the public's **interest**? Give an example of a recent news story that engaged your interest. How did the journalist achieve that?

Mexican bats

5. How can people use the Internet to **expose corruption**?

6. If you want to learn a new language, what do you think is the **key to success**?

7. Have you ever watched a video that has **gone viral**? If so, describe what the video was about.

8. When you are learning a new language, what aspects of language (reading, writing, listening, or speaking) are difficult for your brain to **process** quickly?

THINK AND DISCUSS

Work in a small group. Use the information in the reading and your own ideas to discuss the following questions.

1. **Relate to personal experience.** What are some examples of "celebrity animals" in your country? Explain why they are famous.

2. **Apply knowledge.** Imagine Lucy Cooke came to a place you know well. What animal would she spotlight? Explain your answer.

3. **Summarize.** Choose a quote from Lucy Cooke in Reading 2 that you think best summarizes the article and Lucy Cooke's mission. Explain why you chose this quote.

4. **Express an opinion.** Would you be interested in watching Lucy Cooke's online videos? Why, or why not?

Vocabulary Review

A Complete the paragraph with the vocabulary below that you have studied in the unit.

ambitious project	charismatic personalities	on the brink of	vulnerable to danger
at the end of the day	crucial role	sense of humor	wide audience
buffer zone	in the spotlight		

Baboon

On her television show, *Freaks and Creeps*, Lucy Cooke, uses her funny stories and her _____ **1** to introduce different animals to a(n) _____ **2** of viewers. Baboons are _____ **3** in one episode of the show. Most humans do not think that baboons have _____ **4** —baboons can be violent and aggressive. However, these animals are in danger. In fact, they are _____ **5** extinction. In South Africa, Cooke goes to the Riverside Baboon Rescue Centre. There, she meets Bob Ventor, who is about to release 28 baboons back into the wild. Cooke helps Bob medicate the animals so that they can carry them into an area that has been surrounded by an electric fence. The fenced area is a(n) _____ **6** for the baboons before they enter the wild, and it plays a(n) _____ **7** in their safety. Without the fence, the baboons might run in different directions. If they are separated, they won't be able to help each other, and they will be more _____ **8**.
Viewers of the show watch as Cooke helps with this _____ **9**. The baboons throw things at her, she gets a bump on her head, and she gets shocked by an electric fence. However, _____ **10**, once the baboons are free in the wild, Cooke says that helping them has been a very rewarding experience.

B Compare answers to Exercise A with a partner. Then discuss the following questions.

Would you like to watch the show Freaks and Creeps *about baboons? Why, or why not?*

C Complete the following sentences in a way that shows that you understand the meaning of the words in bold.

1. I hope that someday soon, my dream of _____ **becomes a reality**.

2. One reason for **exposing corruption** is _____.

3. Mother birds **stick around** their nest because _____.

4. When I study, one **effective tactic** I use is to _____.

D Work with a partner and write sentences that include any six of the vocabulary items below. You may use any verb tense and make nouns plural if you wish.

astounding fact	engage someone's interest	just around the corner	let alone
to be onto something	genetic material	a key to success	seek shelter
economic incentive	to go viral		

Connect the Readings

A Use the chart below to take notes on Reading 1 and Reading 2.

ANIMAL CONSERVATIONISTS		
	Alan Rabinowitz	**Lucy Cooke**
Occupation		
Major goal		
How the goal affects humans		
How he or she is working to achieve this goal		
How he or she connects with the public		
The science and technology used		

B With a partner or in a small group, compare answers to Exercise A. Then discuss the following questions.

1. What are the two different ways that Cooke and Rabinowitz champion animals? Do you think one is more helpful than the other? Explain your answer.

2. If you had a chance to donate money or volunteer your time to either the Panthera Foundation or the Amphibian Avenger, which one would you choose? Would you donate money or volunteer? Explain your answer.

C Discuss the following questions with a partner. Use your understanding of the readings and your own ideas.

1. Read the following statements. What were the speakers talking about? How do these statements help you understand the conservationists' missions?

   People are drawn to the animal's beauty, strength, and mystery. (Reading 1, Par. 11)

   I think humor is the sugar coating that helps people swallow the pill. (Reading 2, Par. 3)

   If you remove them, everything else goes haywire. (Reading 2, Par. 6)

2. What is another organization that helps animals? What is its mission? How does it achieve its goals?

FOUR

A gigantic cloud of dust known as a "haboob" advances over the city of Khartoum, Sudan.

FOCUS

1. What are some examples of natural disasters?

2. Have you ever experienced a natural disaster?

3. How can technology help people prepare for a natural disaster?

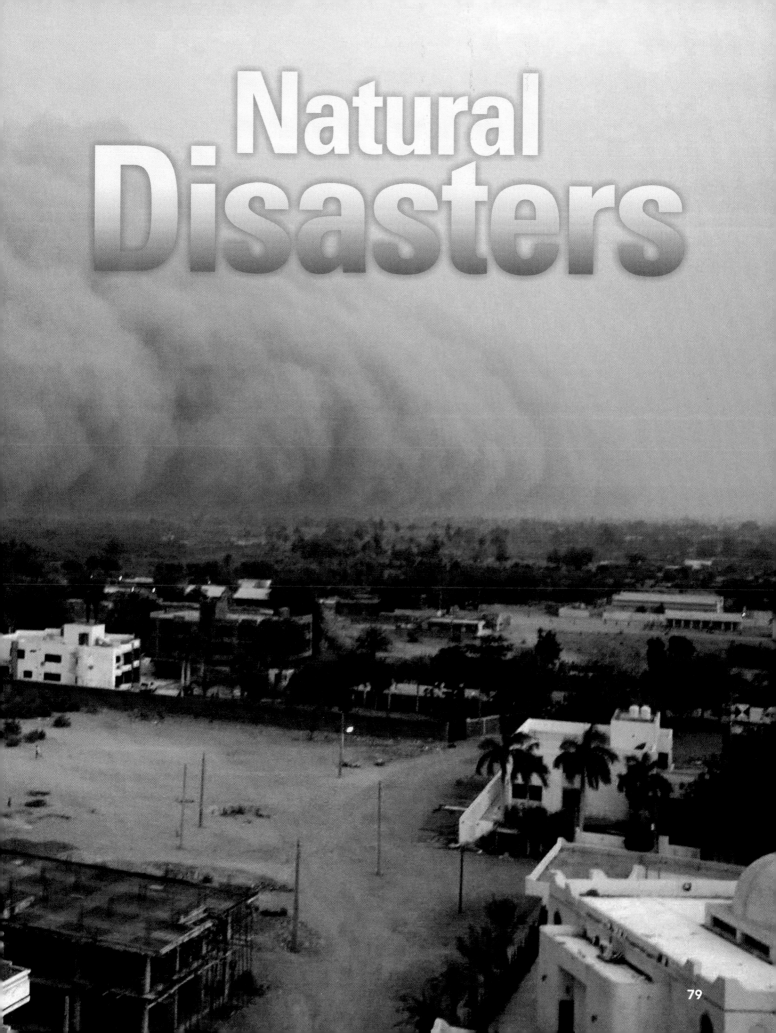

Natural Disasters

Academic Vocabulary

to adjust	an insight	potentially
efficiency	intensity	recovery
to forecast	to monitor	

Multiword Vocabulary

as we know it	on end
to be caught off guard	science fiction
to come to a halt	a time frame
the full extent of	to wreak havoc on

Did you know that storms occur on the sun and that these storms can have damaging effects here on Earth? Find out how scientists are trying to predict solar storms and prevent disaster.

Reading Preview

A Preview. Scan Reading 1. Look for dates and words in italics. Then discuss the following questions with a partner or in a small group.

1. What is a *solar storm*?

2. What happened in 1859?

3. What is *Enlil*?

B Topic vocabulary. The following words appear in Reading 1. Look at the words and answer the questions with a partner.

amateur astronomer	magnetic field
currents	satellite
destroy	solar
electrical grid	sunspot
impact	telescope
interact	transformer

1. Which words are related to outer space?

2. Which words are related to electricity?

3. Which words describe how one thing affects another?

C Predict. What do you think this reading will be about? Discuss each word in Exercise B and predict how it may relate to the reading.

SUN STRUCK

A close-up photo of a solar flare on the sun

I magine today's world with no Internet, no television, no electric lights. How could this happen? One way is through the effects of a *solar storm*.

Solar storms are electromagnetic outbursts that send billions of tons of charged particles[1] toward Earth. They have the potential to destroy our electrical grids as well as all connections that we have with satellites in space. Every credit card purchase, every plane flight, and every cell phone call relies on a satellite connection. The modern world as we know it would come to a halt. This might sound like a scenario from a science fiction movie, but in fact, it is exactly what scientists are trying to prevent right now.

The sun is made of a *plasma*—a material that is not a gas, a liquid, or a solid. Instead, a plasma is made up of charged particles, which make it a powerful conductor of electricity. In addition to these strong electric fields, the sun is also packed with magnetic fields. Magnetic field lines wrap around the sun like an enormous birdcage. The sun's magnetism powers a "solar wind" that flings one million tons of plasma outward every second—plasma that travels at one million miles per hour. Sometimes this event can create powerful plasma explosions called *solar flares*, which release the energy equivalent of hundreds of millions of mega-tons of dynamite.[2] When this energy heads toward Earth, we feel the effects of a solar storm.

Solar storms are not a new phenomenon. They have undoubtedly been happening for billions of years. One of the largest recent solar storms occurred on September 1, 1859, when a 33-year-old amateur astronomer named Richard Carrington adjusted his telescope to project an 11-inch (28-centimeter) image of the sun onto a screen. Suddenly, "two patches of intensely bright and white light" appeared in the middle of a large sunspot group. This was a solar flare, the first sign of the solar storm now known as the *Carrington Event* (see Figure 1).

---

[1] *charged particles:* particles with a positive or negative electrical charge

[2] *dynamite:* a powerful explosive substance

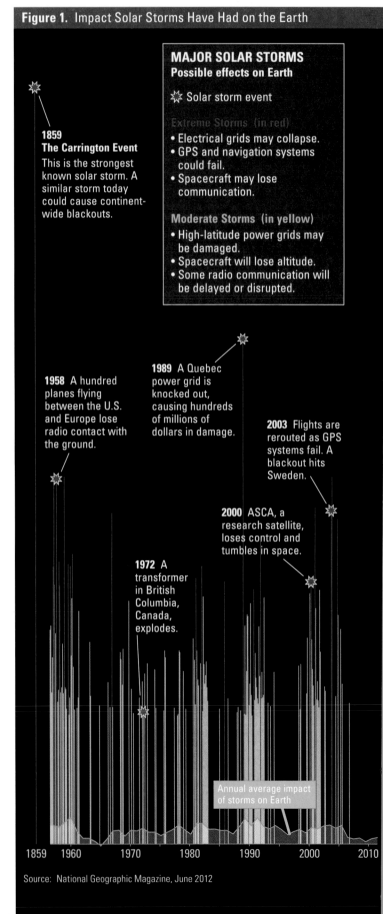

Figure 1. Impact Solar Storms Have Had on the Earth

MAJOR SOLAR STORMS
Possible effects on Earth

✳ Solar storm event

Extreme Storms (in red)
• Electrical grids may collapse.
• GPS and navigation systems could fail.
• Spacecraft may lose communication.

Moderate Storms (in yellow)
• High-latitude power grids may be damaged.
• Spacecraft will lose altitude.
• Some radio communication will be delayed or disrupted.

1859
The Carrington Event
This is the strongest known solar storm. A similar storm today could cause continent-wide blackouts.

1958 A hundred planes flying between the U.S. and Europe lose radio contact with the ground.

1989 A Quebec power grid is knocked out, causing hundreds of millions of dollars in damage.

2003 Flights are rerouted as GPS systems fail. A blackout hits Sweden.

2000 ASCA, a research satellite, loses control and tumbles in space.

1972 A transformer in British Columbia, Canada, explodes.

Annual average impact of storms on Earth

1859   1960   1970   1980   1990   2000   2010

Source: National Geographic Magazine, June 2012

The Carrington Event was due to a powerful 5 solar flare that produced two coronal mass ejections (CMEs)—enormous magnetic eruptions of heated plasma. The first CME probably reached Earth in the normal time frame of 40 to 60 hours. However, this cleared a path through the solar wind for the second CME to make the trip in just 17 hours. The combined strength of these two CMEs compressed Earth's magnetosphere, the area where the planet's magnetic field interacts with the solar wind. This meant the field shrunk from its normal altitude of 40,000 miles to 4,000 miles (64,374 to 6,437 kilometers), leaving the planet more vulnerable to solar activity.

When the electrical currents from the sun 6 hit Earth's magnetic field, it produced intense auroras over much of Earth. Some people thought their cities were on fire. Auroral displays, or bursts of red, green, and purple light, usually seen in the far north, were observed in the skies as far south as Hawaii and Panama. Hikers in the Rocky Mountains of North America thought it was sunrise and consequently got up and started cooking breakfast. The storm also caused electrical currents to surge[3] through telegraph lines.[4] While some telegraph stations were destroyed, others were able to operate using the electricity generated by the storm, which was racing through the telegraph lines.

No solar storm as powerful as the 1859 event 7 has occurred since. As a result, it is difficult to estimate the full extent of the damage that a comparable storm could cause to today's wired world. However, a solar storm doesn't have to be nearly that large to wreak havoc on our planet. A storm on March 13, 1989, provided an insight into just how dangerous even a smaller storm can be. This

---

[3] *surge:* move through something in a sudden and powerful way (often used to speak about water or electricity)

[4] *telegraph lines:* the wires of a system to send messages over long distances

The aurora borealis seen over Alaska, USA

storm was approximately a third less powerful than the Carrington Event. Nonetheless, in less than two minutes, intense currents destroyed a power grid in Canada, which served more than six million customers (see Figure 1).

8 John Kappenman of Storm Analysis Consultants studies the impact of space weather on power grids. According to Kappenman, a solar storm like the 1859 event would be powerful enough to destroy the entire system of power grids. It would take months to manufacture and install new transformers. Satellites would drift silently in space, unable to communicate with us here on Earth. Hundreds of millions of people would be forced to return to a pre-electric way of life for weeks or perhaps months on end. We would have to survive in a world without electric lights, drinkable water, sewage treatment, heating, air-conditioning, gasoline stations, or telephone service. A recent U.S. National Academy of Sciences report estimates that recovery from such damage could cost one to two trillion dollars in the first year alone.

9 There is no way to prevent a solar storm, but accurate predictions may allow us to minimize the damage. When scientists are able to predict a solar storm, steps can be taken in advance to save the electrical grids. Taking the transformers offline, or disconnecting them from the power source, protects the grids for the duration of the storm. While this is inconvenient for the public, a blackout for a few hours is better than one that lasts for a few months.

10 In 1859, the world had very few tools for studying the sun. Today scientists use a number of satellites to constantly monitor our home star. One such satellite is the Advanced Composition Explorer (ACE) spacecraft, launched in August 1997. It monitors the solar wind from a point that is located a million miles closer to the sun than the Earth. While this allows scientists to predict solar flares, they cannot be sure of a storm's intensity until it reaches the ACE satellite, which may be only 20 minutes before it hits Earth.

11 In October 2011, the National Oceanic and Atmospheric Administration (NOAA) introduced

"There is no way to prevent a solar storm, but accurate predictions may allow us to minimize the damage."

a new computer model. Named *Enlil*, after the Sumerian god of winds, this model can predict when a CME will hit Earth but still not more accurately than plus or minus six hours. On March 8, 2012, Enlil predicted a potentially major storm. The storm occurred only 45 minutes later than forecasted. That storm didn't turn out to be very powerful, but it proved the efficiency of the forecasting system. Although the next storm might be more intense, we can hope that with improved technology, we will be able to avoid a world without electricity. Hopefully, we won't be caught off guard.

NASA launches the ACE satellite that will study the effects of the sun on the earth.

READING COMPREHENSION

Big Picture

Ⓐ The following are key words and phrases that could be used to annotate (see page 21) paragraphs 2–11 in Reading 1. Write the correct paragraph number on the line next to each annotation.

_____ **1.** ACE spacecraft = monitor the sun

_____ **2.** smaller solar storm: 1989 storm

_____ **3.** solar flare definition

_____ **4.** the Carrington Event: 1859

_____ **5.** possible solar storm effects today

_____ **6.** Enlil = 2011 computer = accurate forecast

_____ **7.** effects of Carrington Event

_____ **8.** 2 CMEs = Earth more vulnerable after 2nd

_____ **9.** definition and dangers of a solar storm

_____ **10.** a forecasting system can prevent damage

Ⓑ Choose the best answer for each of the following questions.

1. What is the main idea of Reading 1?
   a. Solar storms have been occurring for a very long time.
   b. Scientists are trying to find ways to prevent the damaging effects of a solar storm.
   c. Solar storms cause devastation to electrical grids.

2. Why does the author compare solar storms to science fiction movies?
   a. The author wants to engage the readers' interest.
   b. There is a famous science fiction movie about solar storms.
   c. Science fiction is often about outer space.

3. Which of the following is probably *not* the reason why the author explains what the sun is made of?
   a. Not all readers will know details about the sun.
   b. Too much exposure to sunlight can be dangerous.
   c. In order to understand solar storms, you need to know how they start.

4. Why does the author use the future tense and modals such as *would* and *could*?
   a. No one can be sure what will happen in the future.
   b. The author's research did not include this information.
   c. The author wants the reading to be as current as possible.

5. What do you think the author is most likely to believe?
   a. A solar storm is the most dangerous of all natural disasters.
   b. Technology will protect us against damage from a solar storm.
   c. Another solar storm will occur soon.

Close-Up

Ⓐ Complete the chart below with information from Reading 1.

	1859	1989	In the Future
Effects of a solar storm			

B Scan Reading 1 to find answers to the following questions.

1. Was the Carrington Event the first solar storm? Explain your answer.

2. How quickly do CMEs usually reach Earth after they erupt on the sun's surface?

3. Why was Earth more vulnerable when the second CME reached it in 1859?

4. How can satellites help to minimize the effects of a solar storm?

5. What happened on March 8, 2012?

Reading Skill

Understanding In-Text Definitions

In certain readings, such as scientific readings, there are often key words that are defined in the text. These can be terms that are too specific to be found in a typical dictionary. These key words are often italicized. Their definitions can follow a comma or a dash (—), or they can be signaled by the words and phrases *or*, *that is*, *called*, or *known as*.

Look at the following sentences from Reading 1 that contain the word *plasma*:

> The sun is made of a plasma—a material that is not a gas, a liquid, or a solid. Instead, a plasma is made up of charged particles, which make it a powerful conductor of electricity.

The definition could be written as the following:

> plasma = a material that is not gas/solid/liquid. Charged particles; powerful conductor of electricity.

A Scan Reading 1 and circle the items that signal the definitions of the following terms.

1. solar wind	3. magnetosphere	5. auroral displays
2. solar flares	4. CME	6. offline

B Write a brief definition of each term in Exercise A.

1. solar wind = _____

2. solar flares = _____

3. magnetosphere = _____

4. CME = _____

5. auroral displays = _____

6. offline = _____

VOCABULARY PRACTICE

Academic Words

A Find the words in the box below in Reading 1. Use the context to help you choose the correct words to complete the following sentences.

adjusted (Par. 4)	recovery (Par. 8)	intensity (Par. 10)	forecasted (Par. 11)
insight (Par. 7)	monitor (Par. 10)	potentially (Par. 11)	efficiency (Par. 11)

1. When people started to buy more products online, companies _____ their advertising strategies to keep up with the competition.

2. Nurses are expected to _____ the health of their patients carefully.

3. During training, police officers prepare for a number of _____ dangerous situations.

4. After the hurricane, people were very impressed with the way that the government agency handled the _____. Because of the _____ of the rescue operations, no lives were lost.

5. The meteorologists _____ a snowstorm for yesterday, but we weren't prepared for the _____ of the storm.

6. Detectives tried to gain _____ into how the men were able to rob the bank.

B The words in bold show academic words from Exercise A and words they often appear with. Complete the sentences with your own ideas.

1. The meteorologist **forecasted rain** for Sunday afternoon, so we _____.

2. Extremely hot weather **could potentially** cause _____.

3. Teachers often **monitor the progress** of their students by _____.

4. Movies often portray the **intensity of** people's feelings, such as when _____.

5. Reading novels can provide **insight into** how people _____.

6. After last year's severe flooding, **economic recovery** has been slow coming to the area, and people are _____.

7. The manager of the restaurant was pleased with the **efficiency of** the _____ during the busy lunch hour.

8. It can take some time to **adjust to** new situations such as _____.

Multiword Vocabulary

A Find the multiword vocabulary in bold in Reading 1 and use the context to help you understand the meaning. Then match each item to the correct definition.

_____ **1. as we know it** (Par. 2)

_____ **2. come to a halt** (Par. 2)

_____ **3. science fiction** (Par. 2)

_____ **4. time frame** (Par. 5)

_____ **5. the full extent of** (Par. 7)

_____ **6. wreak havoc on** (Par. 7)

_____ **7. on end** (Par. 8)

_____ **8. be caught off guard** (Par. 11)

a. be surprised by and unprepared for something

b. cause a great amount of disorder or damage

c. stories about events that take place in in the future or other parts of the universe

d. the length of time during which something happens or develops

e. one after another, adding up to a long time

f. stop completely and suddenly

g. the total amount of something

h. how we are used to or familiar with something

B Complete the following paragraph with the correct multiword vocabulary from Exercise A.

It's difficult to even imagine what _____ 1 the devastation would be if a solar superstorm destroyed all of our electrical grids. How long would this last? No one is sure of the _____ 2 , but we could be without electricity for weeks _____ 3 . A solar superstorm would _____ 4 our banking system. No one would be able to use credit cards. Commerce and trade _____ 5 would completely disappear. The ability to buy food or gas using a credit card would _____ 6 . Almost everyone on the planet would _____ 7 since, in this modern age, it is rare to carry large amounts of cash. If this were a _____ 8 story, an action hero might save the day. In this case, the heroes might be the satellites that accurately predict the storm!

Use the Vocabulary

Complete the following sentences with your own ideas. Then share your answers with a partner.

1. **Efficiency** is an important quality for people in professions such as _____ .

2. An example of a time that I was **caught off guard** was when _____ .

3. It is usually easy to **forecast** the weather in _____ because _____ .

4. If you want to _____ , it can be a good idea to set a **time frame** for yourself.

5. A large storm such as _____ **could potentially** do a lot of damage to this area.

6. If everyone lost their _____ , life **as we know it** would **come to a halt**.

7. One example of a **science fiction** movie or book is _____ .

THINK AND DISCUSS

Work in a small group. Use the information in the reading and your own ideas to discuss the following questions.

1. **Relate to personal experience.** Have you ever had an experience where you had to live or manage without electricity? What happened? What did you do?

2. **Summarize.** What did you learn about the sun from this reading?

3. **Analyze.** How could technology help to minimize the effects of a solar storm?

4. **Express an opinion.** Do you think most people are aware of the dangers of solar storms? Why, or why not?

Solar plasma pushing through the sun's atmosphere

Academic Vocabulary

to alert	to facilitate	unprecedented
to broadcast	magnitude	whereas
a colleague	a precaution	

Multiword Vocabulary

at any moment	human nature
at regular intervals	in the wake of
a false sense of security	a preventive measure
to get credit	relatively minor

Reading Preview

A Preview. Look at the photos on pages 90–94 and write three questions about tsunamis that you think might be answered in the reading. Then discuss your questions with a partner or in a small group.

1. _____

2. _____

3. _____

B Topic vocabulary. The following words appear in Reading 2. Look at the words and answer the questions with a partner.

detect	seawall
Earth's crust	seismologist
evacuation route	stabilize
fault	surge
fishing port	warning system
seafloor	waves

1. Which words are related to water?

2. Which words are related to earthquakes?

3. Which words might be related to protecting people in the event of a tsunami?

C Predict. What do you think this reading will be about? Discuss each word in Exercise B and predict how it may relate to the reading.

What would you do if you knew a tsunami was coming to a beach near you? Read about tsunamis and how we can warn people before a tsunami comes ashore.

AFRICA

SOMALIA
Waves up
to 4 feet
(1.2 meters)

7.5 hours

Source: National Geographic Magazine, April 2005

Tracking Tsunamis

INDIA

Andaman
Islands
(INDIA)

THAILAND

•Phuket

SRI LANKA
Waves up
to 45 feet
(13.8 meters)

MALDIVES
Waves up
to 13 feet
(4.0 meters)

S u m a t r a

INDONESIA

EQUATOR

2 hours

3.5 hours

INDIAN   OCEAN

Map showing the time it
took for the tsuami wave
from the underwater
earthquake in Indonesia
in December 2004 to move
across the Indian Ocean

Minamisanriku

On March 11, 2011, Minamisanriku, a quiet [1] fishing port north of Sendai in northeastern Japan, was almost completely washed away.

The disaster started at 2:46 p.m., about 80 [2] miles (about 129 kilometers) east of Sendai in the Pacific Ocean, along a fault line buried deep under the seafloor. A 280-mile- (451-kilometer-) long portion of Earth's crust suddenly moved to the east, parts of it by nearly 80 feet (24 meters).

The earthquake didn't cause much damage [3] to Minamisanriku, but the sea had just begun to swell. Mayor Jin Sato and a few dozen others ran to the town's three-story disaster-readiness center to alert the public to the danger. Miki Endo, a 24-year-old woman working on the second floor, broadcast a warning over the town's loudspeakers:[1] "Please head to higher ground!" Sato and most of his group climbed to the roof. From there, they watched the tsunami pour over the town's 18-foot- (5-meter-) high seawall, destroying everything in its path. Then dark water surged over the building and Endo's broadcasts stopped.

An estimated 16,000 people died that day in [4] Japan, most of them along hundreds of miles of coast. In Minamisanriku, approximately 900 of 17,700 residents were killed or missing, including Miki Endo, whose body was not found until April 23. Sato survived by holding onto a radio antenna on the roof. There were around 30 other people on the roof that night. In the morning, only 10 people remained.

This disaster occurred in a country that [5] leads the world in preparing for earthquakes and tsunamis. It has spent billions of dollars stabilizing old buildings and equipping new ones with shock absorbers.[2] Many coastal towns have high seawalls, and well-marked routes are in place to facilitate evacuation to high ground or to tall, strong buildings. On March 11, government seismologists sent out the first tsunami warning immediately after the earthquake. These preventive measures saved many thousands of lives; Miki Endo herself may have saved thousands.

What Is a Tsunami?

Tsunamis occur somewhere in the world [6] almost every year. Most tsunamis are caused by earthquakes on the seafloor. These commonly occur in the Pacific and Indian Oceans, along faults

---

[1] *loudspeakers:* pieces of electronic equipment that form part of a public address system and transmit sound

[2] *shock absorbers:* devices that reduce the effects of large movements

Minamisanriku, Japan
3:35 p.m., March 11, 2011

called *subduction zones*. An earthquake that begins miles below the seafloor is capable of releasing the energy equivalent of 8,000 atomic bombs.[3] This moves the water above the seafloor and spreads out in long waves that may be a few hundred miles apart. The waves can be dangerous even after they cross the ocean; the tsunami in Japan destroyed boats in several small harbors on the west coast of the United States, and in Antarctica it broke off blocks of ice the size of Manhattan.

Tsunami Precautions

On December 26, 2004, a tsunami occurred in 7 the Indian Ocean, killing nearly 170,000 people in Indonesia. Sixty thousand more died in Sri Lanka, India, and countries as far away as Africa. In the wake of that unprecedented disaster, several countries worked together to expand the use of a tsunami-detecting system. This system consists of an instrument attached to the seafloor, called a *tsunameter,* which is able to detect pressure changes. A tsunameter sends a signal to a surface buoy, which sends the data to a satellite. The satellite then broadcasts the information to warning centers around the world so that people can take the necessary precautions. Although these detectors were invented before the 2004 tsunami, only

---

[3] *atomic bombs:* bombs that cause an explosion by a sudden release of energy that results from splitting atoms

six detectors were in place and there were none in the Indian Ocean. There are now 53 detector buoys operating in the world's oceans, including 6 of a planned 27 in the Indian Ocean.

The Japanese warning system relies not 8 only on tsunameters, but also on *seismometers.* Seismometers help to forecast the scale of a tsunami based on the magnitude and location of the quake. With 1,000 seismometers around the country, Japan has the densest network anywhere in the world. However, in the March 2011 tsunami, the system did not work perfectly. The tsunami forecast warned of waves of 10 feet (about 3 meters) or more, whereas they reached 50 feet (15 meters) in Minamisanriku, and possibly higher elsewhere. Human nature is another factor that can delay reactions to tsunami warnings. This was not the first large tsunami to hit Minamisanriku. In 1960, a 14-foot (4-meter) wave killed 41 people in Minamisanriku. A 5.5-meter high (a little over 18-foot) seawall was built after the 1960 tsunami. Mayor Jin Sato thinks that the seawall gave people a false sense of security. "I think this time many people who lived above the high-water mark of the 1960 tsunami didn't bother to run," Sato says. "Many of them died."

Seismologists' Predictions

Kerry Sieh, director of the Earth Observatory 9 at Singapore's Nanyang Technological University,

Minamisanriku, Japan
3:41 p.m., March 11, 2011

Minamisanriku, Japan
5:54 p.m., March 12, 2011

A seismometer is lowered into the sea off Sumatra Island, Indonesia.

is one of the world's leading paleoseismologists; he studies the geological[4] records for evidence of ancient earthquakes and tsunamis. One way to do this is to study the age of dead coral reefs.[5] When the seafloor rises during an earthquake, it can push a reef above water, killing the corals. By 2003, Sieh and his colleagues had discovered a disturbing history for west central Sumatra.

"We found what we call *supercycles*—clusters 10 of big earthquakes occurring at regular intervals," he says. For at least the past 700 years, pairs of large earthquakes had occurred about every 200 years along a fault near west central Sumatra, with the earthquakes in each pair separated by approximately 30 years. Two occurred around 1350 and 1380, another two in the early to mid 1600s, and yet another pair in 1797 and 1833. In 2003, Sieh realized that it looked like another pair of earthquakes could happen at any moment.

The discovery worried Sieh so much that in 11 July 2004 he and his colleagues began distributing brochures to warn people in the area about

tsunamis. Five months later, *northern* Sumatra was hit by the tsunami, and Sieh's group received a lot of publicity. "We got credit we didn't deserve," he says. "Our forecast was for a different part of the fault." Nonetheless, his original forecast still stands. In September 2007, the first of the anticipated pair of earthquakes occurred. The magnitude 8.4 earthquake caused relatively minor damage; in Padang, capital of the province of West Sumatra, the tsunami was only around three feet (less than one meter). However, Sieh fears Padang may not escape as easily the next time.

"There's never been a more precise forecast of 12 a giant earthquake, period," Seih says. "Our forecast is for an 8.8-magnitude earthquake in the next 30 years. Nobody can say whether it will be 30 seconds from now or 30 months. But we can say it's very likely to happen within 30 years." He adds, "What are you going to do? Move the whole city for something that happens once every 200 years? The fundamental problem is not that scientists don't know enough, and it's not that engineers don't engineer enough. The fundamental problem is that there are seven billion of us, and too many of us are living in places that are dangerous. We've built ourselves into situations where we simply can't get away."

---

[4] *geological:* related to *geology*, the study of Earth's structure, surface, and origins

[5] *coral reefs:* long, narrow masses of coral (a type of very small sea animal), and other substances, that usually sit just above or just below the sea

READING COMPREHENSION

Big Picture

A Read the following pairs of sentences. In each pair, write *MI* next to the main idea and *SD* next to the supporting detail.

1. Minamisanriku

_____ **a.** The disaster in Minamisanriku occurred in a country that leads the world in preparing for earthquakes and tsunamis.

_____ **b.** On March 11, government seismologists sent out the first tsunami warning immediately after the earthquake.

2. What Is a Tsunami?

_____ **a.** An earthquake that begins miles below the seafloor is capable of releasing the energy equivalent of 8,000 atomic bombs.

_____ **b.** Most tsunamis are caused by earthquakes on the seafloor.

3. Tsunami Precautions

_____ **a.** Detectors were invented before the 2004 tsunami, but only six detectors were in place, and there were none in the Indian Ocean.

_____ **b.** After the 2004 tsunami, several countries worked together to expand the use of a tsunami-detecting system.

4. Seismologists' Predictions

_____ **a.** In 2003, Kerry Sieh realized that another pair of earthquakes could happen in Sumatra at any moment.

_____ **b.** Kerry Sieh is one of the world's leading paleoseismologists.

B Complete the following sentences in your own words.

1. The main idea of Reading 2 is _____ .

2. One reason that the author describes the warning systems in Japan is to _____ .

3. For me, one of the most important things to remember about Reading 2 is _____ .

Close-Up

A Choose the word or phrase in parentheses that best completes each sentence.

1. Approximately (16,000 / 17,700) people died in Minamisanriku, Japan, on March 11, 2011.

2. Japan spends (more / less) money than any other country to keep people safe from earthquakes and tsunamis.

3. When an earthquake begins underground, it can have the same powerful force as (8,000 / 800) atomic bombs.

4. According to the reading, there are (6 / 27) detector buoys operating in the Indian Ocean.

5. On March 11, 2011, the waves from the tsunami were (10 / 50) feet high in Minamisanriku.

6. In Sumatra, Sieh and his team found that pairs of large earthquakes occur every (30 / 200) years.

7. In September 2007, the magnitude 8.4 earthquake (did / did not do) a lot of damage.

B Find the following terms in the reading and write a short definition of each one.

1. subduction zone = _____

2. tsunameter = _____

3. seismometer = _____

4. supercycles = _____

Reading Skill

> ### Connecting Visual Material to a Text
>
> As you read, pay attention to the visual material that surrounds a text. In nonfiction readings, visual material such as charts, graphs, diagrams, or photographs can supplement the main reading. Sometimes the reading will reference the visual material. Other times, the text will not mention it at all. However, that does not mean that it isn't important. Visual literacy can be an important tool for understanding a text and providing further information on the topic.
>
> Some techniques for understanding visual material include the following:
>
> - **Read** its title and captions. This will focus your attention on what the visual material is illustrating.
>
> - **Recognize** how the information in the visual material is organized. For example, if there is a chart or map, read the information related to the chart or map carefully.
>
> - **Relate** the visual material to the main text. Notice the extra information that it provides and the information that it clarifies from the text.

A Look at the visual material for this unit. Use the techniques listed above to help you answer the following questions.

1. Look at the map on pages 90–91. What does this map tell you? How does this information help you understand the reading?

2. Look at the three photos on pages 92–93 and read the captions. How do the captions increase your understanding of what happened in Minamisanriku?

3. Look at the photo on page 94 and read the caption. What does the photo tell you? What extra information does the caption provide?

B Look at the visual material for one of the other units that you have already read in this book. Then answer the questions below.

1. What type of visual material is included with the reading?

2. Read the captions and any other information in the visual material. What do they tell you?

3. How does the visual material relate to the main text? Explain your answer.

VOCABULARY PRACTICE

Academic Vocabulary

A Find the words in bold in Reading 2. Use the context to help you match each word to the correct definition.

_____ **1. alert** (Par. 3)

_____ **2. broadcast** (Par. 3)

_____ **3. facilitate** (Par. 5)

_____ **4. unprecedented** (Par. 7)

_____ **5. precautions** (Par. 7)

_____ **6. magnitude** (Par. 8)

_____ **7. whereas** (Par. 8)

_____ **8. colleagues** (Par. 9)

a. not having happened before

b. by contrast; while; but

c. the measure of the strength or importance of something

d. to make a process easier

e. to make people aware of danger

f. to send a message over the air on radio or TV

g. people with whom one works, especially in a profession

h. steps taken in advance to prevent harm

B Work with a partner to choose the best word in the box below to complete each of the following sentences. The words in the box often appear with the academic words in bold.

amount	live	process	sheer	take	to	worked

1. Fire alarms **alert** people _____ the presence of fire with a loud noise.

2. Sometimes newscasters **broadcast** _____ in stormy weather, and you can see them blown about by high winds.

3. The storm was so powerful that it was difficult to comprehend the _____ **magnitude** of the devastation.

4. There has been an **unprecedented** _____ of growth in the alternative energy market as more and more people are interested in solar power and "green" living.

5. Juan and his **colleagues** _____ together to create a new evacuation plan for the city.

6. If someone in your family has a cold, _____ **the precaution** of washing your hands often to avoid any germs.

7. When people apply for a bank loan, a bank teller can help to **facilitate** the _____.

Multiword Vocabulary

A Find the words in the box below in Reading 2. Use the context to help you figure out the meanings. Then complete the definitions with the multiword vocabulary.

preventive measures (Par. 5)	a false sense of security (Par. 8)	got credit (Par. 11)
in the wake of (Par. 7)	at regular intervals (Par. 10)	relatively minor (Par. 11)
human nature (Par. 8)	at any moment (Par. 10)	

1. _____ are steps that can be taken in order to prepare for a potentially dangerous situation.

2. If one thing follows _____ another, it happens after the other thing is over, often as a result of it.

3. If you say that something will or may happen _____ , you are emphasizing that it is likely to happen very soon.

4. If something happens _____ , it happens several times with the same amount of time between each pause.

5. If you _____ for something good, it means that people praised you because they think you were responsible.

6. _____ refers to the natural qualities and ways of behavior that most people have.

7. If something is _____ , it means that compared to other similar situations, it is less important, serious, or significant.

8. If something gives you _____ , it makes you believe that you are safe when you are not.

B Choose the best multiword vocabulary from Exercise A to complete each sentence.

1. Because of her poor health, Basia took _____ before she traveled. She brought her medication with her and bought travel insurance in case she needed to return home unexpectedly.

2. _____ the disaster, our neighbors gave us food and shelter.

3. Worry and jealousy are often a part of _____ , but love and compassion are as well.

4. Cell phones can sometimes give you _____ because they can run out of power when you need them most.

5. The nurses in the hospital usually check on their patients _____ , but the patients can also call when they need something.

6. Our relatives will arrive _____ . They called us from the airport and said that they were on their way.

7. After their class project, Riina complained that Tad _____ for the work that she had done.

8. Reynaldo was in a car accident, but luckily his injuries were _____ , and he did not have to go to the hospital.

Use the Vocabulary

Write answers to the following questions. Use the words in bold in your answers. Then share your answers with a partner.

1. How does the **magnitude** of an event affect its publicity? Give examples of news events to explain your answer.

2. Can you think of a time when someone else **got credit** for something that you did? If so, how did you react? If not, how do you think you would react? Explain your answers.

3. In the place where you live, what systems are in place to **alert** the public **to** danger? Do you think these are adequate? Why, or why not?

4. What is an example of a **preventive measure** that everyone should take **at regular intervals** in their daily life?

5. Storms can be dangerous because, **at any moment**, the weather can get worse. Have you ever been caught off guard in severe weather? Explain your answer.

6. People use the word *whereas* when they want to contrast two things. How could you use *whereas* to contrast your morning routine during the week with your morning routine on weekends?

7. What is one way that language teachers are able to **facilitate** their students' learning?

THINK AND DISCUSS

Work in a small group. Use the information in the reading and your own ideas to discuss the following questions.

1. **Analyze results.** Who said the following? Why did the speaker say it? What were the effects of this announcement?

   Please head to higher ground!

2. **Use prior knowledge.** Who said the following? Do you think this is a common occurrence in scientific research? Why, or why not?

   We got credit we didn't deserve.

3. **Infer meaning.** Who said the following? Why did the speaker say it? What do you think will happen?

   There's never been a more precise forecast of a giant earthquake, period.

4. **Express an opinion.** Who asked the following? Why did the speaker ask it? What do you think the answer is?

   What are you going to do? Move the whole city for something that happens once every 200 years?

Vocabulary Review

A Complete the paragraph with the vocabulary below that you have studied in the unit.

alerts the public	monitor the progress of
at any moment	relatively minor
the efficiency of	sheer magnitude of
human nature	taking precautions
in the wake of	wreak havoc on

CENTRO DE OPERAÇÕES
PREFEITURA DO RIO

The Rio Operations Center

_____ so many recent

__1__

natural disasters around the world, some

tourists are worried about traveling. However,

in Rio de Janeiro, a city on the coast of Brazil,

officials are leading the way in

_____ to keep their city

__2__

secure. Rio's disaster-readiness operations

center was built in 2010, in preparation for the

city hosting a number of high-profile events

such as the 2016 Olympics. Whereas most

cities have offices in different locations, Rio

has one central location. Here, officials learn about and _____ a variety of

__3__

different situations such as fires, floods, and landslides, which can _____ the

__4__

city. Open 24 hours a day, the center has the largest television screen in Latin America, which

actually consists of eighty 46-inch screens where officials can simultaneously watch weather

forecasts and view traffic congestion. Problems that seem _____ at first can

__5__

become dangerous _____. When this happens, the center immediately

__6__

_____, using the media and social networks. The _____

__7__ __8__

the devastation caused by natural disasters can be terrifying. It is part of

_____ to want to avoid potential danger zones. Nonetheless,

__9__

_____ Rio's disaster-readiness center may reassure both tourists and citizens

__10__

that this city is prepared.

B Compare answers to Exercise A with a partner. Then discuss the following questions.

Do you think the operations center will boost tourism for Rio? Why, or why not?

C Complete the following sentences in a way that shows that you understand the meaning of the words in bold.

1. The disaster-readiness center in Rio **broadcasts warnings** about _____.

2. If a hurricane is forecast, one **preventive measure** you can take is to _____.

3. When people move to a new country, it can take time to **adjust to** _____.

4. The **time frame** for a person's **recovery from** surgery usually depends on _____.

D Work with a partner and write sentences that include any six of the vocabulary items below. You may use any verb tense and make nouns plural if you wish.

as we know it	facilitate the process	provide an insight into
at regular intervals	the full extent of	science fiction
come to a halt	get credit	an unprecedented amount of
could potentially cause		

Connect the Readings

A Use the chart below to record information about Reading 1 and Reading 2.

NATURAL DISASTERS		
	Tsunamis	**Solar Storms**
How they (usually) begin		
Effects		
Detection		
Preventive measures		

B With a partner or in a small group, compare answers to Exercise A. Then discuss the following questions.

1. What are the similarities between the ways that a large population could be affected by a solar storm and a tsunami? What are the differences?

2. Imagine that you are asking your government to fund technology that will help to prevent a disaster after a tsunami or solar storm. Explain how the preventive measure in Exercise A will help to save lives.

C Discuss the following questions with a partner. Use your understanding of the readings and your own ideas.

1. After reading this unit, are you more worried or less worried about tsunamis or solar storms? Explain your answer.

2. How are people affected by natural disasters today? How has this changed from 200 years ago? How is it the same?

3. What advice would you give to someone who was concerned about the effects of a natural disaster?

Art
Detectives

1. What are some types of art that you enjoy looking at?

2. How can you tell that a piece of art was created by a particular artist?

3. Why do you think some art costs so much money?

A man studies the cave art in the
Hall of the Bulls in the Lascaux
Caves, Montignac, France.

Academic Vocabulary

to attribute	an exhibit
authentic	an inconsistency
to complement	to indicate
an era	to revolutionize

Multiword Vocabulary

to be found out	in conjunction with
beyond a reasonable doubt	to pass something off as
to cause a sensation	to say the least
a dirty little secret	a work of art

Reading Preview

A **Preview.** Skim Reading 1 by reading the first sentence of each paragraph. Then check (✓) three topics that you think might be in this reading.

_____ **1.** Determining if a painting is a fake

_____ **2.** Creating your own fake

_____ **3.** Technology and fakes

_____ **4.** Historians and fakes

_____ **5.** Great masters

B **Topic vocabulary.** The following words appear in Reading 1. Look at the words and answer the questions with a partner.

apprentice	imitation
art historian	master artist
auction house	masterpiece
expert	museum curator
a fake	workshop

1. Which words are related to people?

2. Which words are related to places?

3. Which words could be used for a piece of art?

C **Predict.** What do you think this reading will be about? Discuss each word in Exercise B and predict how it may relate to the reading.

Did you know that many paintings in museums around the world could be fakes? Learn about high-tech ways to determine whether a painting is by a great master or if it is an expert imitation.

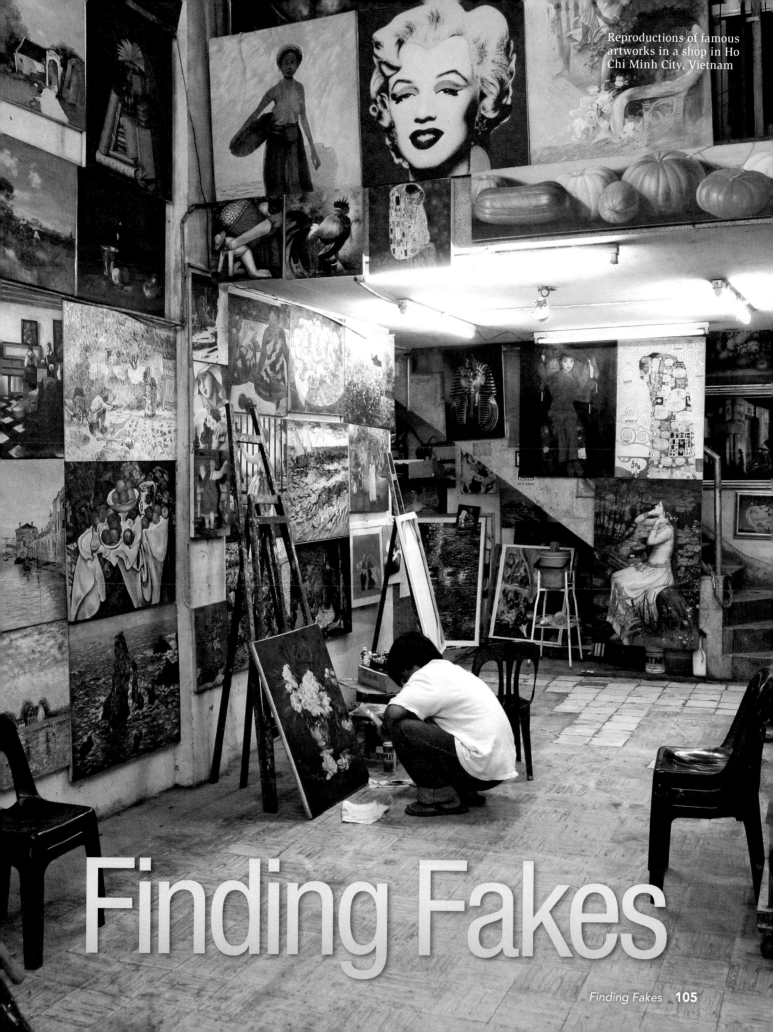

Reproductions of famous artworks in a shop in Ho Chi Minh City, Vietnam

Finding Fakes

A painting by Rembrandt comes up for sale at an auction house in London, England.

1   There is a saying, "Imitation is the sincerest form of flattery." This may be true, but in the art world fakes are unacceptable, to say the least. In fact, selling fake art can be a criminal offense. Paintings by great masters, such as Leonardo da Vinci and Rembrandt, are worth millions of dollars. When a painting is discovered that might have been painted by one of the great masters, it causes a sensation in the art world. However, for every great work, there are also many fakes, deliberate attempts to pass a painting off as that of a master. There are also sincere imitations, paintings that were created in the style of a master painter and later mistakenly attributed to the master himself. Scientists are working on new technology that may aid art historians in answering the question: Masterpiece or masterful imitation?

2   Most master painters have had their works imitated over the years, and some of these imitations have fooled even the experts. The National Gallery of Scotland once reportedly had an exhibit of five paintings of the same subject, all attributed to Leonardo. It turned out that at least three of the works were copies. Today, by some estimates, 15 percent of the art sold at auction houses may not be authentic.

3   Art historians, with their knowledge of the works of a particular artist, are often asked to authenticate art. In addition to their knowledge of the subject, these scholars use science and technology to determine if a work of art was created by a particular artist. The materials used in the painting are often analyzed and X-rayed. Now, art historians may have another technological tool to help their process. Scientists have developed a

new authentication technique that analyzes and classifies paintings based on a digital analysis of the artist's style. "This technique, in conjunction with traditional methods, could play an important role in art forensics,[1]" said Hany Farid, a computer scientist at Dartmouth College in the United States, who works at the forefront of this new technology.

4 The digital authentication technique takes scans of art work that have already been authenticated as being from a master artist. From these scans, it creates a statistical model of the artist's work: a baseline.[2] New paintings can be compared to the baseline to determine their authenticity.

"Today, by some estimates, 15 percent of the art sold at auction houses may not be authentic."

The process works by finding consistencies and inconsistencies in an artist's work. The technique is similar to how a digital camera compresses an image. "Imagine comparing one painting by a very talented artist with a smooth, elegant brush stroke[3] with another painting by an imitator whose strokes are more clunky,[4]" Farid said. The condensed images of the two paintings reveal what the human eye could not see. When the analysis recognizes this difference, the fakes are found out.

5 How well does this work? In an experiment, researchers applied the technique to a set of 13 drawings. The model automatically grouped together the eight authenticated works by the

---

[1] *forensics:* scientific methods used to get information about a crime

[2] *baseline:* starting point to which other things can be compared

---

[3] *brush stroke:* mark made on a surface by a painter's brush

[4] *clunky:* heavy and awkward; not smooth

Computer scientist, Hany Farid (far right), looks at "Madonna with Child" by Perugino at Dartmouth's Hood Museum.

16th-century artist Pieter Bruegel the Elder, separating them from five imitations. Stuart Fleming, author of *Authenticity in Art*, thinks the technology could "revolutionize identification of many sincere imitations of various major artists that occurred during their own lifetimes." In other words, 15th-century paintings that were painted in the same style as, say, Leonardo da Vinci, could be tested to see whether they were actually painted by Leonardo.

6 Nonetheless, some art historians are skeptical about the new technique. "It's an interesting idea. But before curators and art historians will jump in and use this, I think a much larger sample of work has to be tested," said Nadine Oberstein, curator at the Department of Drawings and Prints at the Metropolitan Museum of Art in New York. If the technology turns out to be accurate, she said, it could be used to complement the expertise of scholars. Farid agreed. "What the human eye can see is often very difficult for the computer to extract and vice versa," he said. "What computers are good at, humans are typically not good at."

7 Most importantly, Farid says, such a method could be used to determine, beyond a reasonable doubt, whether more than one person, or "hand" as the scholars say, was involved in creating a painting. This is something that, until now, forensic technology has never been able to address. Many great Renaissance painters had large workshops and painted only portions of their works. They let apprentices paint other parts. This practice has caused scholars to argue over who painted what in many paintings by the great masters.

8 Using his computer model, Farid studied the faces of six individual characters in the painting *Madonna with Child* by the Italian Renaissance painter Perugino (see Figure 1). Three of the faces proved to be statistically similar, while the three other faces were all different. This indicates that at least four hands contributed to the painting. "If further studies prove conclusively that this computer program effectively discriminates between different artistic hands, it will lead to a whole new era in the study of the workshop practice of artists such as Perugino and Peter Paul Rubens," said Katherine Hart of the Hood Museum of Art at Dartmouth College.

9 For now, museum curators and auction houses don't seem as interested in the technology as the scientists are. There may be an obvious reason for that. "If you spent 80 million dollars to buy a painting, I don't think you'd be eager to know that it's a fake," Farid said. "It's a dirty little secret that a lot of paintings are not real."

Figure 1. A Computer Analysis of the Painting "Madonna with Child" by Perugino

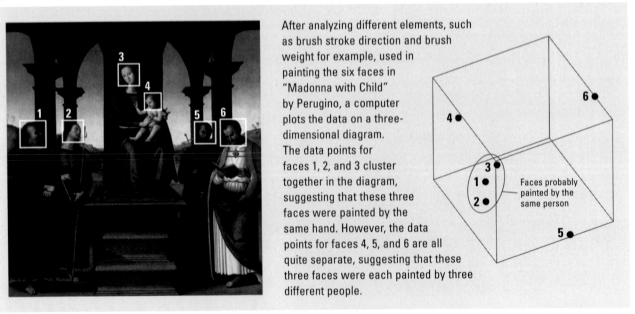

After analyzing different elements, such as brush stroke direction and brush weight for example, used in painting the six faces in "Madonna with Child" by Perugino, a computer plots the data on a three-dimensional diagram. The data points for faces 1, 2, and 3 cluster together in the diagram, suggesting that these three faces were painted by the same hand. However, the data points for faces 4, 5, and 6 are all quite separate, suggesting that these three faces were each painted by three different people.

Faces probably painted by the same person

Source: PNAS, December 7, 2004, vol. 101, no. 49, p. 17008

READING COMPREHENSION

Big Picture

A Choose the best answer for each of the following questions.

1. What is the purpose of paragraph 1?
   a. To talk about the price of paintings
   b. To introduce the fact that there are fakes in the art world
   c. To describe how art historians find fakes

2. What is the main idea of paragraph 2?
   a. Imitations of famous masters' work can fool the experts.
   b. The National Gallery in Scotland had copies of famous masters' work on display.
   c. Many of the paintings sold at auction houses are copies of famous masters' work.

3. What is the main idea of paragraph 3?
   a. Art historians are often asked to authenticate art.
   b. Art historians analyze the materials in a painting using X-rays.
   c. Art historians may have another technological tool to help them find fakes.

4. What would be the best heading for paragraph 4?
   a. New Paintings Are Compared to a Baseline
   b. Fakes Are Found Out
   c. What Is the Digital Authentication Technique?

5. Which sentence best expresses the main idea of paragraph 7?
   a. The first sentence
   b. The second sentence
   c. The third sentence

6. What is the purpose of paragraph 8?
   a. To talk about the importance of Perugino and Peter Paul Rubens
   b. To give an example of how the digital authentication technique can be used
   c. To explain that four hands were used in the painting *Madonna with Child*

B Write a sentence that expresses the main idea of the *whole* reading.

Close-Up

A Scan Reading 1 to find answers to the following questions. Write short answers.

1. According to the author, what is a fake?

2. According to the author, what is a sincere imitation?

3. According to the author, how many paintings in auction houses might actually be imitations of great masters?

4. What does Hany Farid mean when he uses the term *art forensics?*

_____

5. What are two different techniques that art historians use to authenticate art?

_____

6. When scholars talk about "hands" in a painting, what do they mean?

_____

B Work with a partner to create two other questions about this reading. Then ask
another partner or small group to answer the questions.

1. _____

2. _____

Reading Skill

Assessing Problems and Solutions

Readings can have different purposes. One common purpose of a reading is to outline a
problem and then give a solution. In a well-researched reading, you will often find quotes
from people who assess the problem and solution in their own words. Identifying the
problem, the proposed solution, and differing opinions will help you understand a reading.

One way to assess problems and solutions is to ask questions as you read.

For example:
- *What is the problem?*
- *What is the proposed solution?*
- *How would the solution work?*
- *What do people think about this solution?*

A Complete the answers to the following questions with information from Reading 1.

1. What is the problem? *Many paintings of great masters are actually* _____.

2. What is the proposed solution? *A new tool, called* _____, *can* _____.

3. How would the solution work? *The digital authentication technique* _____
paintings based on a digital analysis of _____. *It can create a(n)*
_____ *to use to compare different* _____.

4. What do the following people think about this solution?

   a. *Hany Farid thinks* _____.

   b. *Stuart Fleming thinks* _____.

   c. *Nadine Oberstein thinks* _____.

   d. *Katherine Hart thinks* _____.

B Compare answers to Exercise A with a partner. What is *your* opinion of the digital authentication technique?

VOCABULARY PRACTICE

Academic Vocabulary

A Find the words in bold in Reading 1. Use the context to help you match sentence parts to create definitions.

_____ **1.** If something is **attributed** (Par. 1) to someone,

_____ **2.** An **exhibit** (Par. 2) can refer to

_____ **3.** If something is **authentic** (Par. 2),

_____ **4.** If there are **inconsistencies** (Par. 4) between two things,

_____ **5.** When advances **revolutionize** (Par. 5) an activity,

_____ **6.** If people or things **complement** (Par. 6) one another,

_____ **7.** When something **indicates** (Par. 8) another thing,

_____ **8.** An **era** (Par. 8) refers to

a. a period of time that is known for a particular quality.

b. they don't match each other.

c. people believe that person created it.

d. a public display of works of art or other objects.

e. it strongly suggests the other thing is true or exists.

f. they change completely how it is done.

g. it is real or genuine.

h. they are different but make an effective combination.

B Choose an academic word from Exercise A to complete each of the following sentences. Notice and learn the words in bold because they often appear with the academic words.

1. We are witnessing a **new** _____ of filmmaking as more and more action movies these days are filmed in 3-D.

2. The speech is usually _____ **to** Abraham Lincoln, but, in fact, he didn't write it. Thomas Jefferson did.

3. I thought that the **museum** _____ of modern art was interesting, but I prefer the work of the old masters.

4. There are **a number of** _____ in the suspect's story. The detectives are questioning him further.

5. The research study **clearly** _____ that smoking is bad for your health.

6. When you go on vacation, taking public transportation and eating at local restaurants will give you a more _____ **experience** than staying at a resort and only eating at your hotel.

7. This new type of electric car could _____ **the way** that we drive; cars that need gasoline could soon be a thing of the past!

8. I like the painting. The orange and blue **colors** _____ **each other** well.

Multiword Vocabulary

A Find the words in bold in Reading 1. Use the context to help you complete each definition.

1. When you say **to say the least** (Par. 1) at the end of a statement, you mean that _____ .
   a. other people aren't saying much about a topic
   b. you could have said more on the topic

2. If an event **causes a sensation** (Par. 1), _____ .
   a. people are worried about what will happen next
   b. people are excited and talk about the event

3. If you **pass** a painting **off as** (Par. 1) an original, _____ .
   a. you convince people that it is the original
   b. you use it and the original in the same way

4. When people talk about **a work of art** (Par. 3), they are referring to _____ .
   a. an object such as a painting or sculpture that is created for people to look at
   b. a job that involves teaching or creating paintings or sculptures

5. If one thing is done **in conjunction with** (Par. 3) another, _____ .
   a. the two things happen in a logical sequence, one after the other
   b. the two things are done or used together

6. When people or things **are found out** (Par. 4), _____ .
   a. they are discovered, usually doing something dishonest
   b. they learn new information about a topic

7. You say that something is **beyond a reasonable doubt** (Par. 7) _____ .
   a. when you are certain that it is true and it can't be disproved
   b. when it is more difficult to explain than you had previously thought

8. If someone talks about **a dirty little secret** (Par. 9), _____ .
   a. he or she is talking about something surprising that people talk about for fun
   b. he or she is talking about something dishonest that people try to hide

B Complete the following sentences with the correct multiword vocabulary from Exercise A. In some cases, you need to change the verb or noun form or the article.

1. The newspaper _____ when it was discovered that the journalists had asked their sources to lie in order to make the stories more interesting. Everyone was talking about the newspaper's _____ .

2. At the trial, the judge reminded the jurors that they must be sure _____ that the accused man committed the crime.

3. Tom is passionate about his football team, _____ . He goes to games every weekend and talks about football all week long.

4. The museum has a new art exhibit that includes many _____ from the 1900s to the present.

5. Working _____ the city's officials to celebrate its 200th anniversary, the museum will be open to the public, free of charge, for the month of July.

6. The university student tried to _____ a paper as his own, but he had copied it from the Internet. When he _____, he failed the class and received a stern warning from the dean.

Use the Vocabulary

Complete the following sentences with your own ideas. Then share your answers with a partner.

1. Some people consider the modern **era** to be the "communications **era**" because _____.

2. I can assure you **beyond a reasonable doubt** that _____.

3. If _____ came to speak in my town, it would **cause a sensation** because _____.

4. Many students take a reading class **in conjunction with** a(n) _____ class because they **complement each other** well.

5. When I want to **indicate** that someone should be quiet, I usually _____.

6. I would like to see a **museum exhibit** with **a work of art** by _____.

THINK AND DISCUSS

Work in a small group. Use the information in the reading and your own ideas to discuss the following questions.

1. Summarize. How would you explain the digital authentication technique to someone who hasn't read this reading?

2. Infer meaning. Why does the author say that museum curators and auction houses aren't as interested in the technology as the scientists? How would it affect their business?

3. Express an opinion. Do you think museum curators should spend money to determine whether paintings are imitations or authentic? Why, or why not?

4. Expand the topic. Hany Farid works at the forefront of the technological advances in digital forensics, that is, being an art detective. If you could interview Farid, what questions would you ask him?

Academic Vocabulary

to commemorate	a portrait	a restoration
contemplative	preliminary	vitality
distinctive	to purchase	

Multiword Vocabulary

to attract attention	not to mention
to change hands	to stem from
to make a comeback	to take a closer look
to mark an occasion	thanks to

Reading Preview

A **Preview.** Try to complete the following sentences about the famous artist Leonardo da Vinci. Then scan Reading 2 for the answers.

1. Leonardo da Vinci painted _____.

2. Leonardo da Vinci lived approximately _____ years ago.

3. A painting by Leonardo could be worth _____ of dollars today.

B **Topic vocabulary.** The following words appear in Reading 2. Look at the words and answer the questions with a partner.

art restorer	mysterious	scholar
auction catalog	patron	valuable
collector	poised	vault
frame	royal	

1. Which words are adjectives that can describe a person? Which ones can describe a piece of art?

2. Which words are a place to keep art safe, a way to display a piece of art, or a way to advertise it?

3. Which words are related to people in the art world?

C **Predict.** What do you think this reading will be about? Discuss each word in Exercise B and predict how it may relate to the reading.

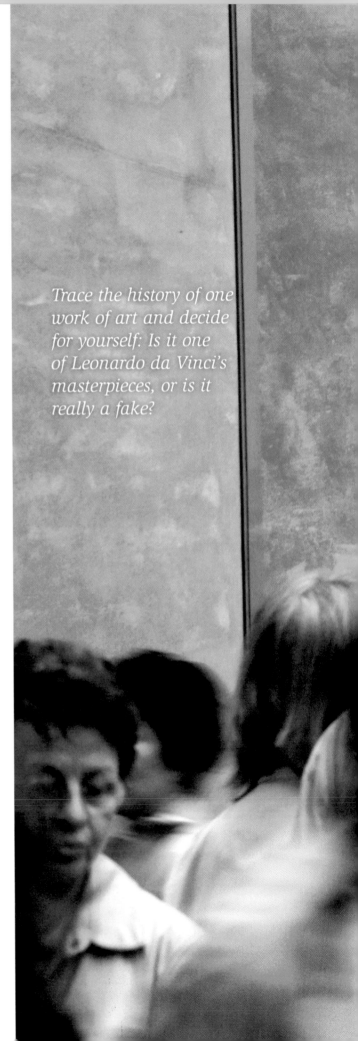

Trace the history of one work of art and decide for yourself: Is it one of Leonardo da Vinci's masterpieces, or is it really a fake?

The Lost Leonardo

Tourists crowd around and take photos of Leonardo da Vinci's *Mona Lisa* in The Louvre museum in Paris, France.

THE LOST LEONARDO

Imagine walking into an art gallery and 1
buying a piece of art for less than $25,000.
Now imagine discovering that its real
worth might be $100 million.

Bianca Sforza didn't attract many 2
stares when she was introduced to the art
world on January 30, 1998. To the crowd
at a Christie's auction in New York City,
she was just a pretty face in a frame.
Nobody knew her name or the name of
the artist who had created her portrait.
The portrait was a colored chalk-and-
ink drawing on vellum,[1] which the
auction catalog described as "early
nineteenth century, German, with
borrowed Renaissance styling."
They assumed that a German
artist had borrowed the distinctive style of the artists of
the Renaissance period, some
400 years earlier. A New York
dealer, Kate Ganz, purchased
the picture for $21,850.

The price hadn't changed 3
almost 10 years later when
a Canadian collector, Peter
Silverman, saw Bianca's
portrait in Ganz's gallery.
He promptly bought it,
suspecting that it might
actually date back to
the Renaissance. Ganz
said that Leonardo da
Vinci may have had
an influence on the
artist, but Silverman started to
wonder: What if this is the work of the
great Leonardo himself?

Discovery of a Leonardo is extremely rare. 4
At the time of Silverman's purchase, it had been
more than 75 years since a previously unrecog-
nized work of art was authenticated as being by
Leonardo. There was no record that the creator of

---

[1] *vellum:* a surface to paint on that is made from the skin
of a calf

the *Mona Lisa* ever made a major work on vellum. There were no known copies of this portrait and no preliminary drawings. If this image was an authentic Leonardo, where had it been hiding for 500 years?

Silverman emailed a digital image of Bianca to Martin Kemp, a professor of art history at Oxford University and a well-known Leonardo scholar. Kemp regularly receives images from people he calls "Leonardo loonies[2]"—people who are convinced that they have discovered a new work of the great master. "My reflex is to say, 'No!'" Kemp said. But the "uncanny vitality" in the young woman's face made him take a closer look. He flew to Zurich, where Silverman kept the 13-by-9¾-inch (33-by-25-centimeter) drawing in a vault. "When I saw it," Kemp said, "I experienced a kind of frisson, a feeling that this is not normal."

"The more Kemp looked, the more he saw what he considered evidence to support that this was drawn by Leonardo's own hand."

That initial shiver of excitement drove Kemp to start his own investigation. He worked with Pascal Cotte of Lumiere Technology in Paris, who created high-resolution images, using a technique called *macrophotography*. This technique takes scans of a painting or drawing and then magnifies parts of it so that previously hidden elements become clearer. Thanks to this technique, Kemp was able to study the different layers of the drawing, from its first strokes to later restorations. The more Kemp looked, the more he saw what he considered evidence to support that this was drawn by Leonardo's own hand. Kemp noticed the beautiful colors, the precise lines, and the way that the girl's hair gathered together. Shaded areas showed distinctive left-handed strokes just like Leonardo's. The girl's expression was poised and contemplative. She had the look of someone who was growing up too fast, which followed Leonardo's idea that a portrait should reveal "motion of the mind."

Kemp needed proof that the portrait had been 7 made during Leonardo's lifetime (1452–1519) and that its history fit with the artist's biography.

Everything pointed to Leonardo. First, carbon dating[3] placed the time that the vellum was made at some point between 1440 and 1650. Then researching the girl's distinctive hairstyle revealed that she must have belonged to the Milanese court of the 1490s. Leonardo lived in Milan at that time and accepted commissions for court portraits. Finally, stitch marks[4] on the edge of the portrait suggested that it came from a book.

Kemp's detective work led him 8 to a name, Bianca Sforza, a daughter of the Duke of Milan. Bianca was married in 1496 to Galeazzo Sanseverino, who was a patron of Leonardo's art. She was 13 or 14 at the time of the portrait, and, tragically, she died just a few months later. Kemp named the drawing *La Bella Principessa*, "The Beautiful Princess."

In 2010, Kemp and Cotte published their find- 9 ings in a book. Some Leonardo scholars agreed, but others were skeptical. Carmen Bambach of New York's Metropolitan Museum of Art said that the portrait simply "does not look like a Leonardo." Another scholar thought the image was too "sweet." Was this a high-quality forgery? Their doubt also stemmed from the portrait's mysterious and sudden appearance. Where had it come from?

Kemp didn't know the answer to this. 10 However, D. R. Edward Wright, a professor of art history at the University of South Florida was following the story with great interest, and he contacted Kemp. Wright suggested that the answer might lie in the National Library of Poland in Warsaw, inside a book called the *Sforziad*. This book commemorated the marriage of Bianca Sforza, and a Leonardo portrait could have been commissioned to mark the occasion. According to Wright, the book reached Poland in the early 1500s, when a member of the Sforza family married a Polish royal.

---

[2] *loonies:* an informal, sometimes offensive, term that refers to people who you think are crazy or eccentric

[3] *carbon dating:* a way to find the age of an object that is very old by measuring how much radioactive carbon it contains

[4] *stitch marks:* marks that show that something has been sewn together

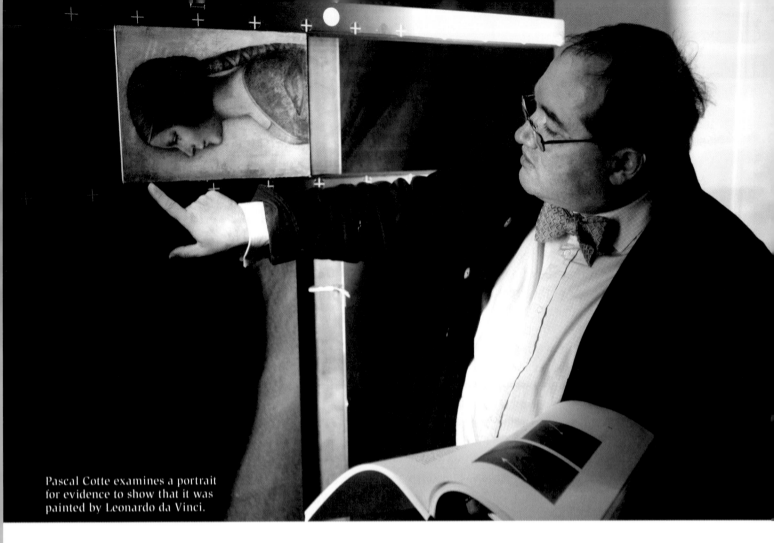

Pascal Cotte examines a portrait for evidence to show that it was painted by Leonardo da Vinci.

Kemp and Cotte received a grant from the National Geographic Society and traveled to Warsaw. When they found the book, they saw that a page had been removed from a place where a portrait would have been appropriate. Cotte's photography was able to enlarge a photograph of the portrait in order to study the small stitch marks on it. These matched up with the marks in the book itself. The moment arrived when they inserted a copy of Bianca's portrait into the open book. It fit perfectly. 11

The route that the portrait took to Christie's is still filled with mystery. The page must have been removed from the book, possibly in the 17th or 18th century when the book was rebound.[5] Little is known about what happened next. At some point, the portrait changed hands and became the property of an Italian art restorer. When he died, his wife put it up for sale at Christie's. 12

Bianca's portrait is not the only Leonardo work making a comeback. His painting *Salvator Mundi* had been lost for centuries, but it was put on exhibit in London in November 2011. Researchers are also looking for Leonardo's *Battle of Anghiari*. This painting was last seen in the mid-1500s, and the researchers are using an endoscope[6] to find out if the painting is hidden behind a wall in the Palazzo Vecchio, in Florence, Italy. 13

Authenticating centuries-old art, especially rare, extremely valuable paintings or drawings, is not an easy process. Reputations, not to mention millions of dollars, are at stake. Scholarly agreement on Bianca's portrait "will take time," says Kemp, "but I have clear confidence in where I am." In 1998, Bianca might not have attracted much attention. But now, if her portrait hangs in a museum as a true Leonardo, everyone will stare. 14

---

[5] *rebound:* had a new cover attached

[6] *endoscope:* a medical device with a small camera that is usually used to look inside the human body

READING COMPREHENSION

Big Picture

A The following are the topics of paragraphs 2–13 in Reading 2. Number them in the order in which they appear in the reading.

_____ **1.** There is still a lot of mystery surrounding how the portrait arrived at Christie's.

_____ **2.** Kemp learned about Bianca Sforza.

_____ **3.** There was very little possibility of this portrait being a Leonardo.

_____ **4.** Researchers are looking for other works by Leonardo as well.

_____ **5.** Kemp started to investigate the portrait, using a technique to magnify the image.

_____ **6.** Peter Silverman suspected that the portrait was by Leonardo.

_____ **7.** Kemp looked for proof that the portrait could have been made by Leonardo.

_____ **8.** Not all scholars agreed that this was a Leonardo.

_____ **9.** The portrait fit into the commemorative book.

_____ **10.** Kemp is usually doubtful about "new" Leonardo works, but he was intrigued.

_____ **11.** Kate Ganz bought a portrait that many people assumed was made by a German artist.

_____ **12.** D. R. Edward Wright helped Kemp find out more about Bianca Sforza.

B Write one sentence that expresses the author's purpose for writing Reading 2.

_____

Close-Up

A Look at the map below. Complete the map with the following information. Write the correct numbers on the lines on the map.

1. Martin Kemp is a professor here

2. Silverman bought the portrait here

3. Silverman kept the portrait here

4. Leonardo was a painter here

5. The book *Sforziad* was found here

6. D. R. Wright is a professor here

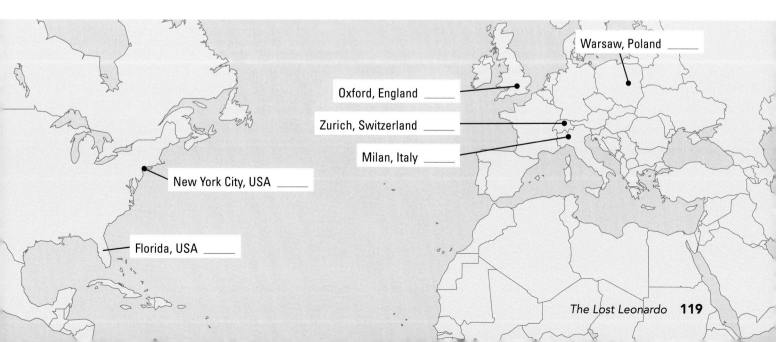

Warsaw, Poland _____

Oxford, England _____

Zurich, Switzerland _____

Milan, Italy _____

New York City, USA _____

Florida, USA _____

B Explain why the following clues led Martin Kemp to believe that the portrait of Bianca Sforza was a work by Leonardo da Vinci. Give details for each clue.

1. The look on the girl's face in the portrait

2. The hairstyle of the girl in the portrait

3. The way the artist painted

4. Leonardo was at the Milanese court

5. The missing page from the commemorative book

C List four reasons why scholars were skeptical about the portrait's authenticity.

1.

2.

3.

4.

Reading Skill

Determining Certainty and Uncertainty in a Text

Successful readers are able to recognize whether the language in a reading shows certainty or uncertainty about a situation, a theory, or an event in the past. Distinguishing what is a fact from what is a possibility allows you to better understand a reading and to create your own opinions about the topic while you read.

The following chart shows vocabulary that can signal certainty or uncertainty in a reading.

	Language of Certainty	Language of Uncertainty
Modal verbs	will, must, have to	can, could, might, should
Verbs	know, find, discover, prove, convince, reveal	assume, believe, suggest, propose, suspect
General words and phrases	proof, evidence, definitely, support, without a doubt	possibly, doubtful, skeptical, need proof, little is known

A Read the following sentences from Reading 2. Circle the language of uncertainty and underline the language of certainty in the sentences. Use the words in the chart to help you.

1. In 2010, Kemp and Cotte published their findings in a book. Some Leonardo scholars agreed, but others were skeptical.

2. Wright suggested that the answer might lie in the National Library of Poland in Warsaw, inside a book called the *Sforziad*. This book commemorated the marriage of Bianca Sforza, and a Leonardo portrait could have been commissioned to mark the occasion.

3. Then researching the girl's distinctive hairstyle revealed that she must have belonged to the Milanese court of the 1490s.

B Compare answers to Exercise A with a partner. Then answer the following questions.

Do you think that the portrait of Bianca Sforza was made by Leonardo da Vinci? Why, or why not?

VOCABULARY PRACTICE

Academic Vocabulary

A Find the words in the box below in Reading 2. Use the context to help you choose the correct word to complete each of the following sentences.

portrait (Par. 2)	purchased (Par. 2)	vitality (Par. 5)	contemplative (Par. 6)
distinctive (Par. 2)	preliminary (Par. 4)	restorations (Par. 6)	commemorated (Par. 10)

1. Alain's _____ characteristic is his height. He is 6 feet 4 inches tall.

2. Nori _____ her textbooks at the bookstore before the start of the school year.

3. Recent _____ have made it possible to see how the statues might have looked in ancient times.

4. Although Abdul's grandfather is over 90 years old, you can see the great _____ in his eyes when he tells stories about his past. He seems like a much younger man when he speaks!

5. The moment of silence _____ the anniversary of the tsunami.

6. Carine has a _____ of her grandmother that was painted by a famous artist.

7. Looking at old photographs can put me in a _____ mood. I like to imagine the past.

8. Before she applied to universities, Kadi did some _____ research to make sure that she would like the universities and their locations.

B The words in bold show the academic words from Exercise A and words they often appear with. Complete the sentences with your own ideas.

1. I would (or would not) like to commission someone to **paint a portrait of** me because

_____ .

2. _____ is a food that has **a distinctive flavor**.

3. Some people prefer to **purchase items** online, but others prefer to go to local stores because

_____ .

4. The **preliminary results** show a connection between diabetes and soda consumption, but the soda
   companies insist that scientists need to do more _____ .

5. Many people attribute their **physical vitality** to every day routines such as _____ .

6. When an old house goes through an **extensive restoration**, the builders sometimes find
   _____ under the floorboards.

7. One way that people **commemorate a victory** in battle is to _____ .

8. People who lead a **contemplative life** are usually _____ .

Multiword Vocabulary

A Find the multiword vocabulary in bold in Reading 2 and use the context to help you
understand the meaning. Then match each item to the correct definition.

_____ 1. **take a closer look** (Par. 5)

_____ 2. **thanks to** (Par. 6)

_____ 3. **stemmed from** (Par. 9)

_____ 4. **mark the occasion** (Par. 10)

_____ 5. **changed hands** (Par. 12)

_____ 6. **making a comeback** (Par. 13)

_____ 7. **not to mention** (Par. 14)

_____ 8. **attracted** much **attention** (Par. 14)

a. became the property of someone else

b. was noticed by a lot of people

c. remember an important event in a specific way

d. becoming successful after a period of failure
or retirement

e. in addition to

f. was caused by something

g. pay attention to the details

h. because of

B Complete the following sentences with the correct multiword vocabulary from
Exercise A. In some cases, you need to change the verb or noun form.

1. The art gallery has a new owner. It has _____ many times
   over the past few years.

2. The gallery doesn't have a lot of business. This _____ the fact
   that it isn't in a good location, so it doesn't _____ from people
   passing by.

3. Sophia went to the art opening, but she didn't buy anything. There weren't any paintings that
   she wanted, _____ the fact that the prices were very high.

4. Yesterday was the museum's 25th anniversary. The museum
   _____ by offering free admission for the day.

5. When a little boy tried to _____ at the painting, he
   accidentally touched it and set off the alarms.

6. No one had heard of the artist in 30 years, but _____ a new
   documentary about her life, she has been _____ . Now she is
   popular once again, and her paintings sell for millions.

Use the Vocabulary

Write answers to the following questions. Use the words in bold in your answers. Then share your answers with a partner.

1. **Thanks to** advances in technology, what are some things that are easier for you to do now than 10 years ago?

2. What is your favorite way to **mark** special **occasions** such as birthdays or anniversaries?

3. How do you usually **commemorate** important events in your life such as graduations, births, and weddings?

4. Before you **purchase** an expensive **item**, do you do any **preliminary** research? Why, or why not?

5. Are you usually a **contemplative** person? Explain your answer.

6. Who is an example of a celebrity who has **made a comeback** recently?

7. What is something that you consider to be a **distinctive characteristic** of your personality?

Leonardo da Vinci

THINK AND DISCUSS

Work in a small group. Use the information in the reading and your own ideas to discuss the following questions.

1. **Summarize.** What was the process that Silverman went through to get the Leonardo drawing authenticated? Include at least three steps in your answer.

2. **Infer meaning.** Kemp talks about "Leonardo Loonies" and says, "My reflex is to say, 'No!'" Why is Kemp's first instinct to say "No" to "Leonardo Loonies"? Why did D. R. Edward Wright follow this story so closely? Explain your answer.

3. **Express an opinion.** Silverman took a chance when he bought the portrait. Would you have done the same? Why, or why not?

Vocabulary Review

A Complete the paragraphs with the vocabulary below that you have studied in the unit.

be found out	paint a portrait
clearly indicate	pass photographs off as
commemorate events	revolutionize the way
a dirty little secret	take a closer look
inconsistencies in	thanks to

A photoshopped picture in a Chilean newspaper of U.S. President Clinton (August 18, 1998)

Five hundred years ago, if people wanted to remember their loved ones, they commissioned an artist to _____. Today, most
1
people take photographs to _____
2
in their personal lives, from births to graduations to weddings. When there is a historic event in the world, people usually view photographs as evidence that the event occurred. However, as digital technology advances, it has become easier to combine two photographs in one, creating scenarios that never really happened. It's _____
3
that some news media try to _____ genuine when they have actually been
4
"photoshopped" to make a celebrity look thinner or a storm look more dangerous. These fakes need to _____. Imagine a photograph of a bombing that has been altered to
5
look larger than it was; it could lead to serious political or international consequences.

Hany Farid, a digital scientist at Dartmouth College in the United States, proposes that we
_____ and examine these photographs. He has created software to find the
6
_____ photographs; if a person's hand is in the sun, while everything else is
7
in the shade, the picture may not be authentic. Farid has devised a system that would give each photograph a score on a scale of 1–5. This could be included next to each photograph to
_____ its level of alteration. _____ Farid, this system
8   **9**
could _____ we look at magazine photographs.
10

B Compare answers to Exercise A with a partner. Then discuss the following questions.

Do you think photoshopped pictures are harmful to society? Why, or why not?

C Compete the following sentences in a way that shows that you understand the meaning of the words in bold.

1. One thing that I know **beyond a reasonable doubt** is that _____.

2. If I could own one famous **work of art**, it would be _____.

3. A recent news event that **caused a sensation** was _____.

4. Two foods that **complement each other** are _____ and _____.

D Work with a partner and write sentences that include any six of the vocabulary items below. You may use any verb tense and make nouns plural if you wish.

attributed to	a distinctive flavor	mark an occasion	physical vitality
change hands	extensive restoration	a new era	to stem from
contemplative mood	in conjunction with		

Connect the Readings

A In this unit, you learned about the different tools that art experts use to determine the authenticity of a painting or drawing. Use information from Reading 1 and Reading 2 to fill out the chart below. Think of one or two questions that each tool could help to answer. One example is done for you.

Tools for Determining Authenticity	Questions
Digital authentication technique	
Macrophotography	
Carbon dating	
Historical background	
Distinctive style	*Are there any preliminary drawings or copies of the work of art?*

B With a partner or in a small group, compare answers to Exercise A. Then imagine that you and your partner or group are interested in buying a painting that you suspect was created by a great master. Discuss the following questions.

1. What tools would you use to determine the authenticity of the painting?

2. Which of the experts in Readings 1 and 2 would you ask for help? Explain your answer.

3. What questions would you ask the experts?

C Discuss the following questions with a partner. Use your understanding of the readings and your own ideas.

1. Have the readings in this unit changed how you look at works of art? Why, or why not?

2. Should the price of a painting be based on its beauty or on its history? Explain your answer.

3. What is a famous work of art that you know well? Describe it. What do you know about its history?

1. Have you ever spent time in the wild?

2. What important survival skills do people need in the wild?

3. Do you know of any amazing stories of survival? What happened?

Stars sparkle in the sky above yellow tents in the little explored Juphal valley in the remote Dolpa region of Nepal.

SURVIVAL SKILLS

Academic Vocabulary

adaptable	a concept	irrelevant
an attitude	to cope	an outcome
a capacity	an equation	

Multiword Vocabulary

to be better off	to let go of
a comfort zone	to make a conscious effort
day-to-day	to obsess about
in the face of	to overcome obstacles

Reading Preview

A **Preview.** Read the first sentence of each paragraph in Reading 1. Then put the following topics in the order in which they appear in the reading.

_____ **1.** Stress and your brain

_____ **2.** How to use a mantra

_____ **3.** A World War II survivor

_____ **4.** An Iraqi journalist

B **Topic vocabulary.** The following words appear in Reading 1. Look at the words and answer the questions with a partner.

acting cool	mind-expanding
adversity	ordeal
combat experience	overwhelmed
focus	paralyzed
hazardous	relaxed
impulsively	surrender

1. Which words refer to a difficult situation?

2. Which words refer to reactions to or results of a difficult situation?

3. Which words suggest that the reading will be about mental states?

C **Predict.** What do you think this reading will be about? Discuss each word in Exercise B and predict how it may relate to the reading.

Do you have the skills that you need to survive in the wild? Read some tips by a survival expert, Lawrence Gonzales. You might find them useful in your everyday life as well!

Mind
Over
Matter

A climber rests after a hard day of climbing near Timbuktu, Mali.

A man makes his way through the Amazon jungle.

Long ago I believed that survival meant 1 having enough equipment to make fire, build shelter, and trap animals to eat in the wild. Then I kept coming across cases in which someone had survived without any equipment. In other cases, someone had all the right tools, but wasn't able to survive. Why was this? Studying survival stories, I realized that how well people cope with adversity can be more important than any type of equipment or training. A person's individual character is an essential element in the equation.

Here are six concepts that have proved 2 helpful to survivors in extreme situations and to people trying to meet the challenges of daily life.

1. Stay Cool

Staying cool is helpful, acting cool isn't. As 3 the head of training for the Navy SEALs[1] once said, "The Rambo[2] types are the first to go." They act impulsively and this, in the real world, can lead them to be the first not to survive. In the book *The Survivor Personality*, Al Siebert explains that in reality, "combat survivors . . . have a relaxed awareness." They notice everything, but pause for a moment to think before they act. True survivors, like most people, get upset when something bad happens, but then they try to figure out what the new reality looks like, what the new rules are, and what they can do about it.

Using technologies like magnetic resonance 4 imaging (MRI), researcher Bruce McEwen has shown that stress can change the shape and chemistry of the brain. This results in trouble remembering, difficulty completing tasks, and altered behavior. In effect, losing your cool makes you stupid. Examine the way you handle pressure: Do you get angry when you're stuck in traffic? Are you able to accept failure, telling yourself that you will do better next time? If you're rejected—in love, in business, in sports— do you obsess about it? Practice being calm in the face of small emergencies, and you'll be better off when you need to deal with large ones.

2. Use a Mantra

In a difficult survival situation, most people 5 need a mantra, a saying that can be repeated over

---

[1] *Navy SEALs:* members of a special U.S. naval unit. *SEAL* stands for *Sea*, *Air*, and *Land*.

[2] *Rambo:* a movie character; a soldier who is strong and fearless, but who often acts impulsively

and over, to focus on what is really important. For Steve Callahan, all alone on a life raft in the open sea for 76 days, his focus was on getting home alive. His mantra was simply the word *survival*. Throughout his ordeal, he'd tell himself things like "Concentrate on now, on survival."

Yossi Ghinsberg, a hiker who was lost in the Bolivian jungle for three weeks, repeatedly used the mantra "Man of action" to motivate himself. A mantra usually has a deeper meaning. Ghinsberg explained his mantra saying, "A man of action does whatever he must, isn't afraid, and doesn't worry." Think about your daily life. What would your mantra be?

3. Think Positively

In the book *Man's Search for Meaning*, Viktor Frankl tells the story of Jerry Long, who was 17 years old when he broke his neck in a diving[3] accident. Long was completely paralyzed and had to use a stick held between his teeth to type. Long wrote, "I view my life as being abundant with meaning and purpose. The attitude that I adopted on that fateful day has become my personal credo for life: I broke my neck, it didn't break me."

Carol Dweck, a professor of psychology at Stanford University, would agree with this sentiment. Dweck studies individual learning habits, specifically how people deal with difficult problems. According to her research, individuals with a "growth mindset" are people who (a) are not discouraged in the face of a challenge, (b) are not afraid to make or admit mistakes, and (c) think positively. These individuals are able to learn and adjust faster and are able to overcome obstacles more easily.

4. Get Out of Your Comfort Zone

Every new challenge you face causes your brain to rewire itself and to become more adaptable. A study at University College London showed that London's taxi drivers possessed unusually large hippocampi, the part of the brain that makes mental maps of our surroundings. London has very strict requirements for taxi drivers. Before becoming a licensed taxi driver, applicants have to pass a test called "The Knowledge," which includes memorizing 320 routes through the city and learning 25,000 streets and 20,000 important landmarks. This process literally expands their minds.

We can all find opportunities for simple mind-expanding exercises. If you're right-handed, use your left hand once in a while. Learn a new mental skill, such as chess, a musical instrument, or a foreign language. Living in a low-risk environment dulls our abilities. So make a conscious effort to learn new things. Force yourself to move out of your comfort zone. Your brain will thank you. And, in a survival situation, it just might save your life.

5. Do the Next Right Thing

Doing the next right thing means that, when overwhelmed, you take some small action, even if it feels like it won't make a difference. Simple, organized tasks can help you think clearly and aid in your survival. "[Survivors] possess the capacity to break down the event they are faced with into small, manageable tasks," writes John Leach, a psychology professor at Lancaster University.

When Private[4] Giles McCoy's ship was torpedoed[5] at the end of World War II, he was sucked under the boat and nearly drowned. He reached the life raft, where sailors were covered in oil and one was "so badly burned that the skin was stripped from his arms," Doug Stanton writes in his gripping account of the event, *In Harm's Way*. Surrounded by sharks, McCoy decided to do something: He cleaned his pistol[6] and gave the other men each a piece to hold as he took it apart. Irrelevant as that task may sound, it

"Every new challenge you face causes your brain to rewire itself and to become more adaptable."

---

[3] *diving:* jumping into water head first, with arms above your head

[4] *Private:* a soldier at the lowest rank in an army or the marines

[5] *torpedoed:* hit by a bomb that travels under water

[6] *pistol:* a small gun

was exactly the right thing to do. Through this simple process, he was able to start thinking clearly. Forcing your brain to think step-by-step in times of crisis and in day-to-day life can quiet dangerous emotions.

6. Surrender, But Don't Give Up

Ahmed Fadaam is an Iraqi jour- 13 nalist and photographer. When he became a war reporter in 2003, he was horrified by the violence and in constant fear of dying. After years of combat experience, he explained the concept of survival by surrender: "Don't be afraid of anything." "If you are afraid, then you have to lock yourself inside your house. But if you want to keep on living, then you must forget about your fears and deal with death as something that is a must, something that's going to happen anyway." In other words, we are all going to die sometime, but we can do our best to ensure that it doesn't happen any time soon.

Photo taken in Iraq in 2004 by Ahmed Fadaam, who was often close to violence and death

Once you surrender and let go of the out- 14 come, it frees you to act much more sensibly. If you are terrified, you are more vulnerable in a hazardous situation. If you are able to keep that core inside of you that says you will never give up, you will be in a better position to survive. A good survivor says, "I may die. I'll probably die. But I'm going to keep going anyway."

READING COMPREHENSION

Big Picture

A The following statements are the main ideas of each of the six survival skills in Reading 1. Write the name of the skill next to its main idea.

Main Idea	Survival Skill
1. Use your brain in new ways. Expanding your mind will help you adapt to new situations.	
2. If the big picture seems overwhelming, focus on small, manageable tasks. This will help you think clearly.	
3. Try not to be discouraged, admit your mistakes, and know that the situation can improve.	
4. Remember that everyone will die eventually, but not necessarily now. Knowing this will help you act sensibly and not out of fear.	
5. Choose a personal saying that you can repeat to yourself. This saying can have a deeper meaning.	
6. Keep calm. Getting stressed can lead to bad decisions.	

B Write a sentence that expresses the main idea of the *whole* reading.

_____

Close-Up

A Complete the following sentences in your own words.

1. The author argues that in a survival situation, a person's _____ can be more important than his or her equipment or training.

2. One example of losing your cool is when you _____.

3. Steve Callahan's mantra was _____.
   Yossi Ghinsberg's mantra was _____.

4. Individuals with a "growth mindset" are people who _____

   _____.

5. The hippocampus is the part of the brain that _____.
   The reason that London Taxi drivers have large hippocampi is because _____

   _____.

6. It was important for Giles McCoy to clean his pistol because _____

   _____.

7. If you say you will never _____, you will be in a better position to survive.

B Compare answers to Exercise A with a partner. Then discuss the following question.

Which of the examples of survival did you find the most intriguing?

Reading Skill

> ### Understanding Argument and Finding Support
>
> When reading a text, it is important to understand the author's purpose, which can be to inform, entertain, or persuade. If the purpose is to persuade the reader, the author needs to present a convincing argument. It's important to recognize each argument in a reading passage and to spot the sentences that support it.
>
> Two common types of support are *anecdotal* (stories or personal opinions) and *research-based*. Recognizing and evaluating support allows you to form your own opinions about an argument in a text.
>
> While reading a persuasive text, ask yourself the following questions:
> - *What is the argument?*
> - *What kind of support does the author provide—anecdotal or research-based?*
> - *How effective is the support? Is it logical? Is it relevant?*

A Read the following statements from the first concept, "Stay Cool," on page 130. Write A next to the statement that provides the argument. Write S next to the statements that provide support.

_____ **1.** As the head of training for the Navy SEALs once said, "The Rambo types are the first to go."

_____ **2.** In the book *The Survivor Personality*, Al Siebert explains that in reality, "combat survivors . . . have a relaxed awareness."

_____ **3.** True survivors get upset when something bad happens, but then try to figure out what the new reality looks like, what the new rules are, and what they can do about it.

_____ **4.** Using technologies like magnetic resonance imaging (MRI), researcher Bruce McEwen has shown that stress can change the shape and chemistry of the brain. . . . In effect, losing your cool makes you stupid.

B Look back at the six concepts, or arguments, in Reading 1. Complete the chart below with the author's anecdotal and research-based support for each argument. The first one is done for you. Note that not all arguments include both types of support.

Argument	Anecdotal Support	Research-Based Support
Stay Cool	*Head of Navy Seals (Rambo)*	*• Siebert (The Survivor Personality)* *• Bruce McEwen (MRI results)*
Use a Mantra		
Think Positively		
Get Out of Your Comfort Zone		
Do the Next Right Thing		
Surrender, But Don't Give Up		

C Discuss the following questions with a partner.

1. Which of the above arguments do you think are the most convincing? Explain your answer.

2. Which of the above arguments do you think are the least convincing? Explain your answer.

3. Do you think the author provided adequate support to persuade readers that survival skills go beyond physical training and special equipment? Why, or why not?

VOCABULARY PRACTICE

Academic Vocabulary

A Find the words in the box below in Reading 1. Use the context to help you choose the correct word to complete each definition.

cope (Par. 1)	concepts (Par. 2)	adaptable (Par. 9)	irrelevant (Par. 12)
equation (Par. 1)	attitude (Par. 7)	capacity (Par. 11)	outcome (Par. 14)

1. If you describe a person or animal as _____, you mean that that person or animal is able to change ideas and behavior in order to deal with new situations.

2. Your _____ toward something is the way that you think and feel about it.

3. Your _____ for something is your ability do it, or the amount that you are able to achieve.

4. _____ are ideas or abstract principles.

5. In a(n) _____, two or more parts have to be considered together so that the whole situation can be understood.

6. If you say that something is _____, you mean that it is not important in the situation.

7. The _____ of an activity or process is the situation that exists at the end of it.

8. If you _____ with a problem or task, you deal with it successfully.

B Choose academic words from Exercise A to complete the following sentences. Notice and learn the words in bold because they often appear with the academic words.

1. Equality in education and the importance of technology are not **new** _____. Educators have been discussing this idea for years.

2. Some people say that computers are a privilege, not a right, but some educators have a **different** _____. Their goal is for every student to have a computer and free Internet.

3. A group of engineers wants to ensure that every student has the necessary technology to succeed. They hope to provide computers to low-income students, but funding is an important **part of the** _____. Without money, this will not be possible.

4. The engineers insist that computer companies have **adequate production** _____ to make computers cheaply and **to** _____ **with** the high demand.

5. Many computer programs are **highly** _____ so that teachers can modify the programs for students to work on at home.

6. They say that arguments such as "there isn't enough money to pay for this" and "students will use the computers for non-school activities" are _____ **details**. The most important thing is that students will be able to have access to the Internet to enhance their education.

7. At the end of this process, there will be a **positive** _____ for everyone. Students will be better educated and ready to join the workforce.

Multiword Vocabulary

(A) Find the words in bold in Reading 1. Use the context to help you complete each definition.

1. When you **obsess about** (Par. 4) something, you _____.
   a. find it difficult to think about anything else   b. feel calm and solve a problem

2. When you take a particular action or attitude **in the face of** (Par. 4) a problem or difficulty, you _____.
   a. show anger   b. react to that situation

3. When you say that someone would **be better off** (Par. 4) doing something, you are _____.
   a. advising that person to do it   b. warning that person to avoid it

4. When people **overcome obstacles** (Par. 8), they _____.
   a. find problems wherever they go   b. successfully deal with difficult situations

5. When you **make a conscious effort** (Par. 10) to do something, it means that you _____.
   a. talk to people about doing something   b. focus your attention on doing something

6. When people talk about their **comfort zone** (Par. 10), they are referring to a place or a situation in which they _____.
   a. try something new and fun   b. are free from stress and worry

7. **Day-to-day** (Par. 12) things or activities are things that happen _____.
   a. as part of ordinary life   b. for a short amount of time

8. If you **let go of** (Par. 14) something, you _____.
   a. stop trying to control it   b. start to try something new

(B) Complete the following sentences with the correct multiword vocabulary from Exercise A. In some cases, you need to change the verb or noun form.

1. As a tourist, driving in large cities such as London and Paris can be overwhelming. You _____ taking public transportation.

2. Whenever you travel to a new country, you should _____ to learn at least a few words of the language.

3. Overseas travel can be educational because it forces people to go outside of their _____ and try new things.

4. When traveling, it is best not to _____ seeing every possible tourist attraction. It's impossible to see everything. _____ any overly ambitious expectations you might be holding onto. That way you'll be able to fully enjoy your experiences.

5. When you are traveling, even _____ tasks such as ordering lunch or finding a restroom can be challenging. However, when you return home, your stories of _____ such as rude waiters or bad directions will seem amusing. Your friends will enjoy hearing about how you reacted _____ such adversity!

Use the Vocabulary

Complete the following sentences with your own ideas. Then share your answers with a partner.

1. When students are asked to _____ in their English class, it can be outside their **comfort zone** at first, but ultimately it can be a very positive experience.

2. Many people **obsess about** _____. They would **be better off** _____ instead!

3. One example of how humans are a remarkably **adaptable** species is the fact that _____.

4. When learning a language, it's important to **make a conscious effort** to _____.

5. Many successful people have had to **overcome obstacles** such as _____.

6. One way to **cope with** rising fuel prices is to _____.

7. One reason that a **positive attitude** can be the key to success is that _____.

THINK AND DISCUSS

Work in a small group. Use the information in the reading and your own ideas to discuss the following questions.

1. **Rank.** Which of the six survival skills from Reading 1 do you think is the most useful to you personally? Explain your answer.

2. **Express an opinion.** Do you think a mantra would be helpful to you? Why, or why not? If you used a mantra in your daily life, what would it be?

3. **Evaluate.** The author claims that learning about these extreme situations can help people meet the challenges of everyday life. Do you think they are applicable to everyday life? Why, or why not?

4. **Use prior knowledge.** These are only six survival skills in this reading. What are other important survival skills that people should know?

5. **Expand the topic.** Which of the books mentioned in Reading 1 would you like to read? Explain your answer.

Academic Vocabulary

to assure	indispensable	a region
daring	minimal	treacherous
essence	a patch	

Multiword Vocabulary

at this rate	to go to extremes
beyond one's wildest dreams	a logical progression
a calculated risk	on behalf of
to check in with	pitch dark

Reading Preview

A Preview. Look at the photos on pages 138–142. Write three questions that you think might be answered in Reading 2 about survival in the Arctic. Then discuss your questions with a partner or in a small group.

1. _____

2. _____

3. _____

B Topic vocabulary. The following words appear in Reading 2. Look at the words and answer the questions with a partner.

airdrops	ice drift	sled
flare gun	polar bear	sponsors
frostbite	satellite images	willpower
fuel	skis	worry

1. Which words could refer to types of supplies or support you would need on an expedition into a remote, cold area?

2. Which words refer to things that might be dangerous?

3. Which words refer to a mental state a person might have when in a remote, cold area?

C Predict. What do you think this reading will be about? Discuss each word in Exercise B and predict how it may relate to the reading.

Join two experienced explorers on a trip to the Arctic. They face polar bears, freezing temperatures, and high winds: will they reach the North Pole, or will they have to turn back?

NORTH POLE

Explorer and extreme adventurer Mike Horn treks across pack ice on the Arctic Ocean.

JOURNEY TO THE NORTH POLE

E xplorers will tell you that in an extreme 1
wilderness such as the Arctic Ocean, one
of the least explored places on Earth, your
life is in danger from the moment you arrive.
After that it's only a matter of how much danger
you are in. This was the case for Børge Ousland,
a Norwegian, and Mike Horn, a South African-
born Swiss. The two explorers landed on Cape
Arkticheskiy, in Siberia, in the pitch dark of polar
winter, in 2006. Their mission was to navigate
their way across the 600 miles (965 kilometers)
to the North Pole, and to do so unsupported—no
dogsleds or airdrops of equipment, no food or
fuel along the way. As they skied their way to
their destination, they pulled sleds that carried
everything they might need.

On the first night in their tent, Børge heard 2
something.

"Mike, is that you?" 3

"Yeah, I'm chewing on a piece of chocolate." 4

Then came a ripping sound—*fwaap!*—fol- 5
lowed by the head of a polar bear. Mike and
Børge quickly moved backward. This scared the
bear, and it ran off with some food. They chased
after it, firing the flare gun, to get the food back.
Each bit of food was necessary, indispensable,
in fact.

When it came time for bed, Børge was ner- 6
vous, but Mike assured him that he was alert
and ready for anything; he knew all the sounds.
Then he immediately fell fast asleep and started
snoring. Børge, however, was wide awake.

"Mike, how can you sleep?" 7

"Børge, if you worry, you die. If you don't 8
worry, you also die. So, why worry?"

The next night, the tent was flapping so 9
noisily in the wind that they didn't hear a polar
bear taking away their rubber boat. They found
it the next morning, 100 yards (91 meters) away,
chewed up, and they had to spend hours repairing it. Two nights, two bears.

After repairing the boat, Børge and Mike 10
took a walk to see whether the ice was stable
enough to travel over. For the duration of their
expedition, the men checked in with Hans
Ambøhl in Switzerland, who relayed information

Mike Horn

Mike Horn skies to the edge of
the ice to find the way forward.

Børge Ousland

about weather conditions. Based on the satellite images provided by the Canadian Space Agency, the ice appeared to be drifting quickly to the southeast—the wrong way—at a rate of half a mile (0.8 kilometers) an hour. Nevertheless, the two men were tired of polar bears. So, as soon as the ice drift calmed down, they took their chances and left.

Børge and Mike had to use the repaired 11 rubber boat to cross the treacherous water, and they camped for the night on a small patch of ice, only a couple of miles away from where they had first started. When they woke up, they found the ice floe[1] had carried them 9 miles (14 kilometers) backward. That's how things went for the next couple of weeks, with everything around them opposite from what it was supposed to be. Instead of frigid weather, there was a Siberian heat wave—temperatures in the teens and twenties. Yet, rather than minimal wind, there was a harsh gale, blowing the wrong way and in their faces. And, finally, as opposed to the ice drifting in a direction that would help them, the floes carried them away from the Pole. Day after day, they'd march north, then slip back toward Siberia while they slept; it was all they could do to hold their position.

There were only a limited number of weeks 12 before the midnight sun would rise over the horizon and begin six months of continuous light to the region. The plan was to get to the North Pole before that. They worried that they'd never make it at this rate, and they would run out of food. So they started walking longer and eating less and, consequently, having distracting food fantasies: blueberry crepes with sour cream for Børge and chocolate-covered marshmallows for Mike.

Sometimes it was all they could do to keep 13 their eyes focused on the ends of their skis and move forward for the next hour, the next minute, the next yard (meter), because it wouldn't do any good to think ahead. It was that rarest of experiences—living completely in the now. *Where am I? What must I do? Can I still feel my fingers?* Sometimes they were happy just to find themselves alive in the tent at the end of the day.

---

[1] *ice floe:* flat piece of ice that floats on its own through the sea

When the two men finally reached their destination, they were utterly exhausted, had frostbite, but were still in one piece. What they had accomplished stands as one of the most daring polar expeditions in recent memory: Setting out in total darkness and surviving physically and mentally. That had been the essence of the trip. Reaching the Pole was a necessary, but almost irrelevant conclusion.

Why would they have put themselves in this position? This was, actually, exactly what they had wanted. Both men had been adventuring since boyhood, taking increasingly higher and higher calculated risks. At some point, they left their comfort zones and never went back. For them, going to extremes that may seem insane was actually a logical progression. They discovered that they could earn a living—writing books, taking pictures, making films, and presenting motivational speeches.[2] Now, they have sponsors: outdoor gear manufacturers, construction outfits, an adventure travel agency, a watch company. Extreme adventure is their livelihood.

Some people say that the two men have a death wish,[3] but this just seems to amuse Mike and Børge. They will tell you that it isn't a desire to be closer to death that attracts them; it's a desire to be closer to life. They've been to the mountaintop. They know that willpower can be built, that ordinary people, like themselves, have abilities beyond their wildest dreams. They're just the ones who are out there, scouting the wilderness on behalf of the rest of us. They aren't marking dots on a geographical map anymore. That was accomplished long ago. What they are doing now is exploring the inner map, the mental and emotional map. What will they learn about themselves from being in a position where nothing matters except staying alive? What, exactly, is the human being capable of? This is what drives them.

14

15

16

---

[2] *motivational speeches:* talks that inspire an audience to do their best, often by sharing the speaker's own stories

---

[3] *death wish:* a conscious or unconscious desire for death

Mike Horn looks out from his tent wearing a headlamp.

READING COMPREHENSION

Big Picture

A The following could be headings for the topics presented in Reading 2. Number them in the order in which they would appear in the reading.

_____ **1.** Trouble on Ice

_____ **2.** Reaching the Pole

_____ **3.** The Mission

_____ **4.** Long Walks with Little Food

_____ **5.** Polar Bear Problems

_____ **6.** Why Are They Doing This?

_____ **7.** Finding a Crossing

_____ **8.** Living in the Moment

B Write one sentence that expresses the author's purpose for writing Reading 2.

Close-Up

A Decide which of the following statements are true or false according to the reading. Write *T* (True) or *F* (False) next to each one.

_____ **1.** On their mission, Børge and Mike brought all of their supplies with them, including food and fuel.

_____ **2.** This was Mike's first expedition as an explorer.

_____ **3.** Mike was more worried than Børge was about bears.

_____ **4.** The men fired a flare gun at a polar bear that was trying to eat their food.

_____ **5.** The men wanted to get to the Pole before the days started getting lighter.

_____ **6.** According to the author, this was the first time explorers have been successful in reaching the North Pole.

_____ **7.** Part of the reason for the expedition was to create geographic maps of the region.

B Compare answers to Exercise A with a partner. Then discuss the following questions.

1. Why did the men communicate with Hans Ambøhl?

2. What made the journey more difficult than they had anticipated?

3. According to the author, what did the two men fantasize about?

4. How do the two men make money from their trips?

Reading Skill

Recognizing Contrasts

As you learned in Unit 2 on page 46, successful readers need to recognize how information is connected in a text. Authors often describe an idea using contrasts—that is, two things that are opposite to each other. Words and phrases such as *but, however, instead of, as opposed to,* and *nevertheless* can signal a contrast. However, signal words and phrases are not always used. Antonyms can be used to signal a contrast instead. For example: *It isn't hot; it is cold.* The contrasting words here are the antonyms *hot* and *cold.* Antonyms, or opposites, can show contrast and help authors emphasize what they want to say.

Look at the following example from paragraph 16 of Reading 2.

> They will tell you that it isn't a desire to be closer to death that attracts them; it's a desire to be closer to life.

The sentence signals a contrast with the antonyms *death* and *life.*

A Read the following statements from Reading 2. Underline the words or phrases that are being contrasted.

1. Instead of frigid weather, there was a Siberian heat wave—temperatures in the teens and twenties.

2. Rather than minimal wind, there was a harsh gale, blowing the wrong way and in their faces.

3. And, finally, as opposed to the ice drifting in a direction that would help them, the floes carried them away from the Pole.

4. They aren't marking dots on a geographical map anymore. That was accomplished long ago. What they are doing now is exploring the inner map, the mental and emotional map.

B Compare answers to Exercise A with a partner. Discuss your choices. Then skim the reading and find one more contrast. What words or phrases signaled this contrast?

VOCABULARY PRACTICE

Academic Vocabulary

A Find the words in bold in Reading 2. Use the context to help you match each word to the definition that is closest to the meaning in the reading.

1. **indispensable** (Par. 5)

   a. necessary

   b. hard to manage

2. **assured** (Par. 6)

   a. guaranteed or promised

   b. ordered or defended

3. **treacherous** (Par. 11)

   a. safe

   b. dangerous

4. **patch** (Par 11)

   a. a small area

   b. a large area

5. **minimal** (Par. 11)

   a. a reduced amount of time

   b. a small amount of something

6. **region** (Par. 12)

   a. a geographical area of a country

   b. different neighborhoods in a city

7. **daring** (Par. 14)

   a. brave, risky

   b. helpful, smart

8. **essence** (Par. 14)

   a. the minor details

   b. the central point

B Choose an academic word from Exercise A to complete each of the following sentences. Notice and learn the words in bold because they often appear with the academic words.

1. The soldiers were captured, but they were able to make a(n) _____ **escape** in the middle of the night.

2. If you are traveling to Paris, this book is a(n) _____ **guide**. It will tell you everything you need to know.

3. The furniture salesman told us that we could assemble the bookcase with _____ **effort**, but we have already been working on it for an hour!

4. In some cities, some people rent or own a small _____ **of land** to grow vegetables.

5. In many countries, people's accents often reflect the **geographic** _____ **of the country** in which they grew up.

6. The company _____ its **customers** that its products were made of high-quality materials and offered refunds to anyone who was not satisfied.

7. _____ **conditions** forced the pilot to turn the plane around. The snowstorm had caused ice to weigh heavily on the wings of the plane.

8. I couldn't understand everything that the speaker said, but the _____ **of** the speech was that everyone has the potential to do amazing things.

Multiword Vocabulary

A Find the multiword vocabulary in bold in Reading 2 and use the context to help you understand the meaning. Then match each item to the correct definition.

_____ 1. **pitch dark** (Par. 1)

_____ 2. **checked in with** (Par. 10)

_____ 3. **at this rate** (Par. 12)

_____ 4. **calculated risks** (Par. 15)

_____ 5. **going to extremes** (Par. 15)

_____ 6. **a logical progression** (Par. 15)

_____ 7. **beyond** their **wildest dreams** (Par. 16)

_____ 8. **on behalf of** (Par. 16)

a. doing things that most people think are unreasonable and possibly dangerous

b. a gradual, reasonable development or next step

c. more than they imagine or hope will happen

d. as a representative for someone else

e. actions that people think might be successful, although they have considered that they might fail, as well

f. without any light at all

g. going at a particular speed

h. talked briefly to someone to let him or her know how you are doing

B Complete the following sentences with the correct multiword vocabulary from Exercise A.

1. Stockbrokers take _____ when they put money in the stock market. They know that not all of their investments will be successful. They could either win or lose a lot of money.

2. When the physicist received the Nobel Prize, she was not able to travel to the award ceremony. Instead, her daughter proudly accepted the award _____ her mother.

3. In England, winter days are short and the nights are long. The sun starts to set at four in the afternoon, and it's usually _____ by five o'clock.

4. Juan Carlos has a habit of _____ . When he proposed to his wife, he wrote "Will you marry me?" on the side of a 30-foot (9-meter) bridge.

5. I need to start making more progress with my English paper. _____ , it will take me two months to finish it!

6. While Grace was traveling, she _____ her mother every day to let her know that she was all right.

7. When Alan and Joan started their company, they didn't know what to expect. But in just five years, it has succeeded _____ .

8. After graduating with a degree in English, Malis began working as a tour guide. She considered this to be _____ in her career path although she hopes to open her own hotel at some point in her life.

Use the Vocabulary

Write answers to the following questions. Use the words in bold in your answers. Then share your answers with a partner.

1. Do you ever watch reality TV shows where people **go to extremes** in order to win a competition? If so, describe one show that you have seen. If not, would you be interested in watching a reality TV show such as this? Why or why not?

2. If you miss an English class, do you **check in with** the teacher or a classmate before the next class? Why or why not?

3. What is the most **daring** thing that you have ever done? Explain your answer.

4. What are two things that you find **indispensable** in your language studies? Explain your answer.

5. How would you describe the **geographic region** where you live? Try to be as specific as possible.

6. Do you prefer sleeping in the **pitch dark** or with some light? Explain your answer.

7. Who are two historical figures who spoke out **on behalf of** people who were suffering in poverty? Describe these two people and what they were able to achieve for others.

8. What do you think is the **essence of** a true friendship? Explain your answer.

THINK AND DISCUSS

Work in a small group. Use the information in the reading and your own ideas to discuss the following questions.

1. **Summarize.** How would you retell the story of Mike and Børge to a friend?

2. **Evaluate.** Read the following quote from Reading 2. What is happening in the story? Why does the author say this is rare? Explain your answer.

   It was that rarest of experiences—living completely in the now.

3. **Express an opinion.** Would you ever want to be part of an expedition? Why, or why not? What are the distinctive characteristics that someone needs to succeed at such an expedition?

4. **Synthesize.** This reading is similar to the reading "The Snow Patrol" on pages 32–34 in Unit 2. Look back at that reading. What are some of the similarities between Mike and Børge and Jesper and Rasmus? What are some differences?

5. **Infer meaning.** How do Mike and Børge fund their expeditions? Why do you think each of their sponsors are involved in their expedition?

Vocabulary Review

A Complete the paragraphs with the vocabulary below that you have studied in the unit.

be better off	part of the equation
checked in with	patch of ice
geographic region	pitch dark
let go of	positive outcome
on behalf of	treacherous conditions

Thomas Ulrich reaches for safety on an expedition to the North Pole.

In 2006, Thomas Ulrich began a solo expedition to the North Pole. This is a _____ where it is impossible

1

to camp on land, so he set up his camp on the ice. But when the _____ broke under him, he was trapped and moving in the

2

wrong direction. As if these _____ weren't bad enough, a storm began. As the

3

winds increased, Thomas had to cut half of his equipment loose and watch it drift away. Thomas _____ Victor Boyarsky over the phone. Victor, his expedition manager in

4

Russia, told Thomas that he would _____ creating a smaller camp with the

5

remains of his old one. Thomas listened to him but saved the pictures that his wife and children had drawn for him. He wanted to hold them if he was about to die, but he also refused to _____ the hope that he would see his family again.

6

Victor made calls _____ Thomas, planning his escape. At first, Russian

7

authorities refused to fly at night, in the _____. However, Victor pointed out

8

that the media had learned of the story; if Thomas died, the public might blame the authorities. When the authorities realized that this was _____, they decided that they

9

needed to act quickly. Thomas was rescued in time.

Thomas's unsuccessful expedition didn't stop him from achieving his dreams. In 2007, he set out with Børge Ousland on a journey from the North Pole to Norway. This time, he was successful, and his expedition had a _____.

10

B Compare answers to Exercise A with a partner. Then discuss the following questions.

How did Thomas's journey differ from Mike and Børge's expedition? How was it similar?

C Complete the following sentences in a way that shows that you understand the meaning of the words in bold.

1. **The essence of** the story in Exercise A is that Ulrich _____.

2. _____ is a type of activity that is outside of my **comfort zone**.

3. When you meet new people, it is a good idea to **make a conscious effort** to _____.

4. Thanks to modern technology, it is possible to _____ **with minimal effort**.

D Work with a partner and write sentences that include any six of the vocabulary items below. You may use any verb tense and make nouns plural if you wish.

at this rate	day-to-day	irrelevant details	obsess about
beyond my wildest dreams	a different attitude	a new concept	overcome obstacles
to cope with	in the face of		

Connect the Readings

A Use the chart below to apply the survival advice in Reading 1 to Reading 2. One example is done for you.

Reading 1	Reading 2
Stay Cool	
Use a Mantra	*I would tell Mike and Børge to repeat, "We can do it!" over and over again.*
Think Positively	
Get Out of Your Comfort Zone	
Do the Next Right Thing	
Surrender, But Don't Give Up	

B With a partner or in a small group, compare answers to Exercise A. Then discuss the following questions.

1. Which of the above skills do you think are the most important in Mike and Børge's expedition? Explain your answer.

2. What do you think is more necessary for survival—mental or physical training? Explain your answer.

3. Choose one of the survival stories from Reading 1. How is it similar to the story in Reading 2? How is it different?

C Discuss the following questions with a partner. Use your understanding of the readings and your own ideas.

1. Has this unit changed your definition of survival skills? Why, or why not?

2. Reading 1 gives techniques on how to prepare now for survival. Which of these could you use in your daily life? Explain your answer.

3. Read the following statements from Readings 1 and 2. What did the speakers mean? Which statement is most meaningful to you? Explain your answers.

> *I broke my neck, it didn't break me.* (Reading 1, Par. 7)

> *. . . if you worry, you die. If you don't worry, you also die. So, why worry?* (Reading 2, Par. 8)

1. Do you know any plants or animals that are used in medicine?

2. Have you ever used a medicine made from plants or animals? What did you use it for?

Nature's Medicine

Academic Vocabulary

to alleviate	to exceed	inconceivable
colloquially	to export	technically
curious	humidity	

Multiword Vocabulary

a clinical trial	in light of
common practice	of choice
to end up	a piece of the action
in full swing	a status symbol

Reading Preview

A Preview. Scan Reading 1 to find answers to the following questions. Then discuss the answers with a partner or in a small group.

1. What are Silang and Yangpin looking for?

2. What does *yarsta gunbu* mean?

3. How much money do the men spend at Zhaxicaiji's store?

B Topic vocabulary. The following words appear in Reading 1. Look at the words and answer the questions with a partner.

ailments	herbalists	skeptics
caterpillars	ingest	stalk
fatigue	poachers	worms
fungus	prescribe	yak herders

1. Which words refer to people?

2. Which words might be found in a medical textbook?

3. Which words are related to plants and animals?

C Predict. What do you think this reading will be about? Discuss each word in Exercise B and predict how it may relate to the reading.

Yartsa, also known as "golden worms," are a traditional cure for many health problems. Learn how the demand for yartsa is transforming one local economy.

Families search for caterpillar fungi in Sichuan Province, China.

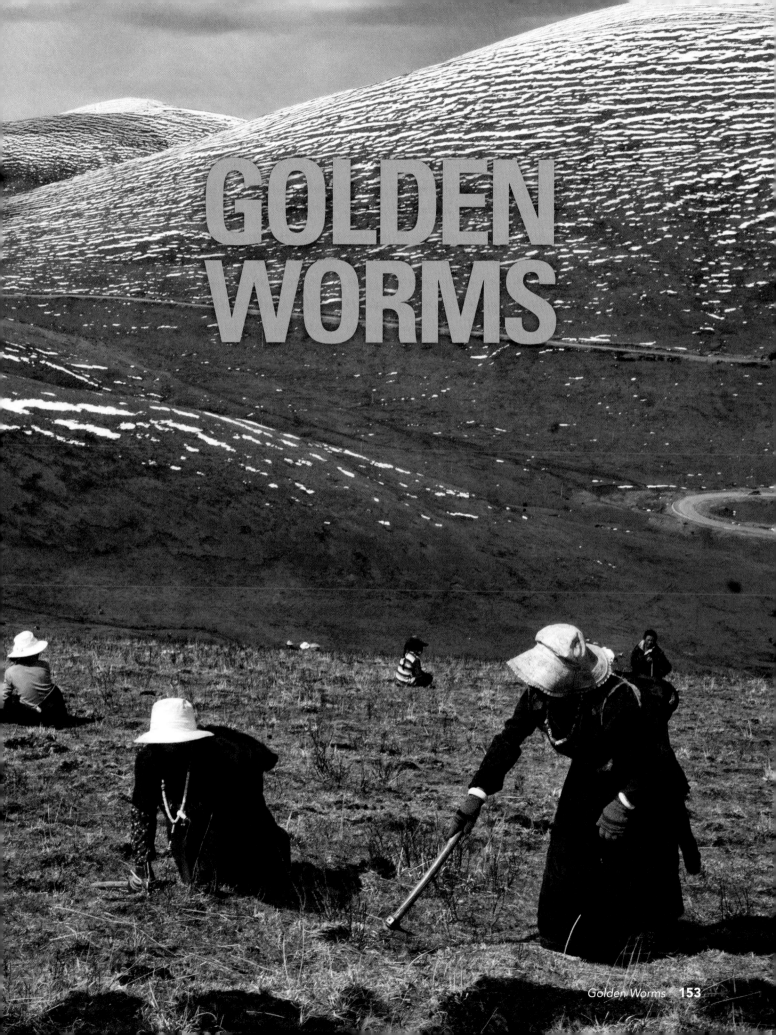

GOLDEN WORMS

Out in the fields, women sort and clean freshly harvested yartsa gunbu.

High on a plateau near the Himalayas, 15,000 feet (4,572 meters) above sea level, Silang Yangpi and his wife, Yangjin Namo, crawl along steep mountain slopes, combing through grass, twigs, and wild-flowers. Along with relatives and friends, they spend 11 hours a day, from early May to late June, searching for a tiny fungus that is believed to have incredible healing powers. They are looking for a thin brown stalk that comes a few inches out of the soil. This stalk is attached to the head of a bright yellow caterpillar. For some, the caterpillar fungus looks like an odd mushroom, but for Silang, 25, and Yangjin, 21, it represents a significant portion of their annual income. Caterpillar fungi have transformed the rural econ-omy, leading to a modern-day gold rush. By the time these arrive at the shops of Beijing, they can be priced at more than twice their weight in gold.

The fungus is called *yartsa gunbu*. This means "summer grass, winter worm," although it is technically neither grass nor worm. It is formed when certain caterpillars are infected by a parasitic fungus called *Ophiocordyceps sinensis*. The fungus eats the inside of the caterpillar, kill-ing the creature, but leaving its exterior intact. In spring, the fungus blooms in the form of a brown stalk that erupts from the caterpillar's head. Though the process occurs underground, as the fungus flowers, it pushes its way out of the ground (see Figure 1). This happens only in the fertile meadows high up in the Himalayan mountains (see Figure 2 on page 156). Although people have tried to farm the fungus, all attempts to do so have failed.

For centuries yartsa gunbu has been thought [3] to possess miraculous medicinal powers. Yaks that eat it, legend holds, become 10 times stronger. One of the earliest known descriptions of yartsa comes from a 15th-century Tibetan text, which describes the "faultless treasure" that "bestows[1] inconceivable advantages" on those who ingest it. Just boil some in a cup of tea or stew in a soup, and all your ailments will disappear.

> *"Caterpillar fungi have transformed the rural economy, leading to a modern-day gold rush."*

The worms, as they're colloquially known, [4] have been prescribed by herbalists to alleviate such problems as back pain, asthma, and fatigue. They are believed to reduce cholesterol, improve eyesight, and even help with hair loss. Bronchitis and hepatitis are some of the other ailments that the worms might cure. There are,

of course, skeptics, and some Western scientists assert that there need to be more clinical trials and more regulation of yartsa. Yet the demand for yartsa has soared in recent years, and it has become a status symbol and the gift of choice at dinner parties even as its cost has also risen. In the 1970s, one pound (0.45 kilograms) of worms cost a dollar or two. In the early 90s, it still cost less than 100 dollars. But by 2012, the same amount was worth a great deal more: $50,000 for a pound of top-quality yartsa.

Due to the demand for yartsa, thousands [5] of yak herders now own motorcycles, iPhones, and flat-screen TVs. As one might expect, many people want a piece of the action. Arguments over worm-picking turf[2] have resulted in violence, including seven murders. In the city of Chengdu, in Sichuan Province, burglars[3] tunneled into

---

[1] *bestow:* to give something formally

[2] *turf:* one's territory or area of authority

[3] *burglars:* thieves who illegally enter a building to steal

Figure 1. The Life Cycle of Yartsa

1 A ghost moth lays eggs on grass, leaves, or ground.
2 A larva hatches and digs into the earth.
3 Microscopic fungal spores wash into the soil and infect the larva.
4 The fungus eats the larva from within, and a brown stalk erupts from the caterpillar's head.
5 Inside the stalk, spores are produced, and the cycle continues.

Source: National Geographic Magazine, August 2012

a shop selling yartsa and stole more than $1.5 million worth of product. In light of these events, the Chinese police have established numerous roadside checkpoints[4] to prevent poachers from sneaking onto hillsides reserved for local villages.

At the end of the long picking day, Silang and Yangjin bring their worms to the local market. Worms are piled in boxes and baskets or spread on pieces of cloth, and carefully examined by yartsa dealers. Their value depends on a number of factors: size, color, and firmness. A crowd gathers to watch the transaction. It is common practice, when preparing to make a purchase, for a yartsa dealer to insult the worms.

"I've never bought such bad worms."

"The color's no good. Too dark."

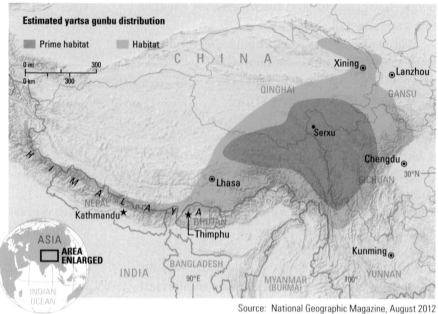

Figure 2. Worm Country

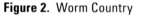

Estimated yartsa gunbu distribution

Prime habitat   Habitat

Source: National Geographic Magazine, August 2012

"I'm going to lose money on these."

Finally, when it's time to do business, the dealer holds out his arm. The sleeve of his coat or a cloth covers his hand. Silang slips his hand inside as well. Then, using finger signals rather than words, the two agree on a price. Hidden from the curious eyes of the crowd, it looks as if a thumb-wrestling match is going on. When a price is agreed upon, the money is passed

---

[4] *checkpoints:* places, usually at borders, where officials stop and examine people and vehicles for security purposes

ginseng root

GINSENG DIGGERS

There are many plants that are used for medicinal purposes. Ginseng, a small flowering plant, is one of the most popular. Ginseng root can be consumed in drinks, pills, candy, and even toothpaste, and is often taken to help the immune system. Other uses include treating cancer and heart disease and reducing stress. Not surprisingly, there is a high demand for wild ginseng.

While most people associate ginseng with the Far East, there has also been a long tradition of digging for ginseng in North America. In the forests of West Virginia, USA, digging for wild ginseng has been a tradition for generations. There's even a nickname for these diggers: *sengers*. However, there are laws for when and how the plants can be picked. The picking season only runs from September to November and only mature plants can be picked. When sengers pick ginseng, they are also required by law to replant the berries where the root once was, so that another ginseng plant will grow in its place.

through the sleeve or cloth. Silang and Yangjin return home, happy. The journey for the worm is just beginning.

The worm may change hands a half dozen or 11 more times before its final destination. Dealers in smaller, more rural markets sell to midsize markets. The best worms usually end up at China's biggest yartsa market. This market operates year-round, is loud and busy, and is spread out over an entire district in Xining.

Many of the largest and firmest "golden 12 worms" are selected by Zhaxicaiji's buyers. Zhaxicaiji is the founder and president of Three Rivers Source Medicine Company, one of China's best-known yartsa brands. Zhaxicaiji, who's now in her late 40s, grew up in a family that raised yaks and sheep and lived in a yak-hair tent. She too crawled along the hills, picking worms. Then, in 1998, she started her yartsa business with $120 of her own money. Now she manages 500 employees and 20 stores; annual sales can exceed $60 million. She plans to expand internationally, to export yartsa to places such as Japan, Korea, and Malaysia. Within a decade, she says, her worms will be sold in the United States.

Far from the hills where Silang and Yangjin 13 search for the little caterpillars, a black Mercedes pulls up to Zhaxicaiji's store in the central Chinese city of Lanzhou. The store occupies a full city block; over the entrance is a giant video screen where commercials advertise the worms. Inside are chandeliers,[5] a fountain, security guards, and vases of fresh-cut flowers. The yartsa is exhibited in dozens of museum-style glass cases, where the temperature and humidity are precisely controlled. Four well-dressed men exit the Mercedes and make their way into the store. They eat walnuts and raisins, drink yartsa-infused water, and make their selections. In a matter of 10 minutes, the men spend $30,000. The yartsa gold rush is in full swing.

---

[5] *chandelier:* a decorative holder hung from a ceiling with metal branches that hold glass lights or candles

Yartsa traders negotiate a deal and exchange money under a cloth.

READING COMPREHENSION

Big Picture

Ⓐ Choose the best answer for each of the following questions.

1. What is the purpose of paragraph 2?
   a. To define the meaning of the term *yartsa gunbu*
   b. To describe how a caterpillar becomes *yartsa gunbu*
   c. To explain why it has not been possible to farm *yartsa gunbu*

2. Which sentence best expresses the main idea of paragraph 3?
   a. The first sentence
   b. The second sentence
   c. The third sentence

3. What would be the best heading for paragraph 4?
   a. An Expensive Cure for Many Ailments
   b. Not Everyone Believes in the Power of Yartsa
   c. The Soaring Cost of Yartsa

4. What is the purpose of paragraph 6?
   a. To show that dealers often insult the worms
   b. To explain that the value of each worm depends on certain factors
   c. To describe how the worms are sold in the marketplace

5. What would be the best heading for paragraph 12?
   a. Who Is Zhaxicaiji?
   b. What Is Three Rivers Source Medicine Company?
   c. How Much Money Does Zhaxicaiji Earn?

Ⓑ Choose the sentence from paragraph 1 that expresses the main idea of the *whole* reading.

Close-Up

Ⓐ Scan Reading 1 and the short extra reading, "Ginseng Diggers," on page 156 to find answers to the following questions.

1. Is yartsa a species of caterpillar? Explain your answer.

   _____

2. How long have people been using yartsa?

   _____

3. What are the examples of ailments that the reading says yartsa is used for?

   _____

4. Does everyone believe that yartsa is a miraculous medicine? Explain your answer.

   _____

5. At the market, how do the dealer and Silang decide on a price for the yartsa? Why do you think this is?

   _____

6. What is the goal that Zhaxicaiji hopes to achieve in the next 10 years?

7. What are some of the laws in West Virginia that protect ginseng plants?

B Work with a partner and write other questions about Reading 1 and "Ginseng Diggers." Then ask another group to answer the questions.

Reading Skill

Understanding Pronoun Reference

Cohesion refers to the way that an author connects information so that it reads smoothly. One technique is to use pronouns, such as *this, these, it, they, his, hers,* and *its,* in order to avoid repeating nouns or noun phrases. Pronouns can refer to ideas as well as to people or things. If you aren't sure what the pronouns refer to, you may miss essential elements of the reading.

Pronouns are almost always backward references, that is, they are referring to something that has already been mentioned in the reading—an *antecedent.* If you aren't sure what the pronoun refers to, look for the nouns or noun phrases in the preceding sentences. Then determine which noun or noun phrase the pronoun is replacing. For example: *The yartsa dealer uses a gold scale. This has been in his family for years.*

This refers to the antecedent, the *gold scale. His* refers to the antecedent, the *yartsa dealer.*

Forward references are less common, but you need to be able to recognize them, too. An explanation directly follows a forward reference. For example: *Those who arrive late to the market may not find the best yartsa gunbu.*

Those is the pronoun, and the relative clause *who arrive late* explains who *those* refers to.

A Read the following sentences from Reading 1, and circle the pronouns. Then draw an arrow from each pronoun to the idea, person, or thing that the pronoun refers to.

1. Caterpillar fungi have transformed the rural economy, leading to a modern-day gold rush. By the time these arrive at the shops of Beijing, they can be priced at more than twice their weight in gold.

2. The fungus is called *yartsa gunbu.* This means "summer grass, winter worm," although it is technically neither grass nor worm.

3. The fungus eats the inside of the caterpillar, killing the creature, but leaving its exterior intact.

4. Though the process occurs underground, as the fungus flowers, it pushes its way out of the ground. This happens only in the fertile meadows high up in the Himalayan mountains.

5. One of the earliest known descriptions of yartsa comes from a 15th-century Tibetan text, which describes the "faultless treasure" that "bestows inconceivable advantages" on those who ingest it.

6. Worms are piled in boxes and baskets or spread on pieces of cloth, and carefully examined by yartsa dealers. Their value depends on a number of factors: size, color, firmness.

B Reread Reading 1, and circle five other examples of pronoun references. Draw arrows to the idea, person, or thing that they refer to. Compare answers with a partner.

VOCABULARY PRACTICE

Academic Vocabulary

A Find the words in bold in Reading 1. Use the context to help you match each word to the correct definition.

_____	**1. technically** (Par. 2)	**a.** according to informal spoken or written language
_____	**2. inconceivable** (Par. 3)	**b.** the amount of moisture in the air
_____	**3. colloquially** (Par. 4)	**c.** according to the facts
_____	**4. alleviate** (Par. 4)	**d.** be more than what is expected
_____	**5. curious** (Par. 10)	**e.** make less difficult or painful
_____	**6. exceed** (Par. 12)	**f.** not able to be imagined
_____	**7. export** (Par. 12)	**g.** interested in knowing about things
_____	**8. humidity** (Par. 13)	**h.** ship something from one country to another in order to sell it

B The words in bold show academic words from Exercise A and words they often appear with. Complete the sentences with your own ideas.

1. **Technically speaking**, a tomato is not a vegetable, it is a _____.

2. It seems **inconceivable that** there is still no cure for _____.

3. Where I am from, _____ is **colloquially known as** _____.

4. Charities such as _____ look for ways to **alleviate suffering and poverty**.

5. Celebrities often wear _____ to hide from **curious onlookers**.

6. One way that a language class can **exceed expectations** is when the class

   _____.

7. This country **exports goods** such as _____ to other countries, for example,

   _____.

8. **Humidity levels** are usually high when there is a lot of _____.

Women sort, clean, and prepare yartsa for sale in a retail store in China.

Multiword Vocabulary

A Find the words in bold in Reading 1. Use the context to help you complete each definition.

1. **Clinical trials** (Par. 4) are _____ .
   a. tests on patients to see if a medical treatment is effective
   b. times when a doctor has to go to court

2. A **status symbol** (Par. 4) is something that shows when a person _____ .
   a. is scheduled for a meeting
   b. has a lot of money or an important place in society

3. When an item is referred to as the gift **of choice** (Par. 4), it means _____ .
   a. it is the gift that most people at the present time prefer from a selection of similar gifts
   b. people are required to make a difficult decision between two gifts

4. If people want **a piece of the action** (Par. 5), they want to _____ .
   a. write about an important story, usually for a newspaper or magazine
   b. take part in an activity, usually in order to make money or become more important

5. **In light of** (Par. 5) means _____ .
   a. as a result of
   b. during

Caterpillar fungus dries in the sun in a bamboo pan.

6. **Common practice** (Par. 6) refers to _____ .
   a. the usual way of doing things
   b. a way of researching material

7. If you **end up** (Par. 11) somewhere, it means that you _____ .
   a. eventually arrive at that place
   b. are unhappy to be where you are

8. If something is **in full swing** (Par. 13), it means that it is _____ .
   a. unsuccessful and almost finished
   b. successful and no longer in its early stages

B Complete the following sentences with the correct multiword vocabulary from the box below. In some cases, you need to change the verb or noun form.

clinical trials	of choice	in full swing	a piece of the action
common practice	end up	in light of	status symbol

1. When we arrived, the party was _____ . Everyone was having a great time.

2. _____ recent storm damage to the park, the city has decided to postpone the outdoor festival.

3. The two women were lost at sea and _____ on a small island in the South Pacific. They survived there for four months before rescuers found them.

4. The drug has gone through five different _____, and it is now ready to be sold to the public.

5. In the 1950s, owning a television was considered a(n) _____; only the wealthy could afford one.

6. In the United States, it is _____ to shake someone's hand when you first meet.

7. When the government began a new program to fund small businesses, everyone wanted

_____ .

8. Health advocates want to promote water as the drink _____ for children, rather than sugary sodas or juices.

Use the Vocabulary

Write answers to the following questions. Use the words in bold in your answers. Then share your answers with a partner.

1. If you left your classroom, walked out of the building, turned left, and walked 500 yards (457 meters), where would you **end up**?

2. Where you live, what is **common practice** to do when you go to someone's house for dinner?

3. What is an example of a **status symbol** that people try to acquire where you live? Why is this a status symbol?

4. Imagine that a friend of yours started a new, successful business. Would you want to get **a piece of the action**? Why, or why not?

5. If you are under a lot of pressure, what is one thing that you usually do to **alleviate** stress?

6. Would you prefer to live somewhere with high **humidity** or low **humidity**? Explain your answer?

7. Why isn't it a good idea for your expenses to **exceed** your income? Explain your answer.

8. What is a situation that might attract **curious onlookers**? Have you ever been a curious onlooker in such a situation? Describe what you saw.

THINK AND DISCUSS

Work in a small group. Use the information in the reading and your own ideas to discuss the following questions.

1. Express an opinion. Would you use yartsa to treat a medical ailment? Why, or why not?

2. Infer meaning. How do you think the yartsa gold rush has changed the villagers' way of life in this area? What are the pros? What are the cons?

3. Summarize. How does a little caterpillar on a hillside arrive at a showroom in Lanzhou as expensive yarsta? Briefly describe the steps in this process.

4. Express an opinion. Do you go to outdoor markets where you live? How do people decide on prices? How does the market described in the reading compare to your own experience?

Academic Vocabulary

advances	to derive	to prolong
composition	to hasten	to trigger
decline	to presume	

Multiword Vocabulary

to be upwards of	on the agenda
to eat away at	to pack a punch
in the near future	to stop in one's tracks
to make a name for oneself	to walk a fine line

Reading Preview

A **Preview.** Read the title of Reading 2. Look at the photos on pages 164–168 and read their captions. Then discuss the following questions with a partner or in a small group.

1. What do you think the title refers to? What kind of bite is it describing?

2. What do all the animals in the photographs have in common?

3. What is Zoltan Takacs's job?

B **Topic vocabulary.** The following words appear in Reading 2. Look at the words and answer the questions with a partner.

antidote	injection	scorpion
arthritis	lethal	sting
blood clotting	lizards	toxins
diluted	promising	venom

1. Which words suggest that this reading is about medicine and health?

2. Which words could be connected to animals?

3. Which words are adjectives and which words are nouns that they might describe?

C **Predict.** What do you think this reading will be about? Discuss each word in Exercise B and predict how it may relate to the reading.

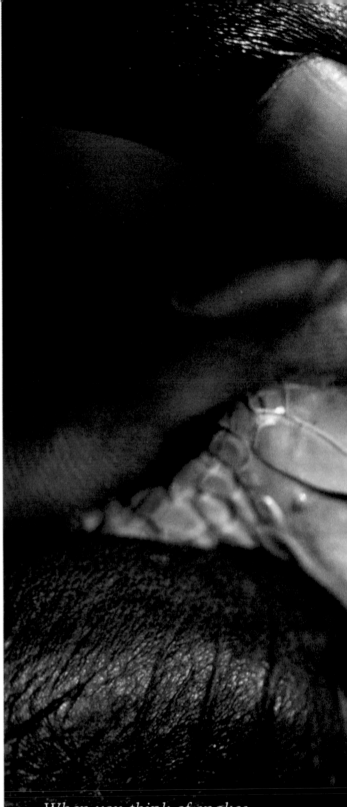

When you think of snakes, do you immediately think of danger? Did you know that snakes can also save lives? Find out how the many varieties of snake venom are being used for medicinal purposes.

A Turkana tribesman in Kenya
milks a green mamba snake for
its poisonous venom.

The Bite
that Heals

On vacation in Mexico, Michael (who does 1 not want to give his last name) jumped into a pool. Suddenly a burning pain ripped through the back of his thigh. He spotted his attacker—a small, ugly, and yellow creature—put it in a container, and promptly sought medical attention. The doctors identified this as a bark scorpion, one of the most poisonous species in North America. The fierce pain from a sting is typically followed by what feels like electric shocks racing through the body. Occasionally, victims die. Luckily for Michael, an antidote was readily available. He was given the injection, was released a few hours later, and in 30 hours the pain was gone.

What happened next could not have been 2 predicted. For eight years prior to the scorpion sting, Michael had endured a condition called *ankylosing spondylitis*, a sort of spinal arthritis. No one knows what triggers this ailment. "My back hurt every morning, and during bad flare-ups[1] it was so horrible I couldn't even walk," he says. Incredibly, just days after the scorpion sting, his back pain disappeared and now, two years later, he remains essentially pain-free. As a doctor himself, Michael is cautious about

overstating the role of the scorpion's venom in his recovery. Still, he says, "if my pain came back, I'd let that scorpion sting me again."

The purpose of venom is simple: to stop a 3 body in its tracks. Venom is a mixture of toxic proteins and peptides—short strings of amino acids[2] similar to proteins. The molecules have different effects, but they work together to pack a punch. Some paralyze areas by blocking messages between nerves and muscle. Some eat away at molecules so that cells and tissues collapse. Venom can kill by clotting blood and stopping the heart or, alternatively, by preventing blood clotting and triggering bleeding. The difference between venom and poison is that venom is injected into the victim's body and poison is consumed. Hundreds of toxins can be delivered in a single venomous bite. Imagine giving your enemy poison, then stabbing him with a knife, before shooting him in the head. That's venom at work.

More than 100,000 animals produce venom, 4 including certain snakes, scorpions, spiders, lizards, bees, octopuses, fish, and cone snails. The composition of the venom of a single snake species varies from place to place and between adults and their young. Not only that, an individual snake's venom may even change with its diet. Although venom is not always lethal, its primary function is to allow an animal to kill, or at least immobilize, its next meal. Humans

---

[1] *flare-ups:* recurrence of symptoms or an onset of more severe symptoms

[2] *amino acids:* the chemical building blocks of protein chains

Scorpion venom is providing promising leads to combat autoimmune diseases.

Zoltan Takacs holds a Jameson's mamba in Africa. Mamba venom toxin is in clinical trial to treat heart failure.

are often accidental victims. The World Health Organization estimates that every year approximately five million venomous bites kill 100,000 people, although the actual number is presumed to be much higher. In rural areas of developing countries, where most bites occur, victims may not be able to get medical treatment or they choose traditional remedies, and thus are not included in this number.

Ironically, the properties that make venom 5 deadly are also what make it so valuable for medicine. Many venom toxins target the same molecules that need to be controlled to treat diseases. Venom works fast and is highly specific. It's a challenge to find the toxin that hits only a certain target, but already top medicines for heart disease and diabetes have been derived from venom. New treatments for autoimmune diseases, cancer, and pain could be available in the near future. So far, fewer than a thousand toxins have been studied for their medicinal

value. "There could be upwards of 20 million venom toxins out there," says Zoltan Takacs, a toxicologist and herpetologist, who has made a name for himself in the field of toxicology. "It's huge. Venom has opened up whole new avenues of pharmacology.[3]"

Venom-based cures aren't a new idea. Cobra 6 venom, applied for centuries in traditional Chinese and Indian medicine, was introduced to the West in the 1830s as a homeopathic remedy[4] for pain. John Henry Clarke's *Materia Medica*, published around 1900, describes the venom as a cure for many ills, even those caused by venom itself. "We should always endeavor to use the same drug to cure as produced the symptoms," the author wrote. Carefully diluted cobra venom

---

[3] *pharmacology:* the science of drugs, which includes drug discovery and design, action, medical use, etc.

[4] *homeopathic remedy:* treating an illness with a small dose of the agent that causes the illness, not considered a science-based method of therapy

was said to relieve asthma, hay fever, headaches, and sore throats, among others. However, it was noted that the amount needed to cure these ailments was only a little less than a lethal dose. Walking such a fine line, physicians may have hastened patients' deaths as often as—or more often than—they prolonged their lives.

Advances in fields such as molec- 7 ular biology continue to give scientists better ways to understand venoms and their targets. Takacs co-invented Designer Toxins, a system that allows researchers to combine toxins and compare their therapeutic values. This can streamline[5] efforts to develop drugs. Takacs recently launched World Toxin Bank, with the goal to create "toxin libraries" that could eventually hold samples of the venom toxins of every animal on Earth.

––––––––––
[5] *streamline:* make something simpler and more efficient

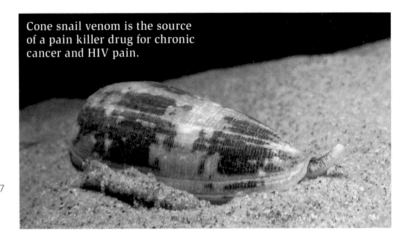

Cone snail venom is the source of a pain killer drug for chronic cancer and HIV pain.

As Takacs says, the medical potential of 8 venom is "mind-blowing." But we're at risk of losing that potential. Snake populations are in decline, and the oceans' changing chemistry could wipe out promising sources of venom, from cone snails to octopuses. The creatures that make nature's deadliest potions should be high on the agenda when conservation decisions are made. Just ask Michael. They can, after all, be lifesavers.

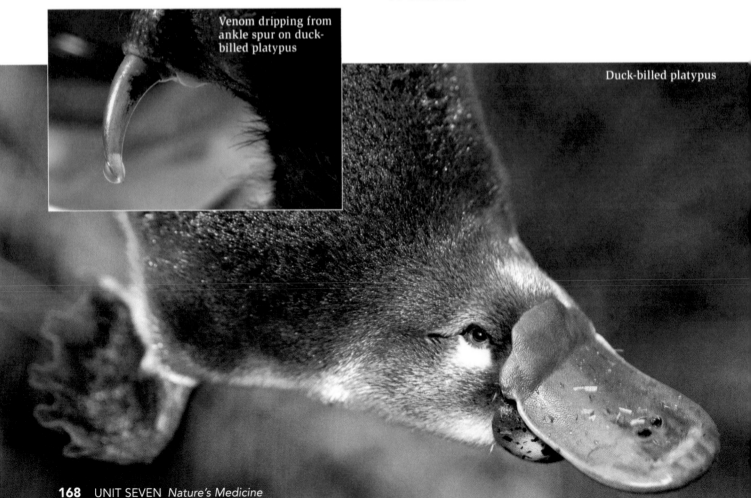

Venom dripping from ankle spur on duck-billed platypus

Duck-billed platypus

READING COMPREHENSION

Big Picture

Ⓐ The following are key words and phrases that could be used to annotate the paragraphs in Reading 2. Write the correct paragraph number on the line next to each annotation.

_____ **1.** Who produces venom / who gets bitten?

_____ **2.** History of venom-based cures: use caution!

_____ **3.** Example of a sting ➔ Michael's story

_____ **4.** Medical advances ➔ designer toxins

_____ **5.** Results of a scorpion sting ➔ no more arthritis

_____ **6.** Venomous creatures at risk

_____ **7.** How venom works

_____ **8.** Venom toxins ➔ medical potential (20 million toxins!)

Ⓑ Complete the following sentences in your own words.

1. The main idea of Reading 2 is _____ .

2. One reason that the author tells Michael's story is to illustrate _____ .

Close-Up

Ⓐ Decide which of the following statements are true or false according to the reading. Write _T_ (True) or _F_ (False) next to each one.

_____ **1.** Michael is a doctor.

_____ **2.** Michael is certain that the scorpion sting is completely responsible for his recovery.

_____ **3.** All venom toxins have the same effect on a person's body.

_____ **4.** Certain types of cone snails and fish produce venom.

_____ **5.** A snake's venom can change depending on what it eats.

_____ **6.** All snakebites are reported to the World Health Organization.

_____ **7.** Approximately five million people are killed by venomous bites every year.

_____ **8.** Zoltan Takacs studies venom toxins for their medicinal value.

_____ **9.** In the 1900s, diluted cobra venom was used to help asthma and headaches.

_____ **10.** In the 1900s, doctors might have killed their patients by prescribing too little venom.

_____ **11.** "Toxin libraries" will have books with information about every toxin in the world.

_____ **12.** The author says that there should be conservation efforts to protect venomous creatures because they could be lifesavers.

B Work with a partner or in a small group. Change the false statements in Exercise A to make them true.

Reading Skill

> ### Categorizing Information
>
> When you read an informational text, there can be so much data that it is hard to keep track of everything. One useful strategy is to categorize information by topic. Sometimes a reading will already have headings to signal different areas of information. Many readings won't have headings, however. When this is the case, you need to determine what the topics are yourself. Take short notes about each topic in order to organize the information for your own comprehension.

A Categorize the information from Reading 2 into the three categories below. Write at least three pieces of information for each category.

Effects of Venom	Uses for Venom	Venomous Animals

B Work with a partner. Choose a reading from an earlier unit that you have already read. How would you categorize information from that reading? Write three categories and then fill in the chart below.

Reading Title: _____

Category:	Category:	Category:

VOCABULARY PRACTICE

Academic Vocabulary

A Read the following sentences from Reading 2. Use the context of each word in bold to match it to the correct definition.

_____ **1.** For eight years prior to the scorpion sting, Michael had endured a condition called *ankylosing spondylitis*, a sort of spinal arthritis. No one knows what **triggers** (Par. 2) this ailment.

_____ **2.** The **composition** (Par. 4) of the venom of a single snake species varies from place to place and between adults and their young.

_____ **3.** The World Health Organization estimates that every year approximately five million venomous bites kill 100,000 people, although the actual number is **presumed** (Par. 4) to be much higher.

_____ **4.** It's a challenge to find the toxin that hits only a certain target, but already top medicines for heart disease and diabetes have been **derived** (Par. 5) from venom.

_____ **5.** Walking such a fine line, physicians may have **hastened** (Par. 6) patients' deaths as often as—or more often than—they prolonged their lives.

_____ **6.** Walking such a fine line, physicians may have hastened patients' deaths as often as—or more often than—they **prolonged** (Par. 6) their lives.

_____ **7.** **Advances** (Par. 7) in fields such as molecular biology continue to give scientists better ways to understand venoms and their targets.

_____ **8.** Snake populations are in **decline** (Par. 8), and the oceans' changing chemistry could wipe out promising sources of venom, from cone snails to octopuses.

a. sustained; kept something going

b. gotten from something else

c. improvements

d. starts a reaction

e. a lowering or decrease

f. sped up

g. how something is put together; its makeup

h. supposed that something is true

B Choose academic words from Exercise A to complete the following sentences. Notice and learn the words in bold because they often appear with the academic words. In some cases, you need to change the verb or noun form.

1. The magazine had an interesting article on ways to _____ **our lives**. Even though we'll all die sometime, most people don't want to _____ **the process**, they want to slow it down.

2. When people have food allergies, seemingly innocent foods such as eggs or nuts can _____ **a reaction**.

3. There has been a(n) _____ **in the number of** people voting in local elections. Only 3,000 people voted in last week's election. The rainstorm is _____ **to be** the cause of the low turnout.

4. There have been recent _____ **in technology** that have led to people spending more time inside. However, **our body's chemical** _____ still requires vitamin D, which is usually _____ **from** sunlight.

Multiword Vocabulary

Ⓐ Find the multiword vocabulary in bold in Reading 2 and use the context to help you understand the meaning. Then match each item to the correct definition.

_____ **1. stop** a body **in its tracks** (Par. 3)

_____ **2. pack a punch** (Par. 3)

_____ **3. eat away at** (Par. 3)

_____ **4. in the near future** (Par. 5)

_____ **5. be upwards of** (Par. 5)

_____ **6. made a name for** himself (Par. 5)

_____ **7. walking** such **a fine line** (Par. 6)

_____ **8. on the agenda** (Par. 8)

a. happening soon

b. in the list of things that someone wants to do

c. became well-known for a specific reason

d. have a strong effect

e. be more than

f. achieving the right balance

g. slowly destroy

h. make something stand still

Ⓑ Complete the following sentences with the correct multiword vocabulary from Exercise A. In some cases, you need to change the verb or noun form or the pronoun.

1. Luan's father _____ in his neighborhood by opening the only store that sold traditional medicine to the public.

2. A terrible secret can _____ you. Over time, it can make you feel more and more miserable. It is better to confess and try to remedy the situation as best you can.

3. When the polar bear approached the camp, Mike shot his flare gun and _____. The bear looked at Mike and then ran away.

4. When interviewing for a job, you have to _____ between proving that you are the best candidate and talking too much about your achievements.

5. Gordana and her husband hope to move to their own house _____, but right now they are living with her parents.

6. Achieving spoken fluency in English is probably high _____ for most students in this class.

7. Officials aren't sure how many people will attend the victory parade, but there could _____ 20,000 people.

8. The coffee from that café really _____. If I have a cup after five o'clock, I can't sleep at night!

Use the Vocabulary

Write answers to the following questions. Use the words in bold in your answers. Then share your answers with a partner.

1. What is one good technique for **prolonging the life** of fruits and vegetables?

2. What is an example of a food that **packs a punch**? What can this mean?

3. When people start talking about a scandal, such as a story about a politician or a celebrity, is it possible to **stop** the story **in its tracks**? Why, or why not?

4. Who is someone who has **made a name for** him**self** or her**self** as a businessperson?

5. What is an example of a recent **advance** that has been made in medicine?

6. What is high **on your agenda** this week? Explain your answer.

7. What is the **composition** of the English class that you are taking right now? That is, how many students are there, where are they from, how old are they, etc.?

8. There is an English expression, "Haste makes waste." What do you think this means? If you **hasten a process**, how can that be a bad thing?

THINK AND DISCUSS

Work in a small group. Use the information in the reading and your own ideas to discuss the following questions.

1. **Infer meaning.** Who said the following? What did the speaker mean? Why is this important?

   There could be upwards of 20 million venom toxins out there.

2. **Analyze.** Who said the following? What did the speaker mean? Why is this important?

   We should always endeavor to use the same drug to cure as produced the symptoms.

3. **Express an opinion.** Who said the following? Why did the speaker say this? If you had the same experience as the speaker, would you say the same thing? Why, or why not?

   If my pain came back, I'd let that scorpion sting me again.

4. **Summarize.** What does the author mean by the following? In your own words, give a more technical explanation of how venom works.

   Imagine giving your enemy poison, then stabbing him with a knife, before shooting him in the head. That's venom at work.

Vocabulary Review

Ⓐ Complete the paragraphs with the vocabulary below that you have studied in the unit.

alleviate suffering	colloquially known as	in the near future	of choice
be upwards of	derived from	inconceivable that	trigger the adverse reactions
clinical trials	in light of		

Most of us are afraid of black mamba snakes, but one day soon, we could be thanking them.

A new drug, _____ black mamba snake venom, may become the new

1

painkiller _____. Scientist Anne Baron leads the study from France's Institute

2

of Molecular and Cellular Pharmacology. Many of today's painkillers can cause serious and

unintended health problems, which are _____ *side effects*. For example,

3

morphine, another painkiller, can cause respiratory distress. Baron says that the venom painkiller

is exciting because it does not _____ of other drugs.

4

As exciting as this is, the black mamba painkiller is still

being tested, and it won't be available any time

_____. Although the drug has only

5

been tested on mice, Baron is confident that it will work

on humans as well. Still, the drug will have to go

through numerous _____ before it

6

is on the market. The cost of such research could

_____ one hundred million dollars.

7

However, _____ the possibilities that the

8

drug offers, it just might be worth it. A drug that can

_____ without causing side effects could make

9

billions of dollars. It isn't _____ someday, when we think

10

of black mambas, we breathe a sigh of relief, rather than hold our breath in fear.

A black mamba

Ⓑ Compare answers to Exercise A with a partner. Then discuss the following questions.

Do you think the black mamba painkiller will become popular? Why, or why not?

Ⓒ Complete the following sentences in a way that shows that you understand the meaning of the words in bold.

1. Where I live, when friends get married, it is **common practice** to _____.

2. I'd like **to make a name for myself** in the field of _____.

3. In most of the world, diseases such as _____ are now **in decline**.

4. One way to **prolong your life** is to _____.

D Work with a partner and write sentences that include any six of the vocabulary items below. You may use any verb tense and make nouns plural if you wish.

advances in technology	hasten the process	presumed to be	technically speaking
exceed expectations	in full swing	status symbol	walk a fine line
export goods	on the agenda		

Connect the Readings

A According to the readings and the Vocabulary Review in this unit, how are yartsa gunbu and snake venom different? How are they the same? Fill out the chart below. Put a check (✓) in the column indicating if the statement applies to yartsa gunbu, snake venom, or both.

	Yartsa Gunbu	Snake Venom
1. Western scientists say that they need to study this more.		
2. There is the potential to make a lot of money from this.		
3. It has been used for centuries.		
4. Its effects can change depending on the animal's diet.		
5. This is sold at a market.		
6. It can only be found in the wild.		
7. It can help with asthma.		
8. If you have too much, it could kill you.		

B With a partner or in a small group, compare answers to Exercise A. Then discuss the following questions.

1. Would you say that yartsa gunbu and snake venom have a lot in common with one another? Why, or why not?

2. If you could research either yartsa gunbu or snake venom, which would you choose to study? Explain your answer.

3. If you were asked to invest money for developing and exporting either yartsa gunbu or snake venom, which would you choose? Explain your answer.

C Discuss the following questions with a partner. Use your understanding of the readings and your own ideas.

1. After reading this unit, has your opinion of snakes and fungi changed? Why, or why not?

2. How important do you think clinical trials are when studying medicine made from plants and animals? Explain your answer.

3. In Reading 2, the author suggests that snake venom could have killed some of the patients that it was trying to cure. Do you think this is more common with traditional medicine than with pharmaceutical medicine? Why, or why not?

Lost at Sea

FOCUS

1. Why did people in the past travel by sea? What were the dangers? What were the rewards?

2. What is an example of a famous shipwreck? What do you know about the event?

177

Academic Vocabulary

accessible	immense	to salvage
to advocate	a lawsuit	sole
heroic	to reassess	

Multiword Vocabulary

at the expense of	a leap of faith
to be reminiscent of	sheer size
to capture one's imagination	to shift one's focus
	state-of-the-art
a change of heart	

Reading Preview

A **Preview.** Read the title of Reading 1. Look at the photos on pages 178–182 and read their captions. Then discuss the following questions with a partner or in a small group.

1. What do you already know about the *Titanic*?

2. Where can you see items from the shipwreck?

3. Why do you think there might be controversy surrounding items that were found from the shipwreck?

B **Topic vocabulary.** The following words appear in Reading 1. Look at the words and answer the questions with a partner.

artifacts	distress	preservation
coward	greed	relics
critical	iceberg	sordid
display	lifeboats	wreck

1. Which words suggest that the reading is about a ship that sank?

2. Which words could be related to a museum exhibit?

3. Which words have negative associations?

C **Predict.** What do you think this reading will be about? Discuss each word in Exercise B and predict how it may relate to the reading.

People around the world are fascinated by the story of the Titanic, *but should the artifacts be taken out of the ocean and put in museums, or should they be preserved underwater?*

The Titanic gets ready for its maiden voyage in 1912 in Belfast, Northern Ireland.

TREASURES
of the *Titanic*

The rusted bow of
the RMS *Titanic*

The story is well known: At 2:20 a.m. on April 15, 1912, the "unsinkable" RMS *Titanic* disappeared beneath the waves. A century later, the *Titanic* still captures our imagination.

The tale of the *Titanic* is a story of superlatives—a ship so strong and so grand, sinking in water so cold and so deep. Some people are awed by the sheer size of the boat itself. Others are fascinated by the stories of the 2,208 people who were on board. It took 2 hours and 40 minutes for the *Titanic* to sink. After the announcement, "Women and children first," one coward tried to escape by jumping into the lifeboats dressed in women's clothing. However, most men were honorable and many were heroic. The captain stayed on the bridge, the band played on, the wireless radio operators continued sending their distress signals until the bitter end. One hundred years later, the stories of how the passengers spent their final moments are still compelling.

Physical reminders of these stories are on display at RMS *Titanic* (RMST) exhibits around the world. More than 25 million people have seen RMST shows and walked through the exhibits in 20 different countries. RMST has salvaged over 5,500 artifacts from the deep. Wandering among the relics, it's possible to see, among other things, a chef's hat, a razor, a set of perfectly preserved dishes, pairs of shoes, bottles of perfume, and a champagne bottle with the cork still in it. They are mostly ordinary objects made extraordinary by the long, terrible journey that brought them here.

In Las Vegas, Nevada, USA, the Luxor Hotel has a semi-permanent exhibition of *Titanic* artifacts brought up from the ocean depths. In the exhibit, visitors pass through a cold, darkened chamber, where they can go up to and touch an "iceberg." Recordings of sighs and groans of shifting metal add to the sensation of being trapped in the belly of a wounded beast. The centerpiece of the exhibit is a 15-ton piece of *Titanic*'s hull.[1] Studded with rivets and ribbed with steel, this piece of the ship is reminiscent of a *Tyrannosaurus rex*[2] at a natural history museum. Impossibly immense and transported at great expense, it is an extinct species hauled back from a lost world.

"One hundred years later, the stories of how the passengers spent their final moments are still compelling."

RMST has the legal rights to the relics found at the site of the *Titanic* wreck, which covers an incredibly large area (see Figure 1). Because they were the first and only company to salvage the wreck, international law states that they have sole ownership. As long as they continue to fund expeditions and preservation efforts, no one else is allowed to take artifacts from the site, or even take photographs. However, over

[1] *hull:* the outside of a ship, without its sails

[2] *Tyrannosaurus rex:* one of the largest known species of dinosaurs

the years many marine archaeologists have had harsh words for the company and its executives, calling them grave robbers, treasure hunters, and worse. Robert Ballard, who first discovered the underwater site of the *Titanic* in 1985, has advocated for the wreck and all its contents to be preserved where they were found. He has been very critical of RMST's methodologies and feels that their effort to salvage artifacts is at the expense of the integrity of the site. "You don't go to the Louvre[3] and stick your finger on the *Mona Lisa*," Ballard said. "You don't visit Gettysburg[4] with a shovel. These guys are driven by a desire to make money while I am more interested in treating the site like a graveyard and giving it the same respect we give the USS ARIZONA[5] in Pearl Harbor. Removing artifacts from the site lessens the impact the site will have on those who will visit it in the future."

In recent years, however, RMST has come under new management. It has shifted its focus away from pure salvage—getting as many relics as possible—toward preservation—treating the wreck as an archaeological site. The company has begun to work in concert with the scientific and governmental organizations that are concerned with

[3] *The Louvre:* The museum in Paris, France where the *Mona Lisa* is on display

[4] *Gettysburg:* The site of a famous battle in 1863 that took place during the American Civil War

[5] *The USS ARIZONA:* a U.S. battleship that sank in 1941

Figure 1. Estimated Area Covered by the *Titanic* Wreck

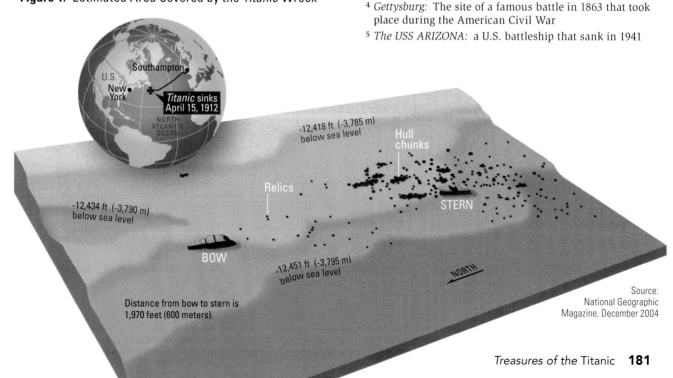

Source:
National Geographic
Magazine, December 2004

preserving the *Titanic*. Christopher Davino, who led RMST from 2009 to 2012, explained the company's new tactic. "For years, the only thing that all the voices in the *Titanic* community could agree on was their disdain[6] of us," he said. "So it was time to reassess everything. We had to do something beyond artifact recovery. We had to stop fighting with the experts and start collaborating with them."

This is exactly what has happened. U.S. government agencies such as the National Oceanic and Atmospheric Association (NOAA) were formerly involved in lawsuits against RMST but, incredibly, are now working directly with the company on various long-range scientific projects, which are focused on protecting the wreck site. Dave Conlin is the chief marine archaeologist at the National Park Service, another agency that had been critical of the company. Conlin commends RMST for their change of heart, saying, "RMST deserved the flak[7] they got in years past,

but they also deserve credit for taking this new leap of faith."

The 2010 *Titanic* expedition that captured the first view of the entire wreck site was organized, led, and paid for by RMST. This ambitious multimillion-dollar expedition used three state-of-the-art robotic vehicles. The team created a massive picture of the site by using high-definition optical cameras that take hundreds of images per second. NOAA archaeologist James Delgado, the expedition's chief scientist, says, "In the past, trying to understand *Titanic* was like trying to understand Manhattan at midnight in a rainstorm—with a flashlight. Now we have a site that can be understood and measured, with definite things to tell us. In years to come, this historic map may give voice to those people who were silenced, seemingly forever, when the cold water closed over them." Hopefully, this new direction will mean that the remains of the *Titanic* will be both protected and accessible to the public for many years to come.

7

8

---

[6] *disdain:* a lack of respect
[7] *flak:* an informal way to describe excessive criticism

Titanic Belfast, a museum in Belfast, Northern Ireland that houses an extensive *Titanic* exhibition

READING COMPREHENSION

Big Picture

A Complete the following sentences in your own words.

1. The purpose of paragraph 2 is to describe _____ .

2. The main idea of paragraph 3 can be found in sentence _____ .

3. The purpose of paragraph 4 is to describe _____ .

4. The main idea of paragraph 5 can be found in sentence _____ .

5. The main idea of paragraph 6 can be found in sentence _____ .

6. The purpose of paragraph 8 is to describe how _____ .

B Write a three-sentence summary of Reading 1.

_____

_____

_____

Close-Up

A Decide which of the following statements are true or false according to the reading. Write *T* (True) or *F* (False) next to each one.

_____ **1.** The *Titanic* sank in the middle of the night.

_____ **2.** There were 2,208 people who died in the *Titanic* shipwreck.

_____ **3.** The members of the band left on the first lifeboats.

_____ **4.** Twenty-five million people have seen the RMST exhibit in Las Vegas, USA.

_____ **5.** One of the RMST exhibits includes a model of a Tyrannosaurus Rex.

_____ **6.** All recent photographs of the *Titanic* underwater are the property of RMST.

_____ **7.** Robert Ballard works for RMST.

_____ **8.** Robert Ballard said that RMST only wanted to respect the wreck site.

_____ **9.** In the past, most scientific and U.S. government organizations were happy with the way that RMST operated.

_____ **10.** The new bosses at RMST started working with other organizations.

_____ **11.** Dave Conlin likes RMST's new approach to the wreck site.

_____ **12.** Before 2010, there were no photographs that showed the entire wreck site.

B Work with a partner or in a small group. Change the false statements in Exercise A to make them true.

Reading Skill

Distinguishing Facts from Opinions

When reading a text, it is important to distinguish between facts and an author's opinion so that you can form your own ideas about the topic. Opinions are often signaled by verbs such as *think* or *believe*, but this is not always the case. Sometimes you will need to look at the context of the sentence to decide if it is a fact or an opinion. One way to help distinguish opinions from facts is to look for *value* words. Value words are used to discuss something *subjectively*. That is, they present a judgment about the topic. Some examples of value words include the following:

Adjectives	ugly, beautiful, interesting, boring, terrific, scary, exciting
Adverbs	disturbingly, wondrously, seemingly
Modal verbs	should, ought to
Verbs	deserve, agree, disagree, worry
Nouns	credit, hero, coward

Note that many adjectives such as ones that express colors or measurements are not always used as value words. Based on the context, they can also describe something *objectively*. Rather than presenting a judgment, they describe a fact; that is, something that can be proven. Look at the two examples from Reading 1 and decide if these are facts or opinions:

> *One hundred years later, the stories of how the passengers spent their final moments are still compelling.*

> *In the exhibit, visitors pass through a cold, darkened chamber, where they can go up to and touch an "iceberg."*

The first example is an opinion although it is presented as a fact. *Compelling* is a value word. Most people find these stories compelling, but not everyone will agree. The second example is a fact because it describes the exhibit objectively; temperature and degree of light can be measured.

A Read the following statements from Reading 1. Decide which are fact and which are opinion. Write *F* (Fact) or *O* (Opinion) next to each one. Then circle the value words that helped you determine that a statement was describing an opinion. Discuss your answers with a partner.

_____ **1.** It took 2 hours and 40 minutes for the *Titanic* to sink.

_____ **2.** However, most men were honorable and many were heroic.

_____ **3.** RMST has salvaged over 5,500 artifacts from the deep.

_____ **4.** They are mostly ordinary objects made extraordinary by the long, terrible journey that brought them here.

_____ **5.** RMST has the legal rights to the relics found at the site of the *Titanic* wreck.

_____ **6.** These guys are driven by greed—just look at their sordid history.

_____ **7.** The team created a massive picture of the site by using high-definition optical cameras that take hundreds of images per second.

_____ **8.** Now we have a site that can be understood and measured, with definite things to tell us.

_____ **9.** In years to come, this historic map may give voice to those people who were silenced, seemingly forever, when the cold water closed over them.

_____ **10.** Hopefully, this new direction will mean that the remains of the *Titanic* will be both protected and accessible to the public for many years to come.

B Reread Reading 1 and underline two more opinions and circle two more facts.

C Discuss the following question with a partner.

Do you think that the author is objective or subjective about the material in this reading? Why, or why not?

VOCABULARY PRACTICE

Academic Vocabulary

A Find the words in the box below in Reading 1. Use the context to help you choose the correct word to complete each of the following definitions.

heroic (Par. 2)	immense (Par. 4)	advocated (Par. 5)	lawsuits (Par. 7)
salvaged (Par. 3)	sole (Par. 5)	reassess (Par. 6)	accessible (Par. 8)

1. When a person is _____, he or she is brave.

2. If an object is _____, it is very large.

3. _____ are legal actions that try to solve a problem through a court.

4. If someone is the _____ survivor, they are the only survivor.

5. When people saved something that was damaged, especially from a fire or a natural disaster, they _____ it.

6. If something is _____, people are able to reach it easily.

7. If a person _____ for something, he or she proposed or supported the idea.

8. To _____ means to think about something again.

B Choose academic words from Exercise A to complete the following sentences. Notice and learn the words in bold because they often appear with the academic words. In one case, you need to change the verb form.

1. Jeremy's _____ **purpose** in life is to make a lot of money. He doesn't care about anything else, but I think he needs to _____ **his priorities**. There is more to life than money.

2. The restaurant is **easily** _____ by public transportation. It is directly across from the subway station.

3. In the 1990s, the movie *Titanic* enjoyed _____ **popularity** and made over $1.8 billion. Jack Dawson, the character played by Leonardo DiCaprio, was a romantic and _____ **figure**.

4. After the company failed to institute safety regulations in their factory, consumers _____ **for change**. They refused to buy products from the company until the factories were safe.

5. When 100 accident victims **filed** _____ in federal court, the company hired a publicity firm to try to _____ **the situation**. The company didn't want consumers to think that they were cruel.

Multiword Vocabulary

(A) Find the words in bold in Reading 1. Use the context to help you complete each definition.

1. If a story in the news **captures** our **imagination** (Par. 1), it means that we are interested, _____ .
   a. but we don't believe the story
   b. and we want to learn more about it

2. If you talk about the **sheer size** (Par. 2) of something, you mean that _____ .
   a. it is very big
   b. the measurements are important

3. If you say that one thing **is reminiscent of** (Par. 4) another, it _____ of that thing.
   a. is the opposite
   b. reminds you

4. If you achieve something **at the expense of** (Par. 5) something else, you do it in a way that might _____ .
   a. cost a lot of money
   b. cause harm to the second thing

5. If an organization has **shifted** its **focus** (Par. 6), it has _____ it is concerned about.
   a. created more interest in something
   b. changed the main thing

6. If someone has **a change of heart** (Par. 7), his or her _____ changes.
   a. attitude toward something
   b. overall physical health

7. If you take **a leap of faith** (Par. 7), you do something even though you are not sure that _____ .
   a. it will succeed
   b. everyone will believe it

8. If you describe something as **state-of-the-art** (Par. 8), you mean that it is the best available because it has been made _____ .
   a. using the most modern techniques and technology
   b. thanks to government funding

(B) Complete the following sentences with the correct multiword vocabulary from Exercise A. In some cases, you need to change the verb or noun form.

1. With gold and silver decorations, the hotel lobby _____ an earlier era, in which guests would wear diamonds to dinner.

2. The company's use of cheap polyester raises their profit margin, but it does this _____ the quality of their products.

3. Marta's boss was not going to give any raises this year, but then he had _____ and gave everyone a small increase in their pay.

4. The _____ of the iceberg made it impossible for the *Titanic* to avoid it.

5. The hospital has _____ equipment and excellent doctors and nurses.

6. Leaving a job to start your own business requires _____ . It can be risky, but it can also be rewarding.

7. The conservation group has _____ from advocating for protection of large areas of land to the creation of smaller, linked areas that can create a path for jaguars across South America.

8. The story of the little girl lost at sea for three days has _____ . We want to know everything we can about her and her story.

Use the Vocabulary

Write answers to the following questions. Use the words in bold in your answers. Then share your answers with a partner.

1. Have you ever done something that required **a leap of faith**? What did you do?

2. What is a common event in people's lives that causes them to **reassess** their **priorities**?

3. Are most buildings in your city or town wheelchair **accessible**? Why, or why not? Are there people in your city or town who **advocate** for the needs of people in wheelchairs?

4. What is a recent news story that has **captured the public's imagination**? What happened?

5. Do you know anyone who has done something **heroic**? Explain your answer.

6. Why do you think some people enjoy watching movies that **are reminiscent of** an earlier era? What are some ways that a movie director can create that feeling?

7. What is one job where it is essential to have **state-of-the-art** equipment? Explain your answer.

THINK AND DISCUSS

Work in a small group. Use the information in the reading and your own ideas to discuss the following questions.

1. **Express an opinion.** Do you think that artifacts from the *Titanic* should remain underwater or should they be exhibited at a museum? Explain your answer.

2. **Analyze.** Who said the following? What did the speaker mean? Why was it important to the story?

   In the past, trying to understand Titanic *was like trying to understand Manhattan at midnight in a rainstorm—with a flashlight.*

3. **Infer meaning.** Why do you think RMST decided to collaborate with scientific and governmental agencies?

4. **Express an opinion.** Do you think the collaboration between the scientists and RMST will be successful? Why, or why not?

5. **Analyze.** Who said the following? What did the speaker mean? Is this an opinion or a fact?

   RMST deserved the flak they got in years past, but they also deserve credit for taking this new leap of faith.

Academic Vocabulary

to contend	goods	to suspend
an encounter	to issue	a venture
to fare	a prospect	

Multiword Vocabulary

as luck would have it	in the vicinity of
by a twist of fate	on the contrary
by the skin of one's teeth	to piece together
in the hope of	a strong indication

Off the coast of Namibia, a 16th century shipwreck is discovered in a present-day diamond mine. Where was the ship going, and what might have happened to the sailors on board?

Reading Preview

A Preview. Skim Reading 2 by reading the first and last sentence of each paragraph. Then check (✓) four topics that you think might be in this reading.

_____ **1.** A ship from the 16th century

_____ **2.** A shipwreck in the middle of the Pacific

_____ **3.** An opportunity to study old ships

_____ **4.** A trading vessel from England

_____ **5.** Archaeological research

_____ **6.** A discovery in the 21st century

B Topic vocabulary. The following words appear in Reading 2. Look at the words and answer the questions with a partner.

cameras	guarded	off-limits
cargo	ingots	personal possessions
coins	lease	spices
geologist	monitor	treasure

1. Which words are things that could be found on board an old ship?

2. Which words could be related to diamond mines?

3. Which words suggest the reading will be about an area with a lot of security?

C Predict. What do you think this reading will be about? Discuss each word in Exercise B and predict how it may relate to the reading.

A 16th-century Portuguese trading vessel fights its way through a violent storm on its way to Africa.

Shipwreck
Discovery

A 16th-century Portuguese trading vessel is headed for the coast of India. The sailors, with a fortune of gold and ivory to trade for spices, hope that this is the trip that will make them rich. However, the ship never reaches India. By a twist of fate, as they sail around Africa, a fierce storm blows them off course and the ship sinks off a mysterious coast sprinkled with diamonds.

This tale would have been lost forever had it not been for an astonishing discovery on a part of the coast of Namibia whose name—*Sperrgebiet*—means "forbidden zone" in German. The *Sperrgebiet* is the site of a very rich and famously off-limits diamond mine. This is a joint venture, called *Namdeb*, between the diamond mining company De Beers and the Namibian government, on the southern part of Namibia's Atlantic coast. One day, in April 2008, while walking on the beach, a company geologist came across what looked at first like a perfectly round half sphere of rock. Curious, he picked it up. It turned out to be a copper ingot, the type traded for spices in the Indies in the first half of the 16th century.

The ingot was the first sign of what is by far the oldest shipwreck ever found on the coast of sub-Saharan Africa, and the richest. Archaeologists later found 22 tons of these ingots beneath the sand, as well as thousands of other artifacts—including swords, muskets,[1] chain mail,[2] and more than 2,000 beautiful, heavy coins—in the vicinity of the site. But the world's archaeologists are even more excited about the ship itself: a Portuguese East Indiaman. The ship,

---

[1] *muskets:* long guns used in the 16th–18th centuries
[2] *chain mail:* armor made out of small links of metal sewn together

A seawall guards the shipwreck of a Portuguese trading vessel off the coast of Namibia.

with its extraordinary cargo of treasure and trade goods intact, had remained untouched in these sands for nearly 500 years.

"This is a priceless opportunity," says 4 Francisco Alves, head of nautical archaeology under the Portuguese Ministry of Culture and one of the many archaeologists who have come to study the shipwreck. "We know so little about these great old ships. This is only the second one ever excavated by archaeologists. All the others were plundered[3] by treasure hunters." The artifacts will now be the property of Namdeb, and treasure hunters are never going to be a problem here. As luck would have it, the site of the shipwreck is on the sands of one of the world's most jealously guarded diamond mines. Far from plundering, Namdeb agreed to suspend their operations around the wreck site and called

in a team of archaeologists, and, for a few weeks, history was mined instead of diamonds.

The sunken ship rests only 20 feet (6 meters) 5 below sea level, on the desert coast. The Atlantic Ocean is held back by a massive retaining wall that leaks a bit at its base. As researchers excavate the ship, cameras monitor their every move. These are a reminder that this is still a diamond mine; loose diamonds could be hidden in the sands that the archaeologists are brushing away. "If it hadn't been for those copper ingots weighing everything down, there would be nothing left here to find," says Bruno Werz, director of the Southern African Institute of Maritime Archaeology. "Five centuries of storms and waves would have washed everything away." Werz and his team have been examining the wreckage by measuring, photographing, and scanning the site with a state-of-the-art laser scanner.

Historians have now pieced together enough 6 information to tell the tale of a long-forgotten voyage. There were a number of Portuguese coins on the shipwreck that had the coat of arms[4] of King João III. These were minted[5] for only a few years, from 1525 to 1538. Finding so many of these coins is a strong indication that the ship was from Portugal and sailed during this 13-year time period. Moreover, the copper ingots suggest the ship was on its way to India to buy spices rather than transporting the spices back to Portugal.

A study of the Portuguese nautical records 7 shows that 21 ships were lost on the way to India between 1525 and 1600. The *Bom Jesus* (*Good Jesus*), which sailed in 1533, was the only one of these that went down anywhere near Namibia. A rare 16th-century book offers a glimpse of the *Bom Jesus*. Issued as a commemorative volume, it contains illustrations of all the fleets that sailed for India each year after 1497. Among the pictures for 1533 is one of a ship disappearing into the waves and the words *Bom Jesus* together with one word: *perdido*—"lost."

The journey of *Bom Jesus* began on Friday, 8 the seventh of March 1533, when a fleet of ships,

---

[3] *plundered:* robbed

[4] *coat of arms:* symbol of a particular noble family
[5] *minted:* physically created money

including the *Bom Jesus*, left Lisbon and sailed out into the Atlantic. These ships were the pride of Portugal, the space shuttles of their day, off on a 15-month journey to bring back a fortune in spices from distant shores. Four months or so after its departure from Lisbon, the fleet was struck by a storm. The *Bom Jesus* disappeared, carrying approximately 300 men, sailors, soldiers, merchants, priests, nobles, and slaves. While there is no record of the shipwreck, this is a likely scenario: Strong winds drove the ship northward along the coast for hundreds of miles. When the ship hit a rock about 150 yards from shore, a large piece of the stern[6] broke off and the *Bom Jesus* was sent to its grave.

Few personal possessions were found among 9 the artifacts. This has led archaeologists to believe that, despite the wreck, many, if not most, sailors made it to land. But then what? This is one of the most inhospitable places on Earth, an uninhabited area of sand and low bushes, stretching for hundreds of miles. It was winter. They most likely had escaped by the skin of their teeth and were cold, wet, and exhausted. There was no hope of a rescue party; nobody in the outside world knew they were alive, let alone where to start looking. Nor was any ship likely to pass this way by chance because the storm had pushed the ship away from the trade routes. The sailors were as lost as if they had been shipwrecked on Mars.

"A winter storm along this coast is no joke," 10 says Dieter Noli, the mine's resident archaeologist. All the same, things didn't necessarily end badly, he says. There would have been plenty of food such as shellfish, seabird eggs, and desert snails. The Portuguese could have met local survival experts—hunter-gatherers known today as *Bushmen*. Winter was the season when Bushmen traveled north along this coast in the hope of finding the carcasses of whales that occasionally washed ashore.

How the Portuguese fared in these encounters 11 would have been up to them. Noli says that they

---

[6] *stern:* the back of a boat

Coins from the wreck of a Portuguese ship found off the Namibian coast could have survived and prospered if they worked together and traded with the Bushmen. "The few small bands of hunter-gatherers along the river had no population-resource pressures to contend with and so no reason to be aggressive to the newcomers. On the contrary, a big, strong Portuguese dom[7]

_____

[7] *dom:* Portuguese nobleman

could well have been seen as an attractive prospect for a son-in-law."

Whatever their final fate, the survivors of the *Bom Jesus* probably did not appreciate the irony of their situation. They'd set off on a great journey in search of their fortune. They ended up in a place rich in diamonds, with no possibility of spending a penny. 12

READING COMPREHENSION

Big Picture

Ⓐ The following are questions that the author attempts to answer in Reading 2. Number them in the order in which the answers appear in the reading.

_____ **1.** Why did the ship probably sink?

_____ **2.** How was the ship preserved and excavated?

_____ **3.** What could have happened to the survivors?

_____ **4.** How was the shipwreck discovered?

_____ **5.** How did researchers determine that the ship was from Portugal?

_____ **6.** How did the shipwreck's location help to preserve the artifacts?

_____ **7.** What was found on the site?

_____ **8.** How did researchers determine the ship's name?

Ⓑ Discuss answers to the questions in Exercise A with a partner. How much can you remember *without* looking back at the reading?

Close-Up

Ⓐ Work with a partner and fill in at least three more pieces of information for each category in the chart below. One example for each category is done for you.

THE *BOM JESUS* SHIPWRECK		
What we know for certain about the shipwreck	**What is very likely to be true based on the evidence**	**What we suspect, but have no real proof that it is true**
The boat is from the 16th century.	*The boat was the Bom Jesus.*	*Storms caused the boat to crash.*

Ⓑ Compare charts with another group. What other information can you add to each category?

Reading Skill

Ⓐ Decide which of the following statements are similes or metaphors. Write *S* (Simile) or *M* (Metaphor) next to each one. With a partner, discuss what each statement is trying to say.

_____ **1.** The diamond shone like a star in the sky.

_____ **2.** The singer has the voice of an angel.

_____ **3.** After seven days at sea, the children were climbing the walls.

_____ **4.** His hands were as cold as ice.

_____ **5.** She looked like she had seen a ghost.

_____ **6.** The book sparked her interest, and she wanted to find out more about shipwrecks.

Ⓑ Read the following statements from Reading 2. Underline the figurative language. Why do you think the author uses this language?

1. These ships were the pride of Portugal, the space shuttles of their day, off on a 15-month journey to bring back a fortune in spices from distant shores.

2. When the ship hit a rock about 150 yards from shore, a large piece of the stern broke off and the *Bom Jesus* was sent to its grave.

3. The sailors were as lost as if they had been shipwrecked on Mars.

Ⓒ Look back at Reading 1 on pages 180–182. Find examples of similes and metaphors. Compare your answers with a partner.

VOCABULARY PRACTICE

Academic Vocabulary

A Find the words in bold in Reading 2. Use the context and the sentences below to match each word to the correct definition.

_____ **1.** Jorge is meeting with potential investors to discuss the company's new **venture** (Par. 2).

_____ **2.** The sale of manufactured **goods** (Par. 3) has increased in the last five years.

_____ **3.** When meteorologists predict a strong hurricane, cities sometimes **suspend** (Par. 4) all public transportation for safety reasons.

_____ **4.** The Postal Service **issued** (Par. 7) a new stamp in honor of the Olympic gold medalists.

_____ **5.** Although the sea was rough, passengers **fared** (Par. 11) better on the second day, and only a few were still seasick.

_____ **6.** Science fiction books often describe **encounters** (Par. 11) with aliens from other planets.

_____ **7.** The Arctic explorers have to **contend** (Par. 11) with difficulties such as polar bears and ice storms.

_____ **8.** The students are excited at the **prospect** (Par. 11) of a night with no homework.

a. did well or badly in a situation

b. activity, especially a business deal, that is exciting but risky

c. possibility of something that will happen in the future

d. stop or delay for a period of time

e. meetings, usually unplanned

f. items that can be bought or sold

g. published, gave, or distributed

h. struggle

B Choose the correct words from the box below to complete the following sentences. Notice and learn the words in bold because they often appear with the academic words.

contend	encounters	fare	goods	issued	prospect	suspended	venture

1. The book describes a journalist's **brief** _____ with different celebrities around the world.

2. The people who _____ **well** in survival situations are usually those who are able to remain calm in the face of danger.

3. During the president's time in office, he has had to _____ **with** many outspoken opponents to his plans.

4. Before a large storm, it is a good idea to buy a lot of **canned** _____ such as tuna fish and soup in case you lose electricity.

5. The company _____ **a statement** apologizing for an offensive advertisement.

6. Faced with the _____ of strong winds and power outages, the company _____ **operations** for the duration of the storm.

7. The two women left their jobs and started their own company. This **joint** _____ ended up making them both a lot of money.

Multiword Vocabulary

A Find the words in the box below in Reading 2. Use the context to help you complete each definition.

by a twist of fate (Par. 1)	pieced together (Par. 6)	in the hope of (Par. 10)
in the vicinity of (Par. 3)	a strong indication (Par. 6)	on the contrary (Par. 11)
as luck would have it (Par. 4)	by the skin of their teeth (Par. 9)	

1. If something is _____ a certain place, it is near it.

2. If there is _____ that something will happen, it means there are signs that make it seem very likely.

3. People use the term _____ when they want to emphasize that the opposite of what has just been said is true.

4. People use the term _____ to describe a situation that had an unexpected outcome that was out of anyone's control. This could be either a good or bad thing.

5. People use the term _____ to describe a situation where others barely managed to succeed in a very difficult situation.

6. If someone _____ the truth about something, he or she gradually discovered information to reach a conclusion.

7. If you do one thing _____ another thing happening, you do it because you think it might cause or help the other thing to happen.

8. People use the term _____ to describe a situation that is fortunate, yet surprising. This term emphasizes that something good happened.

B Choose the answer that best completes each sentence or combination of sentences. Use the information that you have learned in Exercise A to help you.

1. **By a twist of fate**, Joe went for a job interview but instead _____.
   a. got the job
   b. met his future wife

2. Alain's football team won the tournament **by the skin of their teeth** because the other teams _____.
   a. played very well
   b. played very poorly

3. The tourists thought that the shipwreck exhibit was **in the vicinity of** their hotel. Then they discovered that, **on the contrary**, it was _____.
   a. near the hotel
   b. on the other side of the city

4. After the incident, the detectives **pieced together** what had happened by _____.
   a. waiting for more information
   b. speaking to witnesses

5. There is **a strong indication** that the company will hire a new manager very soon because the directors _____.
   a. have been pleased with the current manager
   b. have been interviewing candidates

6. **In the hope of** getting a new job, Soveacha _____.
   a. has been preparing her résumé
   b. has been waiting to hear if she got the job

7. It rained almost every day for a month, but **as luck would have it,** _____ .

a. the weather was beautiful on my sister's wedding day

b. it rained on my sister's wedding day

Use the Vocabulary

Complete the following sentences with your own ideas. Then share your answers with a partner.

1. Many people want to live **in the vicinity of** _____ .

2. Construction workers sometimes have to **suspend operations** when _____ .

3. There is **a strong indication** that the government will _____ this year.

4. One day I woke up late but, **as luck would have it,** I _____ .

5. One interesting **encounter** I have had in my life was when I _____ .

6. I am excited about the **prospect** of _____ in the upcoming year.

7. Most people take this class **in the hope of** _____ .

8. One difficulty that I have had to **contend with** this year is _____ .

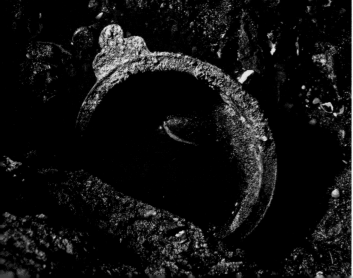

THINK AND DISCUSS

Work in a small group. Use the information in the reading and your own ideas to discuss the following questions.

1. Prior knowledge. If there were survivors in the *Bom Jesus* shipwreck, what advice would you give them?

2. Summarize. How did the researchers find out about the history of the ship?

3. Express an opinion. Were you surprised about the way that Namdeb collaborated with the archaeologists to excavate the shipwreck? Why, or why not?

4. Infer meaning. Why do cameras monitor the excavation process?

5. Analyze. Who said the following? What did the speaker mean? Why was this shipwreck so unusual?

This is a priceless opportunity.

Vocabulary Review

A Complete the paragraphs with the vocabulary below that you have studied in the unit.

canned goods	fared well	a joint venture	shifted its focus
captured the public's imagination	immense popularity	sheer size	sole purpose
a change of heart	in the vicinity of		

The story of Amelia Earhart has

_____ for decades, inspiring movies and
₁

books about her mysterious disappearance. When Amelia

saw her first airplane, at age 10, she was not impressed.

However, in her 20s, she had _____
₂

when she flew in an airplane for the first time. Suddenly, her

entire life _____ and flying became her
₃

mission. She became the first woman to fly across the

Atlantic Ocean and enjoyed _____ with
₄

her many fans all over the world.

On May 21, 1937, when Amelia was almost 40, she began

an around-the-world flight. This was

_____ with her copilot, Fred Noonan.
₅

On July 2, 1937, Amelia and Fred were flying over the

Pacific. They had _____ so far and had
₆

almost finished their journey. They made specified stops

along the way, for the _____ of getting
₇

food and fuel. Amelia didn't take a lot of

Amelia Earhart

_____ with her; she often flew with only tomato juice and soup. The plane
₈

was near Howland Island, their next scheduled stop, when Amelia radioed that they couldn't see

anything in front of them and were running low on fuel. After this, they were never heard from

again. The _____ of the ocean made it difficult for rescue operations. It is
₉

widely believed that the plane crashed in the ocean, somewhere _____ the
₁₀

island. Nonetheless, some people wonder if Amelia and Fred could have landed on a remote island

and survived.

B Compare answers to Exercise A with a partner. Then discuss the following question.

What do you think happened to Amelia and Fred?

C Complete the following sentences in a way that shows that you understand the meaning of the words in bold.

1. Even with **state-of-the-art** technology on airplanes, pilots today have to **contend with**

_____.

2. It isn't wise to focus your attention on _____ **at the expense of** your _____ .

3. Moving to a new country can be **a leap of faith** because _____ .

4. I am excited about **the prospect of** _____ at some time in my future.

D Work with a partner and write sentences that include any six of the vocabulary items below. You may use any verb tense and make nouns plural if you wish.

accessible to the public	by a twist of fate	issue a statement	piece together
advocate for	heroic efforts	on the contrary	a strong indication
as luck would have it	in the hope of		

Connect the Readings

A How are the shipwrecks in Reading 1 and Reading 2 similar? How are they different? Discuss your answers with a partner or in a small group. Then fill in the Venn diagram. Think of at least three items for each circle. Compare diagrams with another group. The first items are done for you.

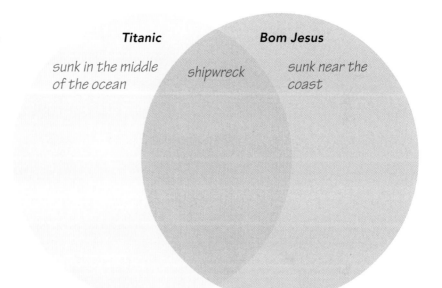

Titanic — sunk in the middle of the ocean

shipwreck

Bom Jesus — sunk near the coast

B With a partner or in a small group, compare answers to Exercise A. Then discuss the following questions.

1. Both of the readings are about collaborations. How are the collaborations similar in the two readings? How are they different?

2. Which shipwreck site would you prefer to visit? Explain your answer.

C Discuss the following questions with a partner. Use your understanding of the readings and your own ideas.

1. Imagine that you discovered a shipwreck while swimming in the ocean. What would you do? What would you hope to discover? Explain your answer.

2. Read the following quote by the German filmmaker, Werner Herzog. What do you think he means by this?

What would an ocean be without a monster lurking in the dark? It would be like sleep without dreams.

3. Would you prefer to see a museum exhibit about shipwrecks or a museum exhibit of paintings by Old Masters such as Leonardo da Vinci? Explain your answer.

Mozambican woman
with painted face

FOCUS

1. What is a legend or story that you remember from your childhood?

2. What are some lessons that legends and ancient cultures try to teach us?

Culture
and
Identity

201

Academic Vocabulary

to demonstrate	to mature	an opponent
to found	to modify	proficient
insufficient	a myth	

Multiword Vocabulary

to grit one's teeth	to look the part
to hone a skill	to make the case
to keep up with	to stretch the truth
a leading role	to talk one's way into

Reading Preview

A Preview. Look at the time line in Reading 1 on page 205. Then discuss the following questions with a partner or in a small group.

1. When was the Shaolin Temple founded?

2. What happened in 1928?

3. When did a lot of Americans learn about the Shaolin Temple? Why?

B Topic vocabulary. The following words appear in Reading 1. Look at the words and answer the questions with a partner.

brand	monks
cash registers	robes
disciples	self-defense
employees	temple
enlightenment	training
karate chop	warfare

1. Which words are connected to fighting?

2. Which words are connected to business and money?

3. Which words suggest that the reading might be about religion and philosophy?

C Predict. What do you think this reading will be about? Discuss each word in Exercise B and predict how it may relate to the reading.

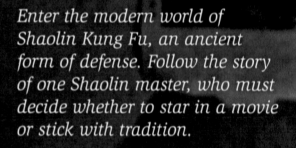

Enter the modern world of Shaolin Kung Fu, an ancient form of defense. Follow the story of one Shaolin master, who must decide whether to star in a movie or stick with tradition.

Kung Fu Battles

A farmer and kung fu master demonstrates a kung fu pose in Henan Province, China.

A monk seeks shelter from a snow shower in the Shaolin Temple.

In a valley just over the Song Mountains, tour buses arrive at the Shaolin Temple. They come from across China—uniformed soldiers on leave, businessmen, retired grandparents on vacation, parents leading children who karate chop the air in excitement—all to see the birthplace of China's greatest kung fu legend.

Here, the popular myth says, is where a fifth-century Indian mystic[1] taught a series of exercises, or forms, that resembled animal movements. He taught these to monks at the Shaolin Temple. The monks adapted the forms for self-defense and later modified these techniques for warfare. As the Shaolin monks fought, they became more proficient as fighters and their fame grew. Over the next 14 centuries, the monks honed their skills and used them in countless battles. Many of these feats[2] are noted on stone tablets in the temple and were used as material in novels dating back to the Ming Dynasty.[3]

Although legends might stretch the truth, we do know that the temple was attacked repeatedly during its long history (see Figure 1). The most devastating blow came in 1928, when an angry warlord burned down most of the temple, including its library. Centuries of information about kung fu theory and training, Chinese medicine and Buddhist scriptures—essentially the temple's soul[4]—were destroyed.

Today, however, temple officials seem more interested in building the Shaolin brand than in restoring its soul. Over the past decade, Shi Yongxin, the 45-year-old abbot,[5] has built an international business empire—including touring kung fu troupes,[6] film and TV projects, and an

---

[1] *mystic:* person who meditates and communicates with spiritual elements in the universe
[2] *feat:* an impressive and difficult achievement

[3] *The Ming Dynasty:* the rulers of China from 1368 to 1644
[4] *soul:* your mind, character, thoughts, and feelings
[5] *abbot:* the head of a group of monks who live together
[6] *troupes:* groups of entertainers such as actors or dancers

online store selling Shaolin-brand tea and soap. Many of the men working the temple's cash registers—men with shaved heads and wearing monks' robes—admit they're not monks but employees paid to look the part. Over tea in his office at the temple, Yongxin makes the case that all of these efforts help to promote awareness of Buddhism. He argues that using the Shaolin brand name in other countries helps to promote Shaolin traditional culture, including kung fu. "We make more people know about Zen Buddhism," he says. Whether it is for enlightenment or riches, the kung fu renaissance[7] is now in full swing.

Evidence of the renewed interest in kung fu   5 can be seen in the city of Dengfeng, just six miles from the temple gates. The city, with a population of 650,000, now has approximately 60 martial arts schools, with more than 50,000 students. These schools include boys, and increasingly girls, from every province and social class, ranging in age from 5 to their late 20s. Some arrive hoping to become movie stars or to win glory as kickboxers. Others come to learn skills that will ensure good jobs in the military, police, or private security. There are also those who are drawn to the ancient wisdom of kung fu.

Hu Zhengsheng is a disciple of Yang Guiwu,   6 a Shaolin master. Hu has just received a call that many martial artists spend their lives hoping for: a Hong Kong producer offering him a leading role in a kung fu movie. It's easy to see why. Hu has a boyishly handsome face and projects a confidence won through years of physical and mental testing. Yet he isn't sure whether to accept the offer. He doesn't agree with how kung fu usually is portrayed in the movies. He views the movie version of kung fu as a mindless celebration of violence that ignores the discipline's focus on morality and respect for one's opponent. He is also concerned that Yang Guiwu's other disciples will lose respect for him if he becomes an entertainer. And he worries about the dangers of fame. Humility[8] defeats pride, Master Yang taught him. Pride defeats man.

On the other hand, a film role would generate   7 publicity and bring much needed money to Hu's small kung fu school. With the blessing of his master, he founded the school eight years ago, in a few cinder-block buildings just outside Dengfeng. Many of the students come from poor families, and Hu charges them only for food. Unlike the big kung fu academies, which stress acrobatics and kickboxing, Hu teaches his 200 boys (and a few girls) the traditional Shaolin kung fu forms that Yang Guiwu passed on to him. Fighting is not the most important lesson of kung fu, Hu explains. His focus is on honor. The skills he is passing on to his students come with great responsibility. In each child, he looks for a willingness to "eat bitterness," an expression that means students welcome hardship and use it to

Figure 1. Shaolin Through the Ages

500 BCE First mention of martial arts in Chinese texts

495 CE Shaolin Temple founded

1300s First mention in Chinese texts of the martial arts skills of Shaolin monks

1552–1554 Shaolin monks help fight off Japanese pirate attacks on Chinese coasts

1700s Temple destroyed by Qing emperors—one of several sackings in its history

1928 Warlord Shi Yousan burns down Shaolin Temple destroying vast library containing ancient martial arts texts

1940s Shaolin monks ambush Japanese soldiers near the temple

1972 Kung Fu TV series begins in USA, introducing Shaolin Temple to Americans

1982 Martial arts champion Jet Li portrays a heroic monk in the film *The Shaolin Temple*, setting off a national Shaolin frenzy

1999 Shi Yongxin installed as the 13th abbot of the Shaolin Temple

2010 Shaolin Temple named UNESCO World Heritage site

Source: National Geographic Magazine, March 2011

---

[7] *renaissance:* a revival of interest
[8] *humility:* modesty; lack of self-importance

discipline their will and help them to strengthen their character.

At night, his students sleep in unheated rooms. No matter what the temperature is, they train outside, often before sunrise. They hit tree trunks to toughen their hands and practice with other students sitting on their shoulders to build leg strength. During drills,[9] coaches use bamboo to hit the legs of any boy whose form is not perfect or whose effort is considered insufficient. When asked if such harsh treatment could upset students, Hu smiles. "It is eating bitterness. They understand it makes them better." **8**

Despite the intensity of the school's training, not many students give up and leave. However, Hu has to continually seek new students to keep up with the rising costs of running the school. Gradually, he has accepted the new teaching trends and has begun offering a few courses in kickboxing and the acrobatic kung fu forms. He hopes to attract new students and then lead them back to kung fu's traditional forms. From his own experience, Hu knows that a boy's idea of kung fu can change as he matures. **9**

When Hu was young, he was obsessed with the kung fu films of Bruce Lee and Jet Li and fantasized about taking revenge on bullies[10] in his village. At age 11, he managed to talk his way into the Shaolin Temple, where he became a servant to the coach of one of the performance troupes. Later the man introduced him to Yang Guiwu. Hu says, "He [Yang Guiwu] taught me the theory behind the moves. Why you must flex your arm a certain way. Why your weight must be on a certain part of your foot." He stands up to demonstrate. A fist strike, he explains, is delivered like a chess move, anticipating a range of possible countermoves. "A student can learn this in a year," he says. "But to do it like this"—his hands and elbows become a blur as he repeats the moves at full speed—"takes many years." **10**

Hu explains that "Shaolin kung fu is designed for combat, not to entertain audiences. It is hard to convince boys to spend many years learning **11**

something that won't make them wealthy or famous." He seems saddened by the thought. "I worry that is how the traditional styles will be lost." A boy appears at the office door to report that a student has twisted an ankle. By the time Hu arrives to check on him, the injured pupil is back on his feet, gritting his teeth as he kicks a heavy bag. Hu nods with a teacher's satisfaction. "He is learning to eat bitterness."

BRUCE LEE

Bruce Lee, born in San Francisco in 1940 and raised in Hong Kong, is perhaps the most famous martial artist in recent history. At the age of 13, Lee began learning *Wing Chun*, a form of Kung Fu, with Master Yip Man. At 18, Lee returned to the United States and attended the University of Washington. During this time, Lee opened his own martial arts school, teaching his version of Kung Fu. Later, Lee combined different techniques to create an entirely new martial arts style called "Jeet Kune Do."

Lee is best known, however, for his screen presence. His roles in the 1966 television series *The Green Hornet* and in such movies as *Enter the Dragon* and *Game of Death* introduced Chinese martial arts to enthusiastic audiences around the world. Unfortunately, Bruce Lee died suddenly in 1973 after complaining of headaches. Although he was so young when he died, Lee has been called one of the most influential people of the 20th century.

---

[9] *drills:* repetitive practice exercises

[10] *bullies:* people who force others to do things by using fear or strength

READING COMPREHENSION

Big Picture

A Choose the answer that best completes each of the following sentences.

1. The purpose of paragraph 2 is to explain _____.
   a. the history of the Shaolin Temple
   b. how kung fu came to be used for fighting
   c. why monks had to fight

2. The main idea of paragraph 4 can be found in sentence _____.
   a. 1
   b. 2
   c. 3

3. The most useful annotation for paragraph 6 would be _____.
   a. Hu Zhengsheng = disciple of Yang Guiwu, Shaolin master
   b. Hu Zhengsheng = handsome and confident movie star
   c. Hu Zhengsheng = entertainment vs. traditional kung fu beliefs

4. The main idea of paragraph 7 is that _____.
   a. Hu's school is different from the larger kung fu academies in Dengfeng
   b. the students at Hu's school are not required to pay a lot of money
   c. fighting is the most important element of kung fu

5. The purpose of paragraph 8 is to show examples of _____.
   a. saving money
   b. "eating bitterness"
   c. outdoor drills

6. The most useful annotation for paragraph 10 would be _____.
   a. H.Z. = early history/how he became a Shaolin master
   b. H.Z. = childhood/why he was obsessed with kung fu films
   c. H.Z. = demonstration/how he learned a fist strike

7. In paragraph 11, the writer probably decided to end the reading with this example because _____.
   a. it explains what happens when a student hurts his or her ankle at the school
   b. it describes another way that Hu's school is very difficult for students
   c. it shows that the next generation is continuing the traditions of kung fu

B Write a sentence that expresses the main idea of the *whole* reading.

Close-Up

A Decide which of the following statements are true or false according to Reading 1 and the short extra reading, "Bruce Lee," on page 206. Write *T* (True) or *F* (False) next to each one.

_____ 1. A fifth-century mystic taught kung fu forms so that the monks could protect the temple.

_____ 2. The author doesn't believe all the stories about the temple.

_____ 3. Everyone who works in the Shaolin Temple is a monk.

_____ 4. The Shaolin Temple has made a lot of money in the past 10 years.

_____ **5.** Dengfeng has many martial arts schools, with a wide variety of students.

_____ **6.** Hu Zhengsheng's main goal in life is to be a film star like Bruce Lee.

_____ **7.** Hu Zhengsheng wants to carry on the traditions that Yang Guiwu taught him.

_____ **8.** Girls are not allowed at the martial arts schools.

_____ **9.** When Hu talks about his students eating bitterness, he means that they are forced to consume food that does not taste good.

_____ **10.** When Hu was young, he applied to many martial arts academies.

_____ **11.** Bruce Lee practiced and taught traditional Kung Fu.

_____ **12.** Before the 1960s and 70s, many people had never seen Chinese martial arts.

B Work with a partner or in a small group. Change the false statements in Exercise A to make them true.

Reading Skill

Analyzing the Pros and Cons of an Issue

Readings often present pros and cons, or arguments for and against different issues. Successful readers will pay attention to the content of the reading and compare and contrast information and the possible outcomes, even if the author has not explicitly presented this information.

In Unit 6 on page 144, you learned about recognizing contrasts. In Unit 3 on page 60, you learned about making inferences. Both of these skills are necessary to analyze the pros and cons of an issue. After you read, think about the main idea of a reading and notice the issues that have been raised. Create a list of pros and cons for each issue, based on the information that the writer has given and your own knowledge. Reflecting on your own opinion can help you reach a deeper understanding of the reading.

A Work with a partner. Read the following statements and add information from Reading 1 or your own knowledge to the charts below.

1. The Shaolin Temple should make Shaolin kung fu into a big business.

Pros	Cons

2. Hu Zhengsheng should take a leading role in a film.

Pros	Cons

B Compare answers to Exercise A with another pair of classmates. Then discuss the following questions.

> *What do you think the Shaolin Temple should do? What do you think Hu Zhengsheng should do?*

VOCABULARY PRACTICE

Academic Vocabulary

A Find the words in bold in Reading 1. Use the context and the sentences below to help you match each word to the correct definition.

_____ 1. The film is based on a Greek **myth** (Par. 2) and tells the story of Hercules.

_____ 2. The book was **modified** (Par. 2) for a younger audience so that they could understand the story.

_____ 3. Joana is a **proficient** (Par. 2) speaker of three languages: Chinese, Spanish, and English.

_____ 4. After all of his training, Juan defeated his **opponent** (Par. 6) easily.

_____ 5. Three friends **founded** (Par. 7) a charity that provides sports education for low-income children.

_____ 6. The court dismissed the case because of **insufficient** (Par. 8) evidence.

_____ 7. As Tad **matures** (Par. 9), he is becoming more and more responsible.

_____ 8. In the workshop, the computer scientist will **demonstrate** (Par. 10) how the new technology can be used.

a. skillful; able to do something well

b. person who plays or fights against another

c. not enough for a particular purpose

d. story from ancient cultures about history, gods, or heroes

e. grows to full size or full mental abilities

f. show how something works

g. changed slightly

h. started and financially supported an organization

B The words in bold show academic words from Exercise A and words they often appear with. Complete the sentences with your own ideas.

1. **Ancient myths** are stories of gods and heroes of long ago. One **popular myth** is

   _____ .

2. When food is **genetically modified**, it means that _____ .

3. When people interview for a job and say that they are **somewhat proficient** at using a type of software, they probably mean that _____ .

4. When a school or university is **founded by** a famous person, the institution often honors that person by _____ .

5. If people are **outspoken opponents** of a political party, it means they _____ .

6. When people complain that they have **insufficient funds**, they mean they _____ .

7. **As** children **mature**, they begin to _____ .

8. One way that students **demonstrate knowledge** of a particular subject is by _____ .

Multiword Vocabulary

(A) Find the multiword vocabulary in bold in Reading 1 and use the context to help you figure out the meaning. Then match each item to the correct definition.

_____ **1. honed** their **skills** (Par. 2)

_____ **2. stretch the truth** (Par. 3)

_____ **3. look the part** (Par. 4)

_____ **4. makes the case** (Par. 4)

_____ **5. a leading role** (Par. 6)

_____ **6. keep up with** (Par. 9)

_____ **7. talk his way into** (Par. 10)

_____ **8. gritting his teeth** (Par. 11)

a. explains why something is correct by providing a good argument

b. resemble a character or a type of person

c. convince someone to allow entry into a particular location

d. refusing to give up even though the situation is very difficult

e. carefully developed their abilities over time

f. able to cope with a change, usually by changing at the same rate

g. a main part in a play or film

h. tell a story that is not completely based on facts

(B) Complete the following paragraph with the correct multiword vocabulary from Exercise A. In some cases, you need to change the verb form or the article.

Brazilian soccer superstar, Pelé

When actor Mark Pareda heard about plans for a new film about the football player Pelé, he knew that he wanted to play _____ 1 . He had spent his childhood in Brazil hearing his grandfather tell stories about Pelé. Mark went to Hollywood even though he didn't know anyone. Luckily, he was able to _____ 2 the film studio. Once inside, he spoke to the producers and _____ 3 for why he should portray Pelé. Everyone could see that he _____ 4 . In fact, he looked exactly like a young Pelé. Mark _____ 5 and made up a story, telling them that that his grandfather was Pelé's cousin. The producers hired him. Before the movie, Mark and his fellow actors _____ 6 through hours of football practice, and they became very good at the game. Sometimes it was so difficult that he wanted to give up, but he _____ 7 and continued. He was able to _____ 8 his training even while preparing his lines for the movie. In the end, everyone agreed that his portrayal of Pelé was very impressive.

Use the Vocabulary

Write answers to the following questions. Use the words in bold in your answers. Then share your answers with a partner.

1. How **proficient** are you in English? Do you think that you are better at reading, speaking, or writing in English?

2. As you **mature**, do you enjoy the same type of movies that you liked 10 years ago, or have your movie preferences changed? Explain your answers.

3. Do you think that students can **make the case** that tests do not always **demonstrate** their ability in English? Why, or why not?

4. Who are some characters from **ancient myths**? What do you know about them?

5. If you had the chance, what type of charity would you like to **found**? Explain your answer.

6. Who plays **the leading role** in your favorite movie?

7. What is one time that you **stretched the truth** a little when telling a story? Explain your answer.

THINK AND DISCUSS

Work in a small group. Use the information in the reading and your own ideas to discuss the following questions.

1. **Infer meaning.** Who said the following? What are the speaker's methods for making this happen? Would Hu agree or disagree with the speaker?

   We make more people know about Zen Buddhism.

2. **Expand.** Who said the following? How is this connected to the reading? Do you think this is a common problem for schools? Why, or why not?

   It is hard to convince boys to spend many years learning something that won't make them wealthy or famous.

3. **Express an opinion.** Would you prefer to visit the Shaolin Temple or Hu Zhengsheng's martial arts school? Explain your answer.

Academic Vocabulary

an aspect	moral	to portray
folklore	to opt	scenic
a medium	a perspective	

Multiword Vocabulary

to be taken with	a jack-of-all-trades
fine arts	to lend itself to
hand in hand with	to pit one's wits against
to have a habit of	to stand out

Reading Preview

A Preview. Scan Reading 2 to find answers to the following questions. Then discuss the answers with a partner or in a small group.

1. What award did Kwame Nyong'o receive?

2. Where did Kwame go to college?

3. Where does Kwame live now?

B Topic vocabulary. The following words appear in Reading 2. Look at the words and answer the questions with a partner.

background artist	initiatives
characters	kick-start
concept designer	magical powers
consultant	novelty
creation	ogre
humor	village
illustrator	

1. Which words might be part of a folktale?

2. Which words refer to the job of computer animation?

3. Which words refer to new and innovative projects?

C Predict. What do you think this reading will be about? Discuss each word in Exercise B and predict how it may relate to the reading.

Meet Kwame Nyong'o, an artist and computer animator in Kenya, Africa. Learn how he became interested in turning ancient fables into animated stories for a new generation.

A still from the animated movie *The Legend of Ngong Hills*, a Maasai folktale

Kwame Nyong'o
FILM ANIMATOR

KWAME NYONG'O: FILM ANIMATOR

Kwame Nyong'o

Hi, Kwame. Thank you for agreeing to be interviewed, and congratulations on winning the award for Best Animation at the African Movie Awards! Can you tell us a bit about *The Legend of Ngong Hills*? 1

Yes. The film is based on a Maasai[1] traditional 2 folktale. Like other peoples in Africa, they have a long tradition of storytelling and folklore. Many of these stories are creation stories—that is, they tell of how things in this world came to exist—and simultaneously teach moral lessons. *The Legend of Ngong Hills* is the creation story of a scenic mountain range on the outskirts of present-day Nairobi. The story is centered around the frightful ogre of the forest, who has a habit of attacking the nearby Maasai village. As the story goes, he falls in love with, and eventually gets trapped by, a beautiful village girl.

---

[1] *Maasai:* an ethnic group that lives in Kenya and Tanzania and continues its ancient traditions

When did you first become interested in 3 **African folktales?**

As a child. I remember being told many stories 4 by African storytellers, reading picture books, and watching films. I was especially taken with the famous West African character Anansi the Spider. Anansi is a fictional character who, in some stories, is human and can change into a spider or vice versa. He's always portrayed as a mischievous character who pits his wits against superior strength, usually with success. In the many different versions of these tales, Anansi weaves his way in and out of trouble and teaches the audience life lessons. This really captured my imagination. From there, I became very interested in African and African Diaspora[2] stories, including African-American folklore such as *John Henry* and *Brer Rabbit*. These folktales tend to lend themselves perfectly to the medium of animation as they often have elements of fantasy like talking animals and magical powers.

---

[2] *African Diaspora:* a term that refers to the communities all over the world of people who have African origins

Why do you think it is important to retell these folktales? 5

Folktales usually shed light on a moral dilemma 6 in the form of metaphor. I think African folktales stand out because they blend creation stories (for example, why the turtle has a broken shell) with a moral lesson (he fell from the sky because he was being too greedy and wanted to eat all the feasts in the heavens). I find that African tales use different degrees of humor to help these lessons be received more easily. As times are changing in Africa and in the African diaspora, the traditional culture of the elders telling stories to the youth is disappearing. I feel it is important to preserve and enhance these stories and culture through this media of film and animation.

> **"*As times are changing in Africa... the traditional culture of the elders telling stories to the youth is disappearing.*"**

How did you get your start in computer animation? 7

Well, I was always a comic and movie fan, and 8 especially interested in the fantasy and science fiction genres.[3] I went to college in the United States, and I opted to be a fine arts major. I was drawn to all the various media available at the time—photography, sculpture, drawing, painting. Although this gave me a firm foundation in fine arts, I had no idea how to apply it toward making a living. I then decided to go back to do a master's[4] at art school. It was there that I discovered that animation blended all my passions from my past experiences into one. At that time, computer animation was just emerging, so I was naturally drawn to it as well.

Since moving back to Kenya 9 in 2000, I've had the opportunity to participate in several exciting animation initiatives. I worked as a trainer for a UNESCO (United Nations Educational, Scientific, and Cultural Organization) sponsored project Africa Animated! that trained over 40 animators across the continent. We produced 19 films, which have won awards at film festivals around the world. This project really acted to kick-start the animation industry on the continent. International animation producers became interested in producing African content. Tiger Aspect (UK), for example, produced the hit children's TV series *Tinga Tinga Tales* right here in Nairobi. The show now airs on channels such as Disney Channel and is distributed in over 40 territories.

How would you describe the computer animation industry in Kenya now? 10

Being back in Kenya has not been without its 11 challenges. In small, emerging industries such as we have here, you kind of need to be a jack-of-all-trades in order to survive financially. Here, I work as a storyboard artist, animator, illustrator, director, producer, teacher, consultant, . . . the list goes on. On the other hand, if I was working in the United States right now, I'd most probably be

Maasai tribesmen in the Mara Region of Kenya perform a traditional storytelling dance.

---

[3] *genres:* specific types of literature, art, or music grouped according to style or subject
[4] *master's:* university degree between a bachelor's degree and a PhD

specialized in a certain aspect of the animation production pipeline,[5] whether it be as a background artist, concept designer, layout artist, etc.

Animation production is typically more [12] expensive than live action, and the local broadcasters don't have the funds to commission animated series work yet. Thus, the few animated series that have been produced for the local market have been funded by NGOs[6] to push their agendas. While this kind of work pays the bills, it almost always lacks creative freedom and novelty.

Good news, though, is that since 2010 [13] we've had high-speed Internet in Kenya. This has opened up huge opportunities in terms of communication and access to new markets. Kenya also has a buzzing tech sector, dubbed[7] the "Silicon Savannah"; it's the hub[8] for tech in

Africa. This sector works hand in hand with animation, as animators need coders and techies[9] to support their creative content.

Finally, what would you like people to take [14] **away from your films? What would be your dream project for the future?**

I would like people to learn just a little more and [15] have just a slightly fresher perspective about a place, people, or thing than they did before. My dream is to create a feature length African period and/or fantasy piece. The history of Africa is so rich and intricate yet very, very little is known of it, and film is such a powerful way to tell these stories.

Thank you very much for speaking with us [16] **today, Kwame.**

Thanks a lot for your interest in my story [17] and what is happening in Africa in terms of animation.

---

[5] *production pipeline:* a series of actions that are necessary in order to create something such as a film

[6] *NGO:* an organization that is not run by the government. It is an abbreviation for "nongovernmental organization."

[7] *dubbed:* when someone or something is given a descriptive nickname

[8] *hub:* an important center for a particular activity

---

[9] *coders and techies:* people who work to create the technology behind the animation

READING COMPREHENSION

Big Picture

A Complete the annotations for each paragraph with your own ideas. The first one is done for you.

1. Paragraph 2: _Legend of Ngong Hills: creation story/Maasai folktale/ogre + girl_

2. Paragraph 4: _____

3. Paragraph 6: _____

4. Paragraph 8: _____

5. Paragraph 9: _____

6. Paragraph 11: _____

B Complete the following sentences with your own words.

1. The purpose of Reading 2 is to show _____.

2. The interviewer asks Kwame about the *Legend of the Ngong Hills* because _____.

Close-Up

A Scan Reading 2 to find answers to the following questions. Write short answers.

1. What is a creation story? _____

2. Who is Anansi? _____

3. Why does Kwame say that African folktales are good material for animated stories?

   _____

4. Why does Kwame say African folktales use humor? _____

5. Did Kwame always want to be a computer animator? Explain your answer.

   _____

6. What was Africa Animated! and how was this an important step in Kwame's career?

   _____

7. How is Kwame's animation work in Kenya different from the work he would be doing if he were in the United States? _____

8. What would Kwame like to produce in the future? _____

B Compare answers to Exercise A with a partner. Write two other questions based on the reading. Then ask your questions to a different partner.

1. _____

2. _____

Reading Skill

Recognizing Different Modes of Writing

Every reading has a purpose: to entertain, inform, or persuade. Often a reading can be a combination of all of these; paragraphs or sections of a reading can present information in different ways, or *modes*, each of which may have a specific purpose in a reading. Successful readers will notice when a writer switches from one mode of writing to another.

The following is a list of different modes of writing that a writer uses.

- *Narrative writing* presents a detailed sequence of events.
- *Persuasive writing* presents information in the hope that the reader will agree.
- *Cause-and-effect writing* shows what happened and what made it happen.
- *Compare-and-contrast writing* shows how two things are similar and different.
- *Steps-in-a-process writing* shows the separate stages of how something happened.

A Match each reading topic with the mode that would most likely be used to write about that topic.

Reading Topics

_____ **1.** A story about a day in Paris

_____ **2.** A blog about why animal conservation is important

_____ **3.** A description of erupting volcanoes and icy fields

_____ **4.** The way that you can prevent a snakebite from killing you

_____ **5.** The reasons why animals are becoming extinct

Modes of Writing

a. Persuasive

b. Narrative

c. Cause-and-Effect

d. Compare-and-Contrast

e. Steps-in-a-Process

B What modes of writing in Exercise A are used in each of the following paragraphs of Reading 2? Write the mode or modes on the line.

1. Paragraph 2: _____

2. Paragraph 4: _____

3. Paragraph 6: _____

4. Paragraphs 8 + 9: _____

5. Paragraphs 11 + 12: _____

6. Paragraph 13: _____

7. Paragraph 15: _____

C Discuss your answers to Exercise B with a partner.

VOCABULARY PRACTICE

Academic Vocabulary

A Find the words in the box below in Reading 2. Use the context to help you choose the correct word to complete each of the following definitions.

> folklore (Par. 2)   scenic (Par. 2)   medium (Par. 4)   aspect (Par. 11)
> moral (Par. 2)   portrayed (Par. 4)   opted (Par. 8)   perspective (Par. 15)

1. The word _____ is related to the right and wrong way of behaving.

2. The word _____ refers to the traditional stories, customs, and habits of a particular community or nation.

3. A(n) _____ is a part of something such as a part of its character.

4. A(n) _____ is a particular way of thinking about something, especially one that is influenced by your beliefs and experiences.

5. If someone is _____ in a certain way, it means that a movie, book, or TV show has represented him or her in that way.

6. If you _____ to do something, you decided to do that in preference to anything else.

7. If an area is described as _____, it means that it has an attractive view of nature.

8. A(n) _____ is a basic material or channel for art or communication such as oil paints, film, sculpture, or animation.

B Choose an academic word from Exercise A to complete each of the following sentences. Notice and learn the words in bold because they often appear with the academic words.

1. This is one of the oldest inhabited areas of the country, and the way of life here is **rooted in** _____ and tradition. I love hearing all of the stories.

2. Trust is an **important** _____ of any friendship. You need to know that the other person is someone you can rely on.

3. Most people feel a _____ **responsibility** to help others in need.

4. The story, told **from the** _____ of an alien from another planet, addressed issues that we face here on Earth.

5. After the oil spill, the oil company insisted that they should not **be** _____ **as** people who are evil. They say they want to do the right thing.

6. Texting is a popular _____ **of communication** among teenagers.

7. The parade was not as busy as usual because the forecast was for rain, and many people _____ **to stay** home instead.

8. We stopped along the road to admire the _____ **view** and take photographs.

Multiword Vocabulary

A Find the multiword vocabulary in bold in Reading 2 and use the context to help you figure out the meaning. Then match each item to the correct definition.

_____ 1. **has a habit of** (Par. 2)

_____ 2. **was** especially **taken with** (Par. 4)

_____ 3. **pits his wits against** (Par. 4)

_____ 4. **lend themselves** perfectly **to** (Par. 4)

_____ 5. **stand out** (Par. 6)

_____ 6. **fine arts** (Par. 8)

_____ 7. **a jack-of-all-trades** (Par. 11)

_____ 8. **hand in hand with** (Par. 13)

a. became very interested in something and wanted to learn more about it

b. competes against someone (in a test of knowledge or intelligence)

c. be very noticeable

d. someone who is able to do a variety of different jobs

e. such pursuits as painting, drawing, music, dance, literature, drama, and architecture

f. does the same thing regularly and often

g. are good for a particular purpose

h. closely connected

B Complete the following sentences with the correct multiword vocabulary in the box below.

fine arts	has a habit of	lends itself to	stands out
hand in hand with	a jack-of-all-trades	pit their wits against	was taken with

1. Francis _____ biting his pencil during tests.

2. The politicians will _____ each other in the debate.

3. Some of the artists studied _____ in college, while others have taught themselves.

4. The Bassetts' house _____ because it is painted purple.

5. Whenever something needs to be fixed, we call my uncle. He's

   _____ .

6. When I saw my first Bollywood movie, I _____ the cinematography and wanted to learn as much as I could about the film industry in India.

7. In professional sports, strength and teamwork go _____ each other. It isn't enough just to be strong—you need to know how to use your strength as well.

8. The library is a quiet, peaceful place that _____ studying.

Use the Vocabulary

Write answers to the following questions. Use the words in bold in your answers. Then share your answers with a partner.

1. What is one particular **aspect** of your life that you would like to change? Explain your answer.

2. Imagine that a film studio wants to make a film about your life. What actor or actress would you like to **portray** you?

3. If you could study anything you'd like in college, would you **opt** to study **fine arts**? Why, or why not?

Still from the animated movie
The Legend of Ngong Hills

4. Do you know anyone who is **a jack-of-all-trades**? If so, who? Describe him or her.

5. What is an example of a **moral** dilemma that many people face today?

6. Television is a **medium** that can connect many people to new ideas. What is a TV show that has changed your **perspective** about a particular topic? Explain your answer.

THINK AND DISCUSS

Work in a small group. Use the information in the reading and your own ideas to discuss the following questions.

1. **Prior knowledge.** Do the folktales that Kwame describes sound like tales that you know? Why, or why not?

2. **Express an opinion.** Are you interested in watching the computer-animated folktales that Kwame produces? Why, or why not?

3. **Infer meaning.** Why do you think children would like hearing about Anansi? Explain your answer.

4. **Summarize.** How did Kwame become a computer animator in Africa? Tell the story in your own words.

Vocabulary Review

A Complete the paragraphs with the vocabulary below that you have studied in the unit.

as they matured	an important aspect	opt to stay	scenic views
founded by	insufficient funds	rooted in folklore	are taken with
hone the skills	keep up with		

The small village of Chincero, Peru, has

_____ overlooking the Sacred Valley

1

of the Incas. It is known for its agriculture, potatoes, and

quinoa, but in recent years the village has faced several

threats. For one thing, many farmers can't

_____ the rising cost of living. For

2

another, a valuable tradition—weaving in the Incan

style—is in danger of disappearing. Now, however, an

effort among women of the village addresses both the

problem of _____ among the poor

3

villagers and the threat to tradition. A weaving

cooperative, _____ a local woman,

4

Nilda Callanaupa, has brought together a group of women

who weave and sell cloth. The cooperative has been a

success. Tourists _____ the colorful

5

cloth and buy from the cooperative, which brings much

needed money into the community.

A traditional Peruvian weaver demonstrates her skill.

Traditional weaving is _____ of local identity and Incan culture. The

6

patterns on the cloth are intricate and are often _____, in the stories of the

7

Incas. Callanaupa was worried that these traditions would disappear. She wanted to do something

so that, _____, the next generation would keep these traditions alive. It takes

8

years to _____ that are needed for this style of weaving. Callanaupa hopes

9

that, with this cooperative, young people will _____ in Chincero, rather than

10

move to the city, and that they will learn more about their Incan culture.

B Compare answers to Exercise A with a partner. Then discuss the following questions.

What were the various objectives that Callanaupa had when she opened her weaving school?

C Complete the following sentences in a way that shows that you understand the meaning of the words in bold.

1. Peruvian textile sellers often **look the part** by wearing _____.

2. When visiting new countries, tourists **have a habit of** buying _____.

3. One craft or skill that I am **somewhat proficient** in is _____.

4. If you look at the weaving cooperative **from the perspective of** the male farmers, they probably think that _____.

D Work with a partner and write sentences that include any six of the vocabulary items below. You may use any verb tense and make nouns plural if you wish.

ancient myth	hand in hand with	outspoken opponent
demonstrate your knowledge	to lend itself to	pit yourself against something
genetically modified	moral responsibility	be portrayed as
grit your teeth		

Connect the Readings

A Refer back to Readings 1 and 2 and fill in the chart below with short answers for each category. One example is done for you.

	Hu Zhengsheng	Kwame Nyong'o
Profession		
Motivation		*Listened to folktales as a child*
Education	*Worked with a performance troupe; Studied with Yang Guiwu*	
Goals		
Difficulties		
Movies		
Moral lessons		

B With a partner or in a small group, compare answers to Exercise A. Then discuss the following questions.

1. Look at the chart above. How are Hu and Kwame similar? How are they different?

2. How could you apply what you have learned from the two readings to promote awareness of a tradition in your country?

C Discuss the following questions with a partner. Use your understanding of the readings and your own ideas.

1. What do you think are the key elements to making something last through time?

2. Do you consider yourself to be more modern or more old-fashioned? Explain your answer.

3. Read the following quote by Albert Einstein. How does it relate to the readings in this chapter? Do you agree with Einstein? Why, or why not?

If you want your children to be intelligent, read them fairy tales. If you want them to be more intelligent, read them more fairy tales.

VOCABULARY INDEX

The following words and phrases are studied in *Reading and Vocabulary Focus 4*. Each vocabulary item is listed according to which unit and reading it appears in. For example, a word or phrase listed as U1 R1 appears in the first reading of unit 1. If a word is in the Academic Word List, it is listed as AWL.

a calculated risk   U6 R2
a change of heart   U8 R1
a jack-of-all-trades   U9 R2
a leap of faith   U8 R1
a piece of the action   U7 R1
abandoned (*adj*) AWL   U1 R1
accessible (*adj*) AWL   U8 R1
accompany (*v*) AWL   U1 R2
accurately (*adv*) AWL   U2 R2
adaptable (*adj*) AWL   U6 R1
adjust (*v*) AWL   U4 R1
advances (*n pl*)   U7 R2
advocate (*v*) AWL   U8 R1
alert (*v*)   U4 R2
alleviate (*v*)   U7 R1
ambitious (*adj*)   U3 R1
annual (*n*) AWL   U1 R1
anticipate (*v*) AWL   U2 R1
as a consequence   U1 R2
as luck would have it   U8 R2
as we know it   U4 R1
aspect (*n*) AWL   U9 R2
assure (*v*) AWL   U6 R2
astounding (*adj*)   U3 R1
at any moment   U4 R2
at regular intervals   U4 R2
at the end of the day   U3 R2
at the expense of   U8 R1
at the very least   U2 R1
at this rate   U6 R2
attitude (*n*) AWL   U6 R1
attract attention   U5 R2
attribute (*v*) AWL   U5 R1
authentic (*adj*)   U5 R1

be better off   U6 R1
be capable of   U2 R2
be caught off guard   U4 R1
be found out   U5 R1
be onto something   U3 R2

be reminiscent of   U8 R1
be taken with   U9 R2
be upwards of   U7 R2
become a reality   U3 R1
beyond a reasonable doubt   U5 R1
beyond one's wildest dreams
   U6 R2
briefly (*adv*) AWL   U2 R2
broadcast (*v*)   U4 R2
buffer zone (*n*)   U3 R1
by a twist of fate   U8 R2
by the skin of one's teeth   U8 R2

capacity (*n*) AWL   U6 R1
capture one's imagination   U8 R1
cause a sensation   U5 R1
cease (*v*) AWL   U1 R1
change hands   U5 R2
charismatic (*adj*)   U3 R2
charity event (*n*)   U1 R1
check in with (*v*)   U6 R2
clinical trial (*n*)   U7 R1
colleague (*n*) AWL   U4 R2
colloquially (*adv*)   U7 R1
come into contact with   U1 R2
come to a halt   U4 R1
come up with (*v*)   U1 R1
comfort zone (*n*)   U6 R1
commemorate (*v*)   U5 R2
commission (*v*) AWL   U1 R2
common practice (*n*)   U7 R1
complement (*v*) AWL   U5 R1
composition (*n*)   U7 R2
concept (*n*) AWL   U6 R1
contemplative (*adj*)   U5 R2
contend (*v*)   U8 R2
convince (*v*) AWL   U2 R1
cope (*v*)   U6 R1
crucial (*adj*) AWL   U3 R1
curious (*adj*)   U7 R1

daring (*adj*)   U6 R2
data (*n*) AWL   U2 R2
day-to-day (*adj*)   U6 R1
decline (*n*) AWL   U7 R2
demonstrate (*v*) AWL   U9 R1
derive (*v*) AWL   U7 R2
dirty little secret   U5 R1
distinctive (*adj*) AWL   U5 R2

eat away at (*v*)   U7 R2
efficiency (*n*)   U4 R1
eligible (*adj*)   U2 R1
encounter (*n*) AWL   U8 R2
end up (*v*)   U7 R1
engage (*v*)   U3 R2
equation (*n*) AWL   U6 R1
era (*n*)   U5 R1
essence (*n*)   U6 R2
evade (*v*)   U1 R2
exceed (*v*) AWL   U7 R1
exhibit (*n*) AWL   U5 R1
export (*v*) AWL   U7 R1
expose (*v*) AWL   U3 R2

facilitate (*v*) AWL   U4 R2
false sense of security   U4 R2
fare (*v*)   U8 R2
fine arts (*n*)   U9 R2
first aid (*n*)   U2 R1
fluctuate (*v*) AWL   U2 R2
folklore (*n*)   U9 R2
for the sake of   U2 R2
forecast (*v*)   U4 R1
found (*v*)   U9 R1
funding (*n*) AWL   U3 R2

generate (*v*) AWL   U1 R1
genetic (*adj*)   U3 R1
get credit   U4 R2
go to extremes   U6 R2

go viral   U3 R2
goods (*n pl*)   U8 R2
grit one's teeth   U9 R1

hand in hand with   U9 R2
hasten (*v*)   U7 R2
have a habit of   U9 R2
have no chance   U2 R1
heroic (*adj*)   U8 R1
hone a skill   U9 R1
human nature (*n*)   U4 R2
humidity (*n*)   U7 R1
humor (*n*)   U3 R2

immense (*adj*)   U8 R1
in a matter of minutes   U2 R2
in a sense   U1 R1
in conjunction with   U5 R1
in full swing   U7 R1
in light of   U7 R1
in secret   U1 R2
in the face of   U6 R1
in the hope of   U8 R2
in the near future   U7 R2
in the open air   U1 R2
in the spotlight   U3 R2
in the vicinity of   U8 R2
in the wake of   U4 R2
incentive (*n*)   AWL   U3 R1
inconceivable (*adj*)   AWL   U7 R1
inconsistency (*n*)   AWL   U5 R1
indicate (*v*)   AWL   U5 R1
indispensable (*adj*)   U6 R2
inevitable (*adj*)   AWL   U2 R1
innovative (*adj*)   AWL   U1 R1
insight (*n*)   AWL   U4 R1
inspector (*n*)   AWL   U1 R2
insufficient (*adj*)   AWL   U9 R1
integrate (*v*)   AWL   U1 R1
intensity (*n*)   AWL   U4 R1
irrelevant (*adj*)   AWL   U6 R1
isolated (*adj*)   AWL   U1 R2
issue (*v*)   AWL   U8 R2

just around the corner   U3 R1

keep something in check   U3 R1
keep up with (*v*)   U9 R1
key to success   U3 R2

lawsuit (*n*)   U8 R1
leading role (*n*)   U9 R1
lend itself to   U9 R2
let alone   U3 R1
let go of (*v*)   U6 R1
lighten the load   U2 R1
logical progression (*n*)   U6 R2
look the part   U9 R1

magnitude (*n*)   U4 R2
make a comeback   U5 R2
make a conscious effort   U6 R1
make a name for oneself   U7 R2
make the case   U9 R1
make the cut   U2 R1
make up one's mind   U2 R2
mark an occasion   U5 R2
mature (*v*)   AWL   U9 R1
medium (*n*)   AWL   U9 R2
minimal (*adj*)   AWL   U6 R2
modify (*v*)   AWL   U9 R1
monitor (*v*)   AWL   U4 R1
moral (*adj*)   U9 R2
myth (*n*)   U9 R1

network (*n*)   AWL   U1 R2
not to mention   U5 R2

obsess about (*v*)   U6 R1
obtain (*v*)   AWL   U2 R2
of choice   U7 R1
of sorts   U1 R2
on behalf of   U6 R2
on end   U4 R1
on the agenda   U7 R2
on the brink of   U3 R2
on the contrary   U8 R2
opponent (*n*)   U9 R1
opt (*v*)   U9 R2
out of the picture   U3 R1
outcome (*n*)   AWL   U6 R1
overcome obstacles   U6 R1

pack a punch   U7 R2
pass something off as   U5 R1
patch (*n*)   U6 R2
persistence (*n*)   AWL   U1 R1
perspective (*n*)   AWL   U9 R2
piece together   U8 R2
pit one's wits against   U9 R2
pitch dark   U6 R2
portrait (*n*)   U5 R2
portray (*v*)   U9 R2
potentially (*adv*)   AWL   U4 R1
precaution (*n*)   U4 R2
precisely the opposite   U1 R1
preliminary (*adj*)   AWL   U5 R2
presume (*v*)   AWL   U7 R2
preventive measure (*n*)   U4 R2
price tag (*n*)   U1 R1
prime (*adj*)   AWL   U3 R1
process (*v*)   AWL   U3 R2
proficient (*adj*)   U9 R1
prolong (*v*)   U7 R2
prospect (*n*)   AWL   U8 R2
purchase (*v*)   AWL   U5 R2

realize one's full potential   U1 R1
reassess (*v*)   AWL   U8 R1
recovery (*n*)   AWL   U4 R1
region (*n*)   AWL   U6 R2
regulate (*v*)   AWL   U3 R1
relatively minor   U4 R2
reliable (*adj*)   AWL   U2 R1
restoration (*n*)   AWL   U5 R2
revolutionize (*v*)   AWL   U5 R1
routine (*n*)   U2 R1

salvage (*v*)   U8 R2
say the least   U5 R1
scenic (*adj*)   U9 R2
science fiction (*n*)   U4 R1
scientific expedition (*n*)   U2 R2
secure (*v*)   AWL   U2 R2
serve a purpose   U1 R2
set out (*v*)   U2 R1
sheer size (*n*)   U8 R1
shelter (*n*)   U3 R1
shift one's focus   U8 R1

simulate (*v*) AWL   U2 R1

sole (*adj*) AWL   U8 R1

solve a mystery   U1 R2

specified (*adj*) AWL   U1 R2

spread out (*v*)   U1 R2

stabilize (*v*) AWL   U1 R2

stand out (*v*)   U9 R2

state-of-the-art   U8 R1

status symbol (*n*)   U7 R1

stem from (*v*)   U5 R2

stepping stone (*n*)   U3 R1

stick around (*v*)   U3 R2

stop in one's tracks   U7 R2

stretch the truth   U9 R1

strong indication (*n*)   U8 R2

submit a proposal   U1 R1

subsequent (*adj*) AWL   U2 R2

surface level (*n*)   U2 R2

surrounded by   U1 R1

suspend (*v*) AWL   U8 R2

tactic (*n*)   U3 R2

take a closer look   U5 R2

take into consideration   U2 R1

talk one's way into   U9 R1

technically (*adv*) AWL   U7 R1

thanks to   U5 R2

the fact of the matter   U2 R2

the full extent of   U4 R1

time frame (*n*)   U4 R1

to say the least   U5 R1

toxic (*adj*)   U2 R2

transformation (*n*) AWL   U1 R1

treacherous (*adj*)   U6 R2

trigger (*v*) AWL   U7 R2

unprecedented (*adj*) AWL   U4 R2

venture (*n*)   U8 R2

viable option (*n*)   U2 R1

virtually (*adv*) AWL   U2 R1

vitality (*n*)   U5 R2

vulnerable (*adj*)   U3 R2

walk a fine line   U7 R2

well suited (*adj*)   U2 R2

whereas (*conj*) AWL   U4 R2

wide audience   U3 R2

work of art (*n*)   U5 R1

wreak havoc on   U4 R1

write something off (*v*)   U3 R1

CREDITS

Text Sources

The following sources were consulted when writing the readings for *Reading and Vocabulary Focus 4*.

6–9: "Miracle above Manhattan," by Paul Goldberger: http://ngm.nationalgeographic.com/2011/04/ny-high-line/goldberger-text/; **16–20**: "Under Paris," by Neil Shea: http://ngm.nationalgeographic.com/2011/02/paris-underground/shea-text/; **26**: "The Lowline," by Justin Davidson: http://nymag.com/news/intelligencer/the-low-line-2011-9/; **32–34**: "The Cold Patrol," by Michael Finkel: http://ngm.nationalgeographic.com/2012/01/sled-dogs/finkel-text/; **42–44**: "The Volcano Next Door," by Michael Finkel: http://ngm.nationalgeographic.com/2011/04/nyiragongo-volcano/finkel-text/; **56–58**: "Path of the Jaguars," by Mel White: http://ngm.nationalgeographic.com/2009/03/jaguars/white-text/; additional source: "A Voice for the Animals," http://www.onbeing.org/program/voice-animals/60/history; **66–69**: "Lucy Cooke, Digital Storyteller/Zoologist," http://www.nationalgeographic.com/explorers/bios/lucy-cooke/; additional source: "The Amphibian Avenger," http://pinktreefrog.typepad.com/; **76**: "Freaks and Creeps: South Africa's Freaky Five," by Lucy Cooke: http://tvblogs.nationalgeographic.com/2012/07/31/freaks-creeps-south-africas-freaky-five/; **82–84**: "Sunstruck," by Timothy Ferris: http://ngm.nationalgeographic.com/2012/06/solar-storms/ferris-text/; **92–94**: "The Calm Before the Wave," by Tim Folger: http://ngm.nationalgeographic.com/2012/02/tsunami/folger-text/; **100**: "Rio Operations Center: Readiness is all," by C40 News Team: http://newswatch.nationalgeographic.com/2012/05/04/rio-operations-center-readiness-is-all/; **106–108**: "Artful Software Spots Fake Masterpieces," by Stefan Lovgren: http://news.nationalgeographic.com/news/2004/11/1123_041123_art_forgery.html/; **116–118**: "Lady with a Secret," by Tom O'Neill: http://ngm.nationalgeographic.com/2012/02/lost-da-vinci/o-neill-text/; **124**: "Photoshopped or Not? A Tool to Tell," by Steve Lohr: http://www.nytimes.com/2011/11/29/technology/software-to-rate-how-drastically-photos-are-retouched.html/; **130–132**: "Everyday Survival," by Laurence Gonzales: http://adventure.nationalgeographic.com/2008/08/everyday-survival/laurence-gonzales-text/1/; **140–142**: "Arctic Dreams and Nightmares," by Marguerite Del Guidice: http://ngm.nationalgeographic.com/2007/01/arctic-trek/del-giudice-text/; **154–157**: "Tibetan Gold," by Michael Finkel: http://ngm.nationalgeographic.com/2012/08/tibetan-mushroom/finkel-text/; **166–168**: "The Bite that Heals," by Jennifer S. Holland: http://ngm.nationalgeographic.com/2013/02/125-venom/holland-text/; **174**: "Could Black Mamba Snake Venom Replace Morphine?" by Kate Andries: http://news.nationalgeographic.com/news/2012/10/121003-morphine-painkillers-black-mamba-snakes-health-science/; **180–182**: "Unseen Titanic," by Hampton Sides: http://ngm.nationalgeographic.com/2012/04/titanic/sides-text/; **190–193**: "Shipwreck in the Forbidden Zone," by Roff Smith: http://ngm.nationalgeographic.com/2009/10/shipwreck/smith-text/; **198**: "The Official Website of Amelia Earhart," http://www.ameliaearhart.com/about/bio.html; **204–206**: "Battle for the Soul of Kung Fu," by Peter Gwin: http://ngm.nationalgeographic.com/2011/03/shaolin-kung-fu/gwin-text/; **214–216**: A personal interview with the author. For more information, visit http://www.kwamenyongo.com; **222**: "Inca Traditions Pay Off for Peruvian Weavers," by Simone Swink: http://news.nationalgeographic.com/news/2002/04/0430_020430_TVincatextiles.html/

Art Credits

Cover: Hidehiko Sakashita/Flickr/Getty Images; **iii (tr)**: RAY CHUI/National Geographic Creative; **iii (cr)**: ROBERT MADDEN/National Geographic Creative; **iii (br)**: Michael Poliza/National Geographic Creative; **iv (tl)**: STR/Stringer/AFP/Getty Images; **iv (cl)**: Sisse Brimberg/National Geographic Creative; **iv (bl)**: Alex Treadway/National Geographic Creative; **v (tr)**: Frans Lanting/National Geographic Creative; **v (cr)**: Randy Olson/National Geographic Creative; **v (br)**: James L. Stanfield/National Geographic Creative; **vi (tl)**: ROBERT MADDEN/National Geographic Creative; **vi (b)**: moodboard/Alamy; **vii (t)**: Benoit Gysembergh/Paris Match/Getty Images; **vii (t)**: Patrick AVENTURIER/Gamma-Rapho/Getty Images;